Higher Education in Music in the Twenty-First Century

In this book, the contributors reconsider the fundamentals of Music as a university discipline by engaging with the questions: What should university study of music consist of? Are there any aspects, repertoires, pieces, composers and musicians that we want all students to know about? Are there any skills that we expect them to be able to master? How can we guarantee the relevance, rigour and cohesiveness of our curriculum? What is specific to higher education in music and what does it mean now and for the future? The book addresses many of the challenges students and teachers face in current higher education; indeed, the majority of today's music students undoubtedly encounter a greater diversity of musical traditions and critical approaches to their study as well as a wider set of skills than their forebears. Welcome as these developments may be, they pose some risks too: more material cannot be added to the curriculum without either sacrificing depth for breadth or making much of it optional. The former provides students with a superficial and deceptive familiarity with a wide range of subject matter, but without the analytical skills and intellectual discipline required to truly master any of it. The latter easily results in a fragmentation of knowledge and skills, without a realistic opportunity for students to draw meaningful connections and arrive at a synthesis.

The authors, Music academics from the University of Glasgow, provide case studies from their own extensive experience, which are complemented by an Afterword from Nicholas Cook, 1684 Professor of Music at the University of Cambridge. Together, they examine what students can and should learn about and from music and what skills and knowledge music graduates could or should possess in order to operate successfully in professional and public life. Coupled with these considerations are reflections on music's social function and universities' role in public life, concluding with the conviction that a university education in music is more than a personal investment in one's future; it contributes to the public good.

Higher Education in Music in the Twenty-First Century

**Edited by
Björn Heile, Eva Moreda Rodríguez and
Jane Stanley**

LONDON AND NEW YORK

First published 2018
by Routledge
2 Park Square, Milton Park, Abingdon, Oxon OX14 4RN

and by Routledge
711 Third Avenue, New York, NY 10017

Routledge is an imprint of the Taylor & Francis Group, an informa business

© 2018 selection and editorial matter, Björn Heile, Eva Moreda Rodríguez and Jane Stanley; individual chapters, the contributors

The right of Björn Heile, Eva Moreda Rodríguez and Jane Stanley to be identified as the authors of the editorial material, and of the authors for their individual chapters, has been asserted in accordance with sections 77 and 78 of the Copyright, Designs and Patents Act 1988.

All rights reserved. No part of this book may be reprinted or reproduced or utilised in any form or by any electronic, mechanical, or other means, now known or hereafter invented, including photocopying and recording, or in any information storage or retrieval system, without permission in writing from the publishers.

Trademark notice: Product or corporate names may be trademarks or registered trademarks, and are used only for identification and explanation without intent to infringe.

British Library Cataloguing-in-Publication Data
A catalogue record for this book is available from the British Library

Library of Congress Cataloging-in-Publication Data
A catalog record for this book has been requested

ISBN: 978-1-472-46732-4 (hbk)
ISBN: 978-1-315-58679-3 (ebk)

Typeset in Times New Roman
by codeMantra

Contents

List of figures and examples	*vii*
List of contributors	*viii*
Introduction	1
BJÖRN HEILE, WITH EVA MOREDA RODRÍGUEZ	
1 **Should there be a twenty-first century 'Complete Kapellmeister'?: the skills, content and purposes of a university music degree**	11
JOHN BUTT	
2 **The learning community, a quodlibet**	30
MARTIN PARKER-DIXON	
3 **Integrative music history: rethinking music since 1900**	55
BJÖRN HEILE	
4 **The many voices of 'art song'**	77
DAVID J. CODE	
5 **The music industries: theory, practice and vocations – a polemical intervention**	112
MARTIN CLOONAN AND JOHN WILLIAMSON	
6 **Writing about music in the 21st century**	126
EVA MOREDA RODRÍGUEZ	
7 **Assessing making and doing**	138
NICK FELLS	

vi *Contents*

8 The teaching of creative practice within higher music education: Guerrilla Learning Outcomes (GLOs) and the importance of negotiation 155
LOUISE HARRIS AND DAVID McGUINNESS

9 On teaching composition: why it can be taught and why that matters 170
BILL SWEENEY

10 A reflective dialogue on teaching composition 179
DREW HAMMOND AND JANE STANLEY

Afterword 195
NICHOLAS COOK

Index 211

Figures and examples

Figures

4.1	The basic types of poetic discourse (as adapted by Renaissance and Romantic theorists from the Greeks)	86
4.2	'Der Erlkönig' as a structure of poetic discourse	87
4.3	Options for strophic setting	88
4.4	Strophic intricies in Müller, 'Gute Nacht'	89
4.5	'Gute Nacht', Schubert's formal alteration to strophes 1 and 2	94
4.6	'Gute Nacht', Schubert's alteration to the final strophe	96
4.7	'Der Leiermann', with implications for strophic setting	97

Music examples

4.1	Schubert, 'Wandrers Nachtlied', op. 96 no. 3, D 768	84
4.2	Schubert, 'Gute Nacht', song 1 from *Die Winterreise*, D 911	90
4.3	Schubert, 'Der Leiermann', song 24 from *Die Winterreise*	98

Contributors

John Butt is Gardiner Professor of Music at the University of Glasgow, Musical Director of Edinburgh's Dunedin Consort and a Principal Artist with the Orchestra of the Age of Enlightenment. Author of five monographs, Butt has written extensively on Bach, the baroque, the historical performance revival and issues of modernity and music. His discography includes some twenty-five recordings as keyboard soloist or conductor. Highlights, as director of Dunedin, include the Gramophone award-winning recordings of Handel's *Messiah* and Mozart's 'Requiem'. His performing career takes him across the world, including the US, Mexico, Hong Kong, Germany, France, Holland, Belgium, Malta, Spain and Norway.

Martin Cloonan is Director of the Turku Institute for Advanced Studies (TIAS), at the University of Turku and was previously Professor of Popular Music Politics at the University of Glasgow. His research interests focus on the political economy of the music industries, especially the live music industry, music policy and issues relating to the status of musicians as workers. He is also coordinating editor for the journal *Popular Music*. Martin chairs the NGO Freemuse, www.freemuse.org, which monitors music censorship across the globe and campaigns for musicians' rights to freedom of artistic expression. He used to manage a band, but is all right now.

David J. Code is Reader in Music at the University of Glasgow, School of Culture and Creative Arts. Previously, he taught at Stanford University on a Mellon Postdoctoral Fellowship, and at Bishop's University in Québec. His research into the work of Claude Debussy, Stéphane Mallarmé, and Igor Stravinsky has appeared in many leading journals including *JAMS*, *JRMA*, *19th-Century Music*, *Journal of Musicology* and *Representations*. In 2010, he contributed a biography of Claude Debussy to the Reaktion Press 'Critical Lives' series on major figures in aesthetic modernism. In recent years, he has also published several essays on the music in the films of Stanley Kubrick, and is currently planning a series of co-edited monographs under the working title 'An Ear for the Movies: Musicality in the Work of Major Directors'. David has received substantial funding for his work from the AHRC (Research Fellowship Scheme;

Collaborative Doctoral Project Scheme) as well as from the British Academy and the Royal Society of Edinburgh.

Nicholas Cook is 1684 Professor of Music at the University of Cambridge, and author of *Music: A Very Short Introduction* (1998), which is published or forthcoming in sixteen languages. *The Schenker Project: Culture, Race, and Music Theory in Fin-de-siècle Vienna* (2007) won the SMT's Wallace Berry Award. His most recently published book is *Beyond the Score: Music as Performance* (2013), while *Music as Creative Practice* is forthcoming. He is currently working on a project entitled 'Music encounters: Studies in relational musicology', supported by a British Academy Wolfson Professorship. He was elected Fellow of the British Academy in 2001.

Nick Fells is a composer, performer, sound artist and Professor of Sonic Practice at the University of Glasgow. His research centres on creative and experimental approaches to sound, particularly the use of computer-mediated sound in performance and in electronic and audiovisual artworks. He is co-director of the Glasgow Sound Network, and a founding member of the composers' collective nerve8 and of the Glasgow Improvisers Orchestra, and plays with a number of other improvising groups. As a performer, he plays shakuhachi and computer-based instruments. His work has been performed in the US, Europe and around the UK, and commissions have included those from the Tramway, Coull Quartet, and Scottish Opera. He was recipient of a Muenchen Kulturreferat Stipendium for an artist residency at Villa Waldberta, Germany, and his work has featured at festivals such as Sónar in Barcelona, Surrounded and Lautwechsel in Munich, Instal and Behaviour in Glasgow, on BBC Radio 3's Late Junction and Hear and Now, at the ISSE Project Room in New York, on Danish TV and on German national radio. [www. nickfells.net]

In his first decade in higher education, **Drew Hammond** has run the gamut of teaching activity, from one-to-one tutorials in jazz piano and composition, undergraduate and postgraduate supervision, scholarly seminars and practical workshops; to large group lectures in subjects ranging from popular music, to modernity and music history, and much more. He has worked extensively in both a research focused university environment, as well as in a performance intensive conservatoire. In the years following his undergraduate studies in the US in the 1990s, he recorded and toured nationally with North Carolina-based ensembles, and spent time working as a private tutor in Boston, Massachusetts. In 2003, he began graduate studies at the University of Glasgow in Scotland, UK, resulting in a PhD in composition in 2009. During this time, he and colleagues founded the Sound Thought postgraduate research exposition at the University of Glasgow, and he was selected as a Sound and Music Shortlist composer. As a composer, Drew has written music for mixed chamber ensembles, symphony, choirs and fixed media, and has taken on a number of recording and production projects.

x *Contributors*

Louise Harris is an electronic and audiovisual composer. She is also Lecturer in Sonic and Audiovisual Practices at the University of Glasgow. Louise specialises in the creation and exploration of audiovisual relationships utilising electronic music and computer-generated visual environments, and her work encompasses fixed media, live performance and large scale installation formats. Louise's work has been performed and exhibited nationally and internationally, including at the Naisa SOUNDplay festival, Toronto, Canada (2011, 2015), Strasbourg Museum of Modern Art, Strasbourg, France (2012, 2013, 2014), Piksel Festival, Bergen, Norway (2012, 2013, 2014), Linux Audio Conference (2013, 2014), Sonorities Festival, Belfast, UK (2014, 2015, 2016), Sweet Thunder Festival, San Francisco, US (2014) and Kiblix Festival, Maribor, Slovenia (2015).

Björn Heile is Professor of Music (post-1900) at the University of Glasgow. He is the author of *The Music of Mauricio Kagel* (2006), the editor of *The Modernist Legacy: Essays on New Music* (2009), co-editor (with Martin Iddon) of *Mauricio Kagel bei den Darmstädter Ferienkursen für Neue Musik: Eine Dokumentation* (2009) and co-editor (with Peter Elsdon and Jenny Doctor) of *Watching Jazz: Encountering Jazz Performance on Screen* (2016) and other publications on new music, experimental music theatre and jazz. He has more projects than he cares to remember, most of which inhabit the twilight zone between the utopian and the doomed.

David McGuinness is a Senior Lecturer in music at the University of Glasgow, and divides his time between historical Scottish music and contemporary work. As director of early music ensemble Concerto Caledonia, he has made thirteen albums, mostly of newly-rediscovered repertoire, and has been a music producer and composer for television and radio, most notably on several seasons of E4's teen drama series *Skins*. In 2007 he produced John Purser's 50-part history of Scotland's music for BBC Radio Scotland, and coordinated the station's observance of No Music Day with the artist Bill Drummond. From 2012 to 2015 he was principal investigator on the AHRC-funded research project Bass Culture in Scottish Musical Traditions, and he is music editor of the forthcoming Edinburgh Allan Ramsay edition.

Eva Moreda Rodríguez is Lecturer in Music at the University of Glasgow, having completed her PhD at Royal Holloway College in 2010. She specialises in the political and cultural history of Spanish music during the twentieth century and is the author of *Music and Exile in Francoist Spain* (2015). Her second book, *Music Criticism and Music Critics in Early Francoist Spain*, was published by OUP in late 2016. Her work has received funding from the Music & Letters Trust, the Carnegie Trust for the Universities of Scotland and the University of Indiana's Lilly Library, among others.

Martin Parker-Dixon is a Lecturer in Music at the University of Glasgow. His PhD was on the Kantian and Marxian aspects of T.W. Adorno's theory of modernist composition. He has published on music technology, avant-gardism and the creative process. Following a serious illness which required a long period of rehabilitation, his research priorities have changed: he is now more concerned with method than content, and is trying to practice writing in an idiom which foregrounds processes of reasoning and logical enquiry into musical phenomena and discourse, rather than pushing a critical theoretic agenda. The chapter in this volume represents one such attempt to provide a logical clarification of the purpose of university-based music education.

Jane Stanley is an Australian-born composer and Senior Lecturer in Music at the University of Glasgow. She specialises in composition for acoustic media. Her music has been performed and broadcast throughout the world, having featured at festivals and conferences including ISCM World Music Days, Gaudeamus Music Week, Asian Composers League, Wellesley Composers Conference, and June in Buffalo. From 2004–2005, she was a Visiting Fellow at Harvard University. Her teachers include Anne Boyd, Peter Sculthorpe, Ross Edwards, Ian Shanahan and Bernard Rands. She has been a composition fellow at Tanglewood Music Center and Aspen Music Festival and School. Her music has been recorded for release by artists in Australia and the UK, and she has received commissions from Tanglewood, Musica Viva, Ensemble Offspring, Bernadette Harvey, Continuum Sax and Halcyon. Her participation in Scottish Crucible in 2011 led to the development of a number of arts–science collaborations. She is a founding member of the Young Academy of Scotland and is a represented composer at the Australian Music Centre. [www.janestanley.com]

Bill Sweeney is a composer, clarinetist and Professor of Music at the University of Glasgow. He has served on the executive committee of the Musician's Union and is currently a member of the classical executive committee of BASCA. He has received commissions from such diverse organisations as the BBC, St Magnus Festival, Musica Nova, Capella Nova, McNaughten Concerts, Theatre Cryptic and the Jim Henson Organisation. His Sonata for Cello and Piano won a BASCA/Radio 3 British Composer Award in 2011. Recent works include "These Lands, This Wall", for the Lammermuir Festival and "Absence" for the Sound Festival and Musiques Démesurées, Clermont-Ferrand. Andrew Clements (*The Guardian*) has commented that

> the influences on his own music have been as wide-ranging as his musical activities. The result is a style that seems to manage to have it both ways, preserving the expressive possibilities and archetypes of the Scottish folk tradition within an idiom that can call on techniques and technology from the whole modernist tradition since 1945.

xii *Contributors*

John Williamson is Lord Kelvin Adam Smith Research Fellow in Popular Music Studies at the University of Glasgow. His recent work has been in the overlapping areas of the music industries, copyright and musical work. He recently co-authored a book on the history of the British Musicians' Union (*Players' Work Time* with Martin Cloonan, 2016) and is currently working on a project mapping the relationship between music and television in Scotland. Prior to completing his doctorate in 2010, he worked in a number of roles in and around various types of (un)popular music as a band and venue manager, promoter and journalist.

Introduction

Björn Heile, with Eva Moreda Rodríguez[1]

Music studies have changed almost beyond recognition in recent years. Not so long ago, the study of Music at a UK university or conservatoire was largely restricted to the western classical tradition, usually with a focus on canonic repertoire, viewed primarily through the lens of style and compositional technique. More recently, a large proportion of applicants to courses in music study some combination of music technology and popular music. Non-western music (under the auspices of ethnomusicology), jazz and traditional music(s) have likewise found their places in the curriculum. This widening of repertoire has been accompanied by a commensurate broadening of critical perspectives: the ideology of aesthetic autonomy that, implicitly or explicitly, underpinned most traditional approaches to music history has given way to critical approaches to cultural and social contexts, including ideologically fraught issues such as gender, sexuality, race, ethnicity and class. Likewise, the almost exclusive concern with compositions ('works') as the embodiment of music history has been or is being complemented by a renewed interest in performance and consumption, bringing with it methodological approaches from such fields as psychology, sociology, anthropology or cultural studies. This diversification of music study has left its traces in official documents. For example, the draft version of the Subject Benchmark Statement for Music by the QAA (Quality Assurance Agency) lists 44 programme codes under W300 '(Music)' from 'W310 (Musicianship/performance studies)' to 'W388 (Popular music composition)', not to mention 'W390 (Music not elsewhere classified)', and 24 alphabetically enumerated areas from 'Acoustics' to 'Song writing' to which a degree programme in music may make reference – a list described as 'indicative rather than prescriptive … [and] not exhaustive' (QAA 2016, 4–7).

These developments are mirrored in most sub-fields. Take, for example, music analysis. When it entered the curriculum in Britain as a fully-formed sub-discipline with a rigorous methodology, two methods ruled more or less supreme: Schenkerian analysis for tonal music and pitch-class set analysis (or set-theoretical analysis) for post-tonal music, the only forms of music that were widely believed to be worthy or in need of analysis. The two most influential textbooks (in Britain), Nicholas Cook's *A Guide to Musical Analysis*

2   Björn Heile

and Jonathan Dunsby and Arnold Whittall's *Music Analysis in Theory and Practice* appeared within a year of each other (in 1987 and 1988 respectively) and gave pride of place to these two methods, among a small number of other analytical traditions. It is revealing that they have never been updated or replaced (although, for various reasons, proper textbooks tend to be a minor feature in UK music higher education in general).[2] The sheer number of variously competing or complementary analytical methods or traditions and the difficulty in discriminating between them would arguably make such an undertaking impossible. It goes without saying that the problem is replicated in teaching: whereas the subject matter of the textbooks by Cook and by Dunsby and Whittall could be covered reasonably well in an introductory course in music analysis, this is no longer an option. Any similar course now would have to make a narrow, and potentially contentious or arbitrary, selection of methodological approaches and repertoires or study the subject from a different perspective altogether. This could include, for instance, focusing entirely on the rationale, objectives and step-by-step analytical procedure of analysis (e.g. by presenting students with a piece and working out what questions one may have of it and how they could be answered). Yet such an approach would jeopardise the link between research and teaching and could effectively confine much of the existing analytical literature, notably that employing formalist techniques, to the dustbin of history.

The same proliferation of subject matter and approach can be observed on the practical side. The traditional focus on instrumental (or vocal) training, composition (pastiche and 'contemporary'), musical techniques (typically harmony and counterpoint) and, in some institutions, conducting, in western classical music has broadened to include equivalent practices in other traditions, such as popular music, jazz, traditional and non-Western performance as well as song writing and arranging (although, as John Butt points out in this volume, in some institutions, such as the University of York, many of these aspects were included from the 1970s). In many if not most institutions, this has also led to the addition of a range of skills to the curriculum that have little or no traditional counterpart, such as improvisation, electronic and digital composition, recording, editing, mixing, production and other studio-based techniques. Finally, the current emphasis on employability and career prospects has led many institutions to offer tuition and/or work placements in the music industries.

Needless to say, this increasing diversity of subject matter and approach reflects the growth and change in student populations. As data published by UCAS (the British University and College Admission Service) shows, undergraduate acceptances in Music almost doubled between 2007 and 2015 from 4,985 to 9,370 (with a seemingly inexplicable jump by almost 50 per cent between 2012 and 2013 not replicated in any other subject), far outstripping overall growth in student numbers (from 413,430 to 532,265 in the same period) (UCAS 2015).[3] All the data suggest that the student body has also become more diverse, with disproportionate increases of international, BME (Black and Minority Ethnic) and disabled students. The figures do not allow clear insight into the class background of applicants, although the percentage of students from independent and grammar schools has declined sharply (the largest intakes are from 'other', 'further education', 'academy' and 'sixth-form college' backgrounds, which does not indicate any particular class but does not suggest conspicuous privilege). What hasn't changed much during this period (although it may have during earlier ones) is the gender balance, with the proportion of women oscillating between 35 and 40 per cent. This continuing male dominance is unusual among arts subjects, and it is difficult to decide whether it is primarily due to the legacy of traditional approaches and attitudes or more recent developments, such as the increasing importance of science and technology, notably in programmes such as music technology and music production.

In other words, the changing nature of music study in UK Higher Education has to be seen at least in part as a response, however imperfect, to the changing demographics of students and, indeed, lecturers. Although much of the resulting diversity of the field may be expressed more in 'vertical' than in 'horizontal' terms – that is to say in increased specialisation of providers, including new providers (Cloonan and Hulstedt 2012), rather than in greater diversity *within* existing programmes and courses – it is probably safe to say that no institution has remained entirely untouched by profound transformations.

Another such transformation is the revolution in information and learning technologies which has profoundly affected both formal and informal education. From Wikipedia through MOOCs, iTunes U and ebooks to instrumental lessons on YouTube, more and more information and learning resources appear to make traditional teaching methods based on the communication of factual knowledge obsolete (although, by the same argument, libraries could have replaced university education at any time). Although the online learning craze appears to have waned and few people now predict that MOOCs will completely replace universities in the foreseeable future, there can be little doubt that elearning has both changed learning and teaching *within* universities and the interactions between formal higher education and informal methods over students' entire learning trajectory (Bothwell and Havergal 2016).

Despite some resistance to these developments, it is astonishing how quickly and smoothly they have taken hold. As a result, most of today's music students undoubtedly encounter a greater diversity of musical traditions and critical approaches to their study as well as a wider set of skills than most of their forebears, and they are being taught and assessed through a greater variety of methods and approaches, using more diverse resources and media. Welcome as these developments are, they come at a price. The overall length of study hasn't increased (at least not in the UK, but in most other countries it is also more likely to have gone down than up), nor has students'

4   *Björn Heile*

capacity for focused learning – indeed, given how many are forced to work to support themselves, the reverse is more likely the case. In addition, today's university entrants tend to be noticeably less well-equipped than their predecessors in the traditional skills of musical literacy and musicianship, to say nothing of music history, theory or organology. Without wanting to indulge in doom and gloom rhetoric, it is not always clear whether what has been gained in breadth consistently balances what has been lost in depth. In other words, something has to give: if it is to be at an intellectual and artistic level appropriate for higher education, we cannot add more material to the curriculum without either sacrificing depth for breadth or making much of it optional. The dangers of either approach are evident: the former is tantamount to dumbing-down, providing students with a superficial and deceptive familiarity with a wide range of subject matter, but without the analytical skills, intellectual discipline and technical facility required to truly master any of it. The latter can easily result in a fragmentation of knowledge and skills, without a realistic opportunity for students to draw meaningful connections between disparate areas and arrive at some sort of synthesis.

What, then, should university study of music include? Are there any aspects, repertoires, pieces, composers and musicians that we want all students to know about; any skills that we expect them to be able to master? In the absence of such prescriptiveness, how else can we guarantee the relevance, rigour and cohesiveness of our curriculum and our learning, teaching and assessment methods, and how can we ensure that our graduates are equipped for future careers in music or other fields and have matured into fully rounded human beings able and willing to make positive contributions to culture and society? Is the current focus on 'graduate attributes' among universities in the UK and elsewhere a step forward in emphasising the *qualities* that students develop over a narrowly conceived (and often rapidly superseded) body of knowledge that they are expected to learn, or does this run the risk of devaluing the actual content and subject matter of academic study? If, after all, studying music is little more than a means to gain 'transferable skills' – connected as they commonly are to the notion of 'employability' that has limited applicability to a field with high levels of self-employment – that can just as well be gained in any other subject, why study it at all? What is specific to higher education in music and what does it mean now and for the future?

These are some of the questions this book addresses. Inspired by a collective publication by the Politics Department of the University of York (Leftwich 2015 [2004]) and, closer to home, a more recent one by the Music Department at Royal Holloway, University of London (Harper-Scott and Samson 2009), the contributors are or were until recently all members of the Music subject unit of the University of Glasgow, which imparts a certain unifying perspective. At the same time, however, they represent six nationalities (seven if one distinguishes between Britain and its constituent nations) and a number of disciplinary and sub-disciplinary backgrounds, and this diversity has similarly left its traces. In addition, the Afterword by Nicholas Cook (University of Cambridge) places the discussion into a wider context. Although we make no claim to universality, the questions we raise and the ideas we entertain are of more general significance. What sets the book apart from previous work is its *integration* of perspectives that typically remain separate, crossing divides, for example, between theory and practice, 'high art' and popular culture, or between teaching and research, as well as those between differing historical periods or theoretical and methodological approaches. Rather than treating them as distinct strands, we regard practical skills, such as performance, composition and sonic arts, and scholarly approaches, such as musicology and critical reflection, as interlinked and we seek to engage in a constant dialogue across these domains.[4] In all cases, the objective is to help students to develop into thinking musicians and/or musical thinkers. Furthermore, as will be clear from a number of contributions, we have long sought to overcome the master-apprentice model of the relationship of lecturers to students, in favour of the model of a learning community built most fundamentally on interactive dialogue. It goes without saying that this model runs counter to the current marketization of higher education with its view of students as consumers, embodied in a reified notion of 'student experience' – whatever lip service is paid to 'innovative' teaching methods such as the 'flipped classroom'. It is thus arguably facilitated by the absence of student fees for Scottish and EU students in Scotland, although that should not undermine its relevance elsewhere.

The breadth of subject matter discussed is matched here by a diversity of approaches in terms of style and genre, ranging from scholarly articles through critical essays, short provocative position statements to dialogues. What this approach highlights is the range of fruitful intellectual and practical engagements with music: what connects (say) historically informed performance practice to the study of the popular music industries or contemporary composition, what they can learn from one another and what a student can gain by engaging with all three. As will become apparent, there are a surprising number of ideas shared between seemingly disparate areas, such as the emphasis on collaboration mentioned in various writings on scholarship, performance and composition alike. We hope that what emerges here is a coherent and value-based vision of music education, beyond compartmentalised and narrow specialisations. Similarly, while we never lose sight of the necessity to prepare our students for a variety of careers within music and beyond, we believe that our responsibility does not end there but extends towards a wider civic role, encapsulated in George Davie's (1961) notion of 'The Democratic Intellect'. In this context, the current (re-)emergence of 'post-truth politics', populism and demagoguery throughout much of the western world may well be partly related to the recent burgeoning emphasis on purely instrumentalist conceptions of education. The authors share the conviction that there can be no enlightened

6 Björn Heile

public and political discourse without an enlightened education system, and any attempt to reduce the value of education to individual earning potential therefore runs counter to the interests of a free, democratic society. Music in higher education cannot solve society's problems, but it can and arguably has to contribute to making a more enlightened society possible.

The perspective adopted throughout this book is that of research-led or research-informed teaching. In other words, one characteristic all authors share is that their teaching is closely related to their own research, allowing students to share in their discoveries, insights and experiences and guiding them in making their own explorations. This is a two-way process, however, requiring lecturers to respond to the needs and interests of students. As the contributions demonstrate, the authors do not simply follow their own idiosyncratic interests or changing disciplinary fashions in their research and recycle the results for teaching purposes, in the vague hope that students will find them interesting and useful. Rather, they pursue a dialogue between teaching needs and research interests, adopting the perspective of students and questioning the wider relevance of their enquiries. For these reasons, this book is not only about narrowly conceived issues of teaching and curriculum but engages the discipline in its totality: teaching, research and the interaction between the two.

The aim of the book, then, is to rethink some of the fundamentals of the discipline. In so doing, we are not aiming for comprehensive coverage of the entire field, but rather to provide some examples, however provisional, of possible responses to the changing intellectual and social climate. Instead of a practical 'How to…' guide setting out the most efficient ways of communicating an unquestioned body of knowledge, we seek to interrogate what students *can* and *should* learn about and from music.

Despite a recent surge in relevant publications, traditionally there has been surprisingly little public reflection on the state of music studies in higher education. Although there are some similarities between our approach and that taken by the authors of *Rethinking Music* (Cook and Everist 1999), we are more concerned with music as an academic discipline, involving teaching and research and practice-based as well as scholarly approaches. Similarly, there is an undeniable overlap with the aforementioned *Introduction to Music Studies* (Harper-Scott and Samson 2009). However, whereas the latter addresses present and future potential undergraduate students, our book is primarily targeted at fellow academics and postgraduate students. Furthermore, the *Introduction* takes traditional sub-disciplines for granted, providing pithy and interesting snapshots on 'Music History', 'Theory and Analysis', 'Sociology of Music', 'Early Music', 'Jazz', 'Popular Music', 'Performance', 'Composition' etc. By contrast, we take a more critical approach to the way disciplinary knowledge and skills have historically been constituted, while seeking both to illuminate the intersections between sub-disciplines and approaches and to probe the continuing relevance of the divisions between them. Another group of existing publications largely concentrates on more practical advice about teaching and assessment methods, ranging from 'How to...' guides for aspiring university teachers (e.g. Conway and Hodgman 2009; Davis 2012) – which, by their nature, rarely question established approaches and a relatively stable, seemingly authoritative curriculum – to others that strive to renew pedagogic practices and approaches. Among the latter, one of the most interesting is Haddon and Burnard (2016), which only appeared when the present book approached its completion. Indeed, we share many of the assumptions and goals with the authors represented in this latest contribution – which also includes a chapter by our own Louise Harris. One key difference, however, is that whereas that book is primarily concerned with the nitty-gritty of teaching and assessment techniques, ours is more about the wider questions of what to teach and why. In other words, Haddon and Burnard (2016) fits within education as a discipline (it is indeed shelved under 'education' in the University of Glasgow Library) in ways the present book does not.

John Butt opens the volume by outlining the history of higher education in Music in the UK, pointing out that this history is much shorter than is generally thought. As he explains, the curriculum was based on a

> "Kapellmeister" style of education, training all undergraduates in progressively demanding skills of harmony, counterpoint and associated stylistic composition, together with challenging aural tests and keyboard skills ... [enabling students] to practise the role of a generally competent musical organizer, director or teacher, able to undertake a whole range of expected (and indeed unexpected) leadership roles.

Given that the careers the 'Kapellmeister' education was geared towards are not a realistic or even attractive option for the majority of students, Butt asks what function this tradition can still serve in the modern academy, arguing that

> the retention of at least some aspects of the "Kapellmeister" tradition has the potential to give us insight into the workings of a music that remains contemporary – through its fragile ubiquity – while also embodying something of our cultural roots and values.

A concern for the history and tradition of the university in general and music teaching in particular is also critical for Martin Parker-Dixon, who envisages lecturers and students forming a 'learning community' and engaging in 'rigorous argumentation ... about the art of music ... as an object of serious intellectual enquiry'. Significantly, for Parker-Dixon, practice-based work, such as composition and performance, should be subject to the same criteria and standards as scholarly work, so there should be no categorical distinctions between theory and practice or, for that matter, between lecturers and students. In his contribution, Björn Heile tackles another historical division, that between popular and classical music, arguing that the two

8   *Björn Heile*

can and should be discussed in relation to one another under the auspices of an 'integrative music history'. As examples, he provides the contrasting consequences of the introduction of recording to the performance practice of jazz and classical music in the interwar period, and the more comparable responses to the student rebellions of 1968 in the fields of classical contemporary composition, jazz and rock.

A broadly similar approach pervades David Code's chapter, which approaches the Romantic *Lied* from a post- or para-canonic perspective that begins by finding value in the linguistic and musical strangeness it might now carry for most modern-day students (as opposed to the presumed familiarity with which it would once have entered a traditional 'classical' music education), and proceeds to view it through the prism of select performances and compositional appropriations whose various voices can be heard to invite similarly creative responses from us twenty-first century listeners. The focus on the curriculum (broadly speaking) is continued by Martin Cloonan and John Williamson, who argue for the inclusion of a critical perspective of the music industries. According to them, this is necessary not solely for the benefit of students' employability and career prospects or to meet employers' demands, but by providing insight into the music industries' working practices, without which the music produced cannot be properly understood. It is this critical dimension that empowers students to act as active participants in musical culture (whatever their career).

Eva Moreda Rodríguez opens a thematic focus on skills with a reflection on writing and a proposal to complement traditional academic genres, such as essays, with genres that were made possible by web 2.0 technologies, such as blogs and wikis. Such an approach, she argues, would help students to see the connections between academic study and real life and teach them skills that are undoubtedly useful in contemporary workplaces. Over and above this, however, technological innovations such as hypertext provide useful ways of connecting different aspects of music and musical experience (such as scores, sketches, audio or audiovisual recordings) as well as an innovative and creative mode of explanatory or critical commentary that is impossible to achieve in traditional paper-based writing. As so often, our communication technologies reflect aspects of their wider social and cultural contexts. Next, Nick Fells introduces the idea of 'generative practice', which emphasises 'the synthesis of practice from multifarious other sources: materials, sounds, works, personal histories, motivations, and repeated or repeatable processes and operations' – as opposed to the idea of creation out of nothing suggested by the more widely used term 'creative practice'. Generative practice, then, covers both composition and performance, but isn't contained by either of these terms; nor is it particularly concerned with their separation in traditional teaching practices. Moreover, in sympathy with Parker-Dixon's approach, Fells argues that generative practice crucially relies on critical thought, and that its assessment is therefore based on similar if not the same criteria as (other) academic work.

Like Fells, Louise Harris and David McGuinness are concerned with the teaching and, crucially, assessment of creative practice. Like Parker-Dixon, they develop their ideas in a dialogue, albeit an actual dialogue, not a Socratic one, in the process coining such concepts as 'Guerrilla Learning Outcomes (GLOs)' and 'unassessables'. While these may be partly tongue-in-cheek, the 'six principles for effective learning in creative practice' on which they close are anything but. In actual fact, as touched on throughout this book, there is little here that is limited to creative practice: arguably, these principles are valuable for all learning and teaching in higher education. Note too the importance Harris and McGuinness place on a collaborative learning community, uniting lecturers and students, reinforcing the point made by Parker-Dixon about scholarship. The discussion of creative practice is continued by Bill Sweeney, who argues for a stronger consideration of the *process of creating*, including exploration and experimentation, as opposed to the *product*, which, inevitably, is the focus of assessment. As a consequence, he expresses scepticism about the importance of compositional style. The discussion of the learning and teaching of composition is concluded by a conversation between Drew Hammond and Jane Stanley who reflect on the wider role of composition in music study and higher education as a whole, considering that only a small minority of students are likely to continue with composition after their undergraduate studies. This inevitably raises questions about the value of composition for other activities – in music and beyond – and about the ideals, models and repertoires composition teaching is, directly or indirectly, based on.

The book is brought to a close by Nicholas Cook's Afterword, in which he usefully contextualises the volume as a response to the encroachment of neo-liberalism in the academy, epitomised by the Browne Report (Browne 2010). While he appears to be broadly sympathetic with this agenda, he sounds noticeably more sceptical about the high modernist values that he identifies (again, not without justification) as the common ground shared by most if not all the authors. Instead, he goes further than most of the other contributors in his embrace of diversity, arguing that the traditional skills training that Butt characterises as the 'Kapellmeister model' is 'undeliverable' and that 'the idea of a core applicable across all music degree programmes is wrong-headed'. But, then, as Cook also writes, '[t]he point of this book is not to prescribe solutions but to offer an example of what happens when you think in a sustained manner about the problems'.

Notes

1 The editors and contributors wish to thank two anonymous reviewers for their valuable comments on the proposal for and draft version of this book.
2 It is noteworthy, for instance, that even a theoretical approach as influential as neo-Riemannian analysis still awaits a pedagogical adaptation. Students have to be referred to the original formulations of the theory, which are anything but straightforward and reader-friendly.

10   *Björn Heile*

3 However, a more detailed look shows that this increase is concentrated in London, the South of England and Wales and that growth was more modest in the North of England, Northern Ireland and, particularly, Scotland (from 455 in 2007 to 515 in 2015). Furthermore, it is conceivable that part of the growth is associated with relatively new private providers, such as the Institute of Contemporary Music Performance (ICMP), the Liverpool Institute for Performing Arts (LIPA) or the Brighton Institute of Modern Music (BIMM).

4 In this text, as is common practice, 'scholarly' is used as the antonym to 'practice-based' or 'practice-led' research or 'practice-as-research'. Needless to say, this is not to suggest that these latter approaches may not involve scholarly methods.

Bibliography

Bothwell, Ellie, and Chris Havergal. 2016. 'Moocs Can Transform Education – But Not Yet'. *Times Higher Education (THE)*. July 21. www.timeshighereducation. com/features/massive-open-online-courses-moocs-can-transform-education-but-not-yet.

Browne, John. 2010. 'Securing a Sustainable Future for Higher Education: An Independent Review of Higher Education Funding and Student Finance [Browne Report]'. www.gov.uk/government/publications/the-browne-report-higher-education-funding-and-student-finance.

Cloonan, Martin, and Lauren Hulstedt. 2012. 'Taking Notes: Mapping and Teaching Popular Music in Higher Education'. Higher Education Academy. www.heacademy.ac.uk/resource/taking-notes-mapping-and-teaching-popular-music-higher-education.

Conway, Colleen Marie, and Thomas M. Hodgman. 2009. *Teaching Music in Higher Education*. New York: Oxford University Press.

Cook, Nicholas, and Mark Everist, eds. 1999. *Rethinking Music*. Oxford and New York: Oxford University Press.

Davie, George Elder. 1961. *The Democratic Intellect: Scotland and Her Universities in the Nineteenth Century*. Publications : History, Philosophy and Economics (University of Edinburgh), no. 12. Edinburgh: Edinburgh University Press.

Davis, James A., ed. 2012. *The Music History Classroom*. Farnham, Surrey: Ashgate.

Haddon, Elizabeth, and Pamela Burnard. 2016. *Creative Teaching for Creative Learning in Higher Music Education*. New York: Routledge.

Harper-Scott, J. P. E., and Jim Samson. 2009. *An Introduction to Music Studies*. Cambridge: Cambridge University Press.

Leftwich, Adrian, ed. 2015. *What Is Politics?: The Activity and Its Study*. Cambridge: Polity.

QAA. 2016. 'Subject Benchmark Statement Music: Draft for Consultation'. www.qaa.ac.uk/en/Publications/Documents/SBS-Music-consultation-16.pdf.

UCAS. 2015. 'UCAS Undergraduate End of Cycle Data Resources'. www.ucas.com/corporate/data-and-analysis/ucas-undergraduate-releases/ucas-undergraduate-end-cycle-data-resources.

1 Should there be a twenty-first century 'Complete Kapellmeister'?

The skills, content and purposes of a university music degree

John Butt

University music education in the UK over the last century has enjoyed a peculiar history that is not directly shared by any other country. As becomes clear on closer examination, the tradition seemingly embodied within this history is in many respects of considerably shorter duration than many might believe, and it was only securely in place in the years following the Second World War. This fact also relies on a further characteristic of the British situation from *c.*1945–2000, namely the provision of free university education to those deemed suitable to benefit from it, as part of the welfare state, which was instituted directly in the wake of the Second World War (and towards which many interwar trends were pointing). Nevertheless, provision of fees and maintenance by Local Education Authorities was not completely established until the Education Act of 1962 (Education Act 1962).

In its most traditional form (that is, what would have been perceived as 'traditional' *c.*1975, and with most departments emulating what they saw as 'Oxbridge' norms), university music tuition reflected a 'Kapellmeister' style of education, training all undergraduates in progressively demanding skills of harmony, counterpoint and associated stylistic composition, together with challenging aural tests and keyboard skills. Music history was added to this, usually as an uncritical, factually based discipline aimed at teaching basic knowledge of the classical canon, and often borrowing unashamedly from the publications of the burgeoning 'music appreciation' industry in the US over the same period, notably the well-nigh ubiquitous source of pre-digested music history (Grout 1960/2014). Acoustics was sometimes included, as if to remind students of music's traditional association with the physical sciences and also perhaps to prove that music was a 'proper' science. Notation and paleography often also played a role, usually involving study of Renaissance mensural practices and particularly of English music, which had been undergoing revival since the late nineteenth century. Later additions to this core were composition (whether stylistic, free or modernist), analysis (traditionally in the Tovey mould, but increasingly dominated by Schenker from the 1970s onwards) and historical performance practice.

12 *John Butt*

This latter was initially an extension of organology (occasioned by the wonderful instrument collections surviving in the ancient universities and associated museums), but in the 1950s and 1960s it was very much guided towards a rethinking of attitudes towards earlier repertories, particularly by the pioneering and entirely idiosyncratic work of Thurston Dart. Performance itself was often excluded (that was the job of the conservatories, or, in the case of Oxbridge, the richer constituent colleges, many of which offered prestigious organ and choral scholarships). Sometimes performance was grudgingly appended to the curriculum, perhaps as an option that was examined but not necessarily taught under the direct supervision of the faculty or department concerned.[1] With all these skills mastered in the course of a three- or four-year university degree (together with a secondary school syllabus that directly interlocked with the university curriculum), it was assumed that the graduate would be fit to practise the role of a generally competent musical organiser, director or teacher, able to undertake a whole range of expected (and indeed unexpected) leadership roles. Perhaps never before had Mattheson's (1739/1981) ambitions for the education of the 'Complete Kapellmeister' been so fully realized on the level of a national curriculum.[2]

One obvious observation: with the increased marketization of higher education from the 1980s onwards, together with the dramatic growth of student numbers (well beyond the previous expansion enshrined by the Robbins Report of 1961–3: Robbins 1963),[3] the specialization demanded by the 'Kapellmeister' degree soon became unviable. If music was to survive as an academic subject it had to be adapted to a much broader range of interests. Moreover, the social liberalism that is often an unsung corollary of monetarist economic policy meant that there was increasing unease about the narrow focus on western classical music (and it may not be entirely coincidental that some of the UK departments that have closed since the 'Thatcher revolution' were among those that cleaved most closely to the classical tradition).[4] Together with the new intellectual imperatives spurred by the American 'new musicology' of the 1980s and 1990s, the field of music suddenly became richer in its range of world and popular music, together with the methodologies by which these could be explored (Cook and Everist 1999). The 'critical turn', much heralded by Joseph Kerman (1985), went beyond the initial imperative to evaluate and discern social meaning in the classical repertory, towards a much more complex network of evaluation and hermeneutics within which 'classical' values were strictly relativized. Now, to many, the 'Kapellmeister' degree seemed absurdly abstract, on a par with, say, stylistic composition in Latin, and relevant only to a very small component of the overall 'markets' and 'industries' of music. Of course, there was something of a time lag between the changes in research direction and in the content of teaching, even in America, where 'new musicology' was most prevalent, but where the institutionalized approach to classical music appreciation has continued to endure. British musicology was a little slower to adapt to the new methodologies, although some distinctive voices soon emerged (as exemplified by Cook and Everist 1999). However, teaching content could still be very traditional in terms of stylistic techniques and adherence to the classical canon, even by the turn of the twenty-first century. But whatever the rates of change, virtually no department has remained unaffected by the broadening of musical study. Now the immediate question is whether what remains of the 'Kapellmeister' degree is worth preserving or even restoring, and whether, now that so many other – largely excellent – aspects of music have gained syllabus space (such as cultural or philosophical critiques, but also a much extended range of music and creative practices), anything worthwhile has been lost.

Any answer to this question will require some understanding of how and why the 'Kapellmeister' degree developed in the first place, particularly given that it does not go back as far as many traditionalists might like to believe. Music, it is true, had a very prestigious place in the medieval curriculum as an essential component of the 'scientific' quadrivium, which constituted the larger part of the seven liberal arts; the three 'trivial' subjects, which were the more practical arts such as rhetoric and dialectic, significantly did not include music. Thus the 'ancient' universities (i.e. the two in England, four in Scotland and the one Elizabethan foundation in Ireland, all dating from before 1600) would have promoted the study of the music theory in Boethius and Aristotle, since the proportions and relationships embodied in music were considered central to the understanding of the medieval cosmos together with the human body and its spiritual harmony. Some of this understanding persisted into the seventeenth century, supplemented with newer discoveries and theories concerning the science of sound (i.e. the emerging field of acoustics). But particularly interesting is what now seems like an unhelpful disconnect between the prestigious role of music as theory, linking the cosmos and the human in spiritual harmony (*musica mundana* and *musica humana*) and its more lowly position as a practical art (*musica intrumentalis*). Most of the ancient universities were closely associated with (or situated near) choral foundations, which were responsible for preserving and promoting both monophony and polyphony (famously so, in the case of St Andrews, given its role in the preservation of early polyphony), but this activity seems to have been an essentially different sphere from the academic, liberal arts, one.

Nevertheless, music of a more practical nature eventually did make its way into the university, but not as part of the central BA syllabus (MA in Scotland), rather as an entirely separate degree. The first specific music degrees in the world belong to Renaissance Cambridge (BMus and DMus established in 1463/4) and Oxford was not far behind with equivalent qualifications. These awards could be gained through a compositional submission, which might involve many years of preparation. But residency and a structured course of study were not generally required. In short, composition was clearly becoming acceptable as an aspect of musical science, but it was only

14   *John Butt*

admitted as a supplement to the BA curriculum and not as a component or substitute. As Cudworth and Andrewes (no date, section 1) and Wollenberg (no date, section 5) outline, only in the nineteenth or early twentieth centuries did residency become essential to the acquisition of music degrees and only then were written examinations in specific compositional techniques instituted.

A closer relationship between theoretical and practical music was instigated with the appointment of the first professors of music (Oxford in 1626 and Cambridge in 1684), who were expected to retain a scientific interest in music but also provide leadership in composition and other practical aspects of music. For many years, these figures were associated with college or university organist roles, so one might assume that their work in composition probably accorded with the sort of music they performed in their respective chapels, right into the 1920s. Likewise, the next generations of cathedral and church organists usually came through the Oxbridge system, even though the centrality of religion to university life had slumped during the Enlightenment era.

All this demonstrates a peculiarity of British music: the more-or-less intact survival of the Anglican choral tradition through the ages of revolution and Enlightenment, industrialization and the birth of the modern state, and right into the twenty-first century. In no other European country was there such a continuous tradition and, given its association with the ancient universities, it is not surprising that the professoriate and recipients of the music degrees were so often associated with the church and its music (certainly in England and 'Anglican' Ireland, if not in Scotland, where the universities had become Presbyterian institutions, albeit with some regard for traditional church music). A further factor concerns the important role of the provincial cathedral and church organist in Britain, which grew in the nineteenth century when such figures effectively became the directors of music for entire regions (in the comparative absence of the professional orchestras and opera houses that were already spreading across the entirety of German and Italian lands, McCrea 1998, 288–90). Organists were not only conductors of provincial choral societies and orchestras, they also became a primary means by which the latest orchestral repertory was transmitted to audiences beyond the main centres, in the guise of organ transcriptions (very much facilitated by the increasingly orchestral specifications of the English romantic organ, Thistlethwaite 1990). In short, nineteenth-century British musical culture was dominated by broadly educated musicians who tended to have a first degree in a range of arts subjects and one of the coveted music degrees of Oxbridge (and Dublin, and later, Durham and Edinburgh).

If this short history suggests that some aspects of the 'Kapellmeister' tradition do indeed stretch back towards the institution of music degrees back in the seventeenth century, it needs to be stressed that full degree programmes in music (i.e. beyond the 'second' degrees that were generally taken without a full formal course of study) are of considerably later vintage. Indeed, full degrees in music were available only in Scotland before the Second World War. The first faculty of music was set up under the approval of Queen Victoria in Edinburgh in 1894, following several decades of intermittent music tuition from the Reid Professors of the Theory of Music (first appointed in 1839). The Reid Professor who successfully inaugurated the full degree in music was Frederick Niecks, a German-born Scot who was astonishingly visionary in his approach. Although he was clearly influenced by the newly inaugurated discipline of musicology in Germany, Tovey noted in 1920 that Niecks's scheme still had no parallel in Europe. His rich syllabus (of which students were to take 'not less than eighty Lectures') was designed to educate students in the 'how and why of things', and it ranged from performance, through advanced harmony and counterpoint, form and orchestration, to study of analysis, history and acoustics; moreover, students had to pass examinations in languages, rhetoric and literature (Farmer 1947, 395).[5] This BMus degree essentially became the model for later music degree programmes throughout the UK, with Glasgow first following suit in 1930–1.[6] Most surprising is perhaps the fact that the ancient English universities were rather later in developing faculties of music, together with the associated single-honours undergraduate degrees: Oxford's dates from 1944 (Wollenberg no date, section 5) and Cambridge's from 1947–8 (Cudworth and Andrewes no date, section 1). Most other prestigious degrees in music date from later still, with that of a 'plateglass' university such as York dating from 1964 (Griffiths and Paynter no date), around the same time as that of King's College London (despite the latter having had a professor of music for several decades, Breen 2015, 3).

The 'Kapellmeister' education served particular ends, not least those of the lecturers who were appointed between the 1940s and the 1960s, all of whom tended to be well-rounded practitioners of some kind, often connected with the church (predominantly Anglican) and/or regional music culture. To them, 'academic' meant the study and practice of stylistic compositional techniques, done wherever possible without a keyboard, to cultivate the 'inner ear'. This was to provide a solid and essential musicianship, which would sustain musical culture in a way that practitioners from conservatories could not necessarily offer. The students were being prepared for the sorts of jobs that helped perpetuate the very tradition to which they belonged: church and cathedral music, the organist as a regional focus of classical music, broadcasting and concert promotion and, perhaps most significantly, school teaching. Although many of the more 'establishment' figures in classical music culture came from independent schools (which were most likely to be able to afford the resources and time in the curriculum for learning harmony, counterpoint, keyboard skills and advanced performance), this was also the period when pupils from state schools were most intensively educated in classical music and – if particularly talented – could become fully qualified to proceed to a university or conservatory education in music. National exams (whether A Levels or Scottish Highers) tested the skills of a prospective

16   *John Butt*

Kapellmeister, and given that 48 per cent of graduates in the Humanities in 1963 went into teaching (Robbins 1963, 92, table 34), it is easy to see how the system sustained itself and indeed gave the impression that it had already lasted for many years. Graduates with this sort of training in music were also in a position to inform the public about classical music culture and fit in directly with the Reithian values of the BBC, the 'Third Programme' of which became the world leader in the broadcasting of classical music.

There is an irony to this situation that perhaps cannot be stressed too strongly: this burgeoning of classical music culture, championed by the universities and filtering into the rest of the educational culture came at the time of the greatest government investment and ownership in public services across the board. In other words, what might today often be considered a particularly privileged and 'elitist' culture was officially made available to any suitably qualified person during the era of the welfare state. Indeed, the championing of 'high culture' was a very common feature of much discourse on the socialist and democratic left. If populist art was not necessarily to be condemned (other than perhaps for its explicit commercialization), the aspiration to have access to – and participate in – cultures such as classical music was frequently expressed, as in for instance the *Policy for Music in Post War Britain* by the Workers' Music Association (1945).

If many in the older generation (and many younger figures besides) see this period as a golden age from which we have deviated, it is perhaps worth noting Thomas Piketty's (2014, 96–9, 126–9) observations about the general trends in western capitalism since 1700.[7] Within this broader history it is clear that the period stretching from after the First World War to the 1970s is the exception rather than the rule in terms of the support for public services in the western world (and, one might also obviously add, this also applies to the Soviet bloc, which flourished during precisely the same period). The economy during this period was devastated by two world wars and the Great Depression, and the need for urgent and repeated rebuilding inspired a trend for considerable public spending. This was also the period in which capital in general had the lowest value, while growth in national economies was at its greatest. Without entering into greater economic detail, it seems clear that the 'elite' culture of classical music was most central to public education and culture precisely when the country as a whole was least wealthy and had the greatest debt (and this was also the time when the gap between rich and poor was at its narrowest point). Only when the situation has reverted to the capitalist 'norm' (in terms of the larger historical trends), does this culture seem 'elitist' and contrary to the 'cost-effective' imperatives of the market. A perfectly democratic desire for pluralism and a non-judgmental embrace of popular culture by the academy and arts funders are covertly supported by the neo-liberal order.

On the other hand, lest golden-ageism encourages us to succumb to a narrative of decline, it is important not to underestimate the gains to music education in recent years. Not only is it now possible to study virtually any form of music (in other words, representing a more democratic attitude towards the choice of culture), but also the methodologies that can be applied to music, from the empirical-scientific side to all forms of cultural theory on the other, are richer than ever before. We should also surely acknowledge that the numbers who succeeded in gaining the skills to undertake university study were still very small and that many other aspects of post-war culture were extremely repressive compared with the situation today (particularly in attitudes towards minorities, gender roles and sexuality).

Before returning to our present situation and the question of how much of the 'Kapellmeister' tradition might be preserved or restored, it is worth exploring further how much the pre-1980s culture of university education differs from that of the present. The seminal document here is the Robbins Report (Robbins 1963), the first comprehensive survey of Higher Education in the UK (1961–3), which set the model for the next two decades. It resulted in an enormous expansion in university provision (even while fees and maintenance were still funded by the Local Education Authorities). Reading this report today may well remind many lecturers of what they *thought* a university was meant to be, its academic ethos perhaps seeming so self-evident that one might imagine oneself temporarily waking from an ongoing nightmare.[8] In 1963, academic freedom was deemed not 'a privilege but rather as a necessary condition for the proper discharge of the higher academic functions as we conceive them' (230). In comparison with the educational policy documents of the last twenty years – suffused as they are with the faux-academic language of management manuals – much of the tone of Robbins reads like scholarly criticism: 'To do justice to the complexity of things, it is necessary to acknowledge a plurality of aims' (Robbins 1963, 6). Many might be surprised today to learn that this report was commissioned by Harold Macmillan's Conservative government and that Lionel Robbins himself was hardly a figure of the left.

On the other hand, some of its opening statements chime directly with the sort of language that often accompanies seemingly conservative justifications for classical music (and 'high' culture in general):

> The aim should be to produce not mere specialists but rather cultivated men and women. And it is the distinguishing characteristic of a healthy higher education that, even where it is concerned with practical techniques, it imparts them on a plane of generality that makes possible their application to many problems – to find the one in the many, the general characteristic in the collection of particulars. It is this that the world of affairs demands of the world of learning.
>
> (Robbins 1963, 6)

The notion of 'cultivated' citizens is also tied to 'a common culture and common standards of citizenship' (Robbins 1963, 7), which is of course very difficult to imagine in the pluralistic climate of the twenty-first century, however

18   *John Butt*

desirable the complementary requirement 'to compensate for any inequalities of home background' may still obviously be. The emphasis throughout is on fostering the talents of each individual citizen and building society and the economy from the needs and achievements of the constituent people rather than vice versa (and the authors of the report have no hesitation in seeing education in the Soviet Union as one of several models to emulate in certain respects, Robbins 1963, 74).

The classical economists, great supporters of education, had precisely the imprudence of neglecting education in mind when they invented the phrase 'human capital'. And, provided we always remember that the goal is not productivity as such but the good life that productivity makes possible, this mode of approach is very helpful (Robbins 1963, 204).

Interestingly, Robbins does not advocate an ossification of established disciplinary norms, but encourages institutions to experiment with the contents of their courses, coordinating subject areas across the country without compromising the ideals of academic rigour or freedom. Robbins also encourages the development of multidisciplinary courses (rather along the lines of the traditional Scottish MA course) while not destroying the intensity of single-discipline study where this continues to be appropriate. Whichever way the future programmes are taken, it is crucial that the 'essential aim of a first degree course should be to teach the student how to think'. This implies that specialist skills are essentially transferrable and that the net result of developed thought is more important than the specifics of the knowledge pursued. Moreover, even single specialist disciplines contain a 'variety of discipline' in themselves, so that even the most intensive of single-subject courses need not necessarily be as narrow as is sometimes believed. It is therefore assumed that students with a desirable education will be in a position to adapt to whatever the external circumstances of society and economy might demand: 'The urge to knowledge for its own sake, pursued in depth, is one that inspires students of many levels of ability' (Robbins 1963, 90–1). The overall trend, then, is towards innovation within the bounds of academic freedom and experimentation, but with no imperative to tailor degrees to the specific and changing economic or social needs of the day. At its best, this type of education would seem to encourage 'timeless' academic values whilst admitting innovations based on the developing state of each discipline. Whatever the strength or weakness of the Robbins report there is no doubt that it had a pronounced effect, most obviously on the building of new universities and the increase in the number of places (which has continued right up to the present).

If the assumptions of Robbins are correct, it might be possible to surmise that the 'traditional' music degree – like any other – is going to be useful regardless of its apparent narrowness and precise content. The various skills involved will all conspire to encourage the students to develop the quality of their thinking as far as possible and thus enable them to negotiate a range of future circumstances. One might even trace something of the remnants

A twenty-first century 'Complete Kapellmeister'? 19

of the 'liberal arts' education of the Middle Ages (of which music theory was a part) whereby a traditional syllabus is assumed to give one the skills to negotiate all the challenges of the present. But, if there is one thing that distinguished the 'Kapellmeister' type of music degree from others in the arts or sciences, it is in the music-specific skills that clearly had a vocational function (thus the university music degree was perhaps closer to the sort of targeted programme taught in conservatories than most other arts courses). The 'Kapellmeister' spent so much time learning musical skills that he (sic) generally had little time to cultivate any interest in other fields (and indeed was often antagonistic towards the new critical movements in the other arts and indeed towards free intellectual inquiry in general).

Some figures in the music field in the early 1960s were already picking up on the notion that traditional music degrees might be too narrow, particularly in the wake of the Robbins recommendations. Foremost here was the activity of Thurston Dart, who took up the challenge of developing the new department of music at King's College London in 1964 (having found the Cambridge system too intransigent). He made his positive reaction to Robbins, and concomitant turn away from the traditional Kapellmeister degree, absolutely clear:

> And what ought the story of [music degrees'] future to be, post-Robbins... in an age when the organ-loft is no longer the principal repository of musical talent up and down the country? When musical scholarship can stand beside scholarship in any other branch of humane learning, as a proper subject for advanced study? When composing, performing, interpreting, teaching and researching are seen to be sister elements in music, and no longer rival suitors for public esteem?
>
> (Breen 2015, 21)

Dart's ambition was to make the study of music thoroughly compatible with study of other subjects, through the development of a whole range of degree programmes in which music could be taken as a subsidiary subject. Moreover, even for the music-intensive BMus degree, he insisted that students had to take one-fifth of their courses in other subjects (Breen 2015, 26–7). This dedicated music course was also broadened to include subjects such as ethnomusicology, electronic music and the history of music pedagogy. The traditional 'Kapellmeister' style subjects such as composition, counterpoint, orchestration and fugue were no longer to be compulsory components. Rather as Joseph Kerman was beginning to advocate in the US, Dart believed that music needed to participate in much broader discourses, and that university music education should be 'through' music rather than necessarily 'in' it (Breen 2015, 31). While by no means averse to the western classical tradition, Dart believed that this needed to be seen through the new eyes of historically informed performance, and that it needed to be coordinated with a much broader array of world music and new approaches to composition.

20   *John Butt*

If Dart's reaction against the 'Kapellmeister' tradition took him towards a normalizing of music's relation with other subjects (his first degree was in mathematics, after all), Wilfrid Mellers (whose first degree was in English) took an even more flamboyant approach towards music and its place in the broader culture, at the University of York. Here, a full music degree was instigated at precisely the same time as Dart's in London. Mellers was likewise not concerned with traditional musical techniques but lectured extensively on the relation of the music of composers such as Bach, Couperin and Beethoven to much broader human concerns. Unlike Dart (who, despite a strong advocacy of electronic music, wondered whether composition as a vocational art ought to perhaps be taught elsewhere), he was particularly keen to appoint lecturers who were creative composers or practical musicians. Perhaps most significantly of all, he was the first major figure in British music study to admit popular music as an unquestioned subject of serious academic study, producing critical analyses of Beatles releases almost as soon as they appeared (East and Rumson no date).

A further twist to the 'Kapellmeister' tradition was that which was instigated by the imperatives of musical high modernism during the post-war decades. This almost inevitably set itself against the Anglican musical culture that lay behind traditional music degrees, and particularly against the sorts of music it tended to approve and promote in the last half of the twentieth century. To the modernist, the latest church idioms of Herbert Howells and other Anglican stalwarts (together with their French 'co-conspirators' in suffocating conservatism, such as Maurice Duruflé) must have seemed entirely complacent and philistine.[9] A particularly telling example of this attitude was embodied in Alexander Goehr's Cambridge from the late 1970s, where the faculty of music became something of a parallel, if not antagonistic, world to the college culture of vanguard Anglicanism. Advanced composition and theoretical analysis were the leading intellectual subjects, but supported by a fully integrated history of the entire western high art tradition, world music, acoustics and the traditional 'Kapellmeister' arts of aural and keyboard skills, harmony, counterpoint and examination fugue. Here, in effect, the traditional degree was refreshed and reaffirmed, but purged of its more utilitarian, churchy, functions, and now combined with education in the entire culture of canonic classical music (together with at least some of its 'others'). All this was designed to serve the imperatives of an essentialist historical progress in the Hegelian tradition.

Programmes conditioned by this ideology were also typical of those American departments that were dominated by late modernist imperatives in the post-war era (after all, the US greatly benefited from the influx of Austro-German high modernists just before the Second World War, not least Schoenberg himself).[10] In this environment, an abstract study of counterpoint (usually of the Fuxian species variety) was seen as an essential foundation both for voice-leading analysis (most of Schenker's students were working in the US) and for composition in the most advanced serialist idioms. Although this type of curriculum shares much with the British 'Kapellmeister' variety, it tends to lack the exercises in stylistic imitation and base itself around abstract rules of harmony and counterpoint, largely in the belief that the underlying principles of great music are universal and only superficially inflected by historical change. Only the 'internal' historical development of music really matters. It is perhaps this formalist approach to music as an autonomous art that made so many US departments prime targets for the 1980s revolution in 'new historicism' and 'new musicology'; in other words, a complete turn away from the abstract and universal to the historical and culturally contingent, away from the sanctity of autonomous musical logic towards human meaning, away from the belief in unconscious historical urges governing the acceptable developments of musical language, and towards the uncovering of hidden cultural prejudice.

To sum up the situation as it stood in the UK from the 1960s to the late 1980s: the Robbins recommendations both permitted the 'Kapellmeister' tradition to continue, at least as long as there were faculty who saw it as the essential ethos of a music degree, and they also allowed maverick academics to take programmes in new directions. The opportunity to broaden the scope of what could be covered by a music degree was clearly in place by 1963, but it was not until several decades later that this became more of an imperative.

The first factor in the need for change was the dramatic increase in the number of students studying at university, with a third of the available population enrolled by 2010 (see above). As Robbins states, in 1962 only about 8 per cent of the eligible population was in full-time higher or further education (9.8 per cent of men and 7.3 per cent of women). If universities only are considered, these figures reduce to 5.6 per cent for men and 2.6 per cent for women, thus a total of 4 per cent of the population. If the part-time further education figures are included (which are not generally relevant for music degrees), the proportion was slightly better, at least for men, at 22.4 per cent, with women still only at 7.9 per cent (Robbins 1963, 17–21). Therefore, although there was clearly something very laudable about suitable students being fully educated in classical music culture regardless of their background or means, the numbers (with only 4 per cent of the total population going to university) were still extremely small.

Moreover, if a music degree is designed to produce a generation of music directors, leaders and teachers, there is an obvious limit to the number actually needed (even if the number of students possessing the necessary talent or attainment is somehow increased). So, increasing student numbers would automatically bring in students who were not necessarily suited to the range of 'Kapellmeister' careers, but who might otherwise benefit from some sort of study of music (not least in music beyond the classical sphere). In order for music to survive as a subject within the numbers game of contemporary higher education, the quantity of eligible students undoubtedly has had to be raised; it has also become imperative to raise the proportion of music

22   *John Butt*

students coming from the state sector, something which further skewed the intake against the intensity of 'pre-Kapellmeister' skills in which many private schools excel.

It is precisely the diversity of what might count as a degree in music that is the essential message of the *Subject benchmark statement for music*, issued by the Quality Assurance Agency for Higher Education in 2002 and then in a revised version in 2008, which was further amended in 2016 (QAA 2008, 2016). The statement is addressed both to conservatoires and universities, which itself shows a much more generous opening of disciplinary boundaries than had been common during the previous century. This was surely conditioned partly by the need for solidarity within the community of music HEIs, providing a united front against a sequence of governments that were (and continue to be) considered by many in music and academia, to be hostile to any endeavour that does not provide firm quantitative results.[11] It is clear from the structure of the document and the categories it covers that its template was designed by the QAA as a way of providing benchmarks for measuring the quality of the institutions, their disciplinary coverage and teaching, and of the students and the skills they attain.[12] But, in terms of the actual content of the document, it is difficult to imagine any area of study, or type of study, being excluded from a music degree. Indeed, the authors resolutely refuse to prescribe any fixed parameters for the study of music: 'subject areas within music are constantly evolving and each HEI creates its own subject boundaries' (QAA 2008). To put it bluntly, a government or university official engaging this document as a pretext for curtailing musical activity in an HEI, on account of the irrelevance or datedness of the programme concerned, would find little of support here. In fact, much of the benchmark statement reads rather more like a celebration of the range and diversity of music education in the UK, and it could almost be used as a manifesto for music's role in education in general.

In most respects, it is difficult to argue with such a positive manifesto: 'music is intrinsically interdisciplinary and multidisciplinary, international and multicultural'. The authors trace the ancient Greek heritage of music in both poetic inspiration and meditation on the cosmos, together with an outline of its traditional place within the quadrivium. It also traces the diversification of music provision from the standard models of conservatoire and university, as established in the early and late nineteenth centuries, respectively (QAA 2008: 6–7). There is clearly an attempt to make a strong case for music's centrality to the human condition, as if this document were a modernization of the ancient system that gave music such a privileged position: 'The diversity inherent in music degrees gives rise to perhaps the broadest skill base in any subject, with students frequently crossing the boundaries between the arts and humanities, the social sciences and the physical sciences' (QAA 2008: 13).

There is perhaps only one telling omission regarding the range of skills that may be acquired by the student, and this relates to the traditional discipline of stylistic composition (and indeed the notion of full competence in western harmony and counterpoint). The only mention of this comes under the umbrella of composition, as a creative and largely individualised art: 'Some elements of compositional craft and technique may be developed through exercises using historical exemplars and by historical and aesthetic reflection' (QAA 2008: 16). In other words, stylistic disciplines might have value for a composer learning from the experience of impersonating past idioms, but no longer is this seen as essential for performers or those working in text-based study of music. Apart from a brief reference to the role of exercises designed to cultivate familiarity with 'traditional concepts' (QAA 2008: 12) in relation to the study of music theory and analysis, it is striking how much the traditional 'Kapellmeister' components relating to stylistic compositional techniques are underemphasized.

On the other hand, with the notion of music's unique place at the crossroads of so many disciplines and enhancing a multitude of career pathways, it could be argued that this document (and the culture that it so enthusiastically describes) represents an updating of the 'Kapellmeister' ideal. Although no student could possibly embody all the possible skills relating to music, it seems that most will come with a broad range of transferrable skills, which provide them with a remarkable versatility and the ability to cope with a wide range of situations. In short, there would be a strong case for describing today's music graduates as all-rounder twenty-first-century 'Kapellmeisters', but now with a much broader concept of 'the musical', enabling them to enter a far wider range of careers, both within the arts and beyond.

To the degree that the benchmark statement accurately describes the diversity and richness of music in UK higher education, it is difficult to complain about the overall picture. Nevertheless, there is the clear possibility that some courses might now be sacrificing depth of coverage for openness and breadth of approach. Even with the best will in the world, it is unlikely that many students will be graduating with the type of musical literacy that sustained the older 'Kapellmeister' tradition. And this also implies that the number of graduates with a deep immersion in the classical tradition is likely to have greatly decreased. It is now essentially (and not necessarily wrongly) one tradition among many, no longer the music that is held up as the peak of 'civilized' culture.

This trend is also replicated at the secondary education level, where there is a marked reduction in classical musical skills and the admission of a much broader range of music. In the Scottish context, school leavers intending to study music might now have little or no experience in western art music and are expected to only possess theory and practical skills of 'Grade 4 or above' ABRSM level (SQA 2014).[13] Without this drastic reduction in traditional requirements – many have claimed – music as a subject would not have survived at all in school. And, just as the 'Kapellmeister' style of education was self-generating (in that a very large proportion of music graduates

24   *John Butt*

themselves became teachers), now the process works in reverse, by which many school pupils are now being taught by teachers who are trained in few of the traditional skills and indeed might have very little enthusiasm for the western classical tradition.

Therefore, if anything of the 'Kapellmeister' tradition is to survive in the university context, it has to be taught from very first principles at university level (as indeed it has always been in the US, where high school education was never influenced by what Dart would have described as 'organ-loft' culture). The question then becomes one of how much effort ought to be put into this 'remedial' education, particularly given that even if this took up the entirety of the curriculum, the overall level of attainment would most likely be much lower than it was during the four decades after the Second World War. In other words, a balance would have to be found between new and often very rigorous skills that were absent from the traditional music degree, and any desirable remnants of the 'Kapellmeister' system.

Music in the classical tradition is often assumed to require a greater level of specialist skill and training than most of the other arts. It is arguably 'less natural' than most other forms of music and requires a sort of technological immersion that is not unlike that found more generally in western industrialization from the eighteenth century onwards. In other words, individuals generally no longer understand the whole process of production, technology, municipal administration and currency. Most of us use mobile phones, without the slightest knowledge of the range of technologies that make them work – we do not generally consider them to be magical, but rather the product of an enormous range of embedded knowledge and practice. With classical music, those who appreciate it do not necessarily have any knowledge whatever of its detailed construction, and are only aware of its emotional or intellectual effect. Indeed, part of the skill of a composer is surely to make a piece of music convincing and moving for the untutored listener. The same goes for performers, many of whom have little knowledge of the essentials of tonal harmony and counterpoint, even if they are at the top of their field. It is, of course, possible for some performers to gain from this sort of knowledge and skill, but not a necessary condition (the same might also be true of many genres of composition). And perhaps it is worth noting that classical music has thrived as a public (and private) art since the seventeenth century, without its consumers necessarily knowing much about its techniques. What is important for its survival is perhaps some sort of 'connoisseurship' (just as in art history, where even the trained connoisseur might have mastered very little of the technique of painting). Might it then be possible that the short period of universal 'Kapellmeister' style education, from *c.* 1945–90, was not actually as vital to music culture as it is sometimes believed?

This situation engenders further oddities: if all the rules of tonal composition are historically contingent (i.e. some valid for several hundred years, others for only a few years or in a certain place), what is the point of learning them today? An affirmative answer must lie in the view that learning the skills and parameters of possibility within one culture will give us an experience that can be applied to the rigorous mastery of another type of music. Even so, this attitude would tend to privilege the music that comes with some sort of theory and that tends to expect a disciplined approach to creativity. Furthermore, although we may all understand and enjoy tonal music of the classical tradition, and can follow its various historical changes and developments, no longer do we have a contemporary 'state of the language' for contemporary art music. The move towards diversity has affected composition as much as it has the study of music as a whole. Without a unitary range of parameters by which to judge musical achievement (something that the world of quality assurance and research 'excellence' has made a sort of imperative), the diversity both within art and other music poses a problem for critical judgment. Perhaps the best that can be hoped for is that education in both skills and criticism accustoms students to search for the markers of quality that are somehow appropriate for each particular genre. Here the popular music field provides an interesting context: the language, so far as the tonal tradition is concerned, can be very conservative and often crude, something that anyone could (indeed, should?) pick up without tuition. But its virtues surely lie much more in its performative elements, its lyrics and its interaction with technology and current cultural concerns. Therefore, it would surely be incorrect to discuss it on anything like the same terms as the classical tradition (whether negatively, as a sort of degradation, or positively, as something 'more natural' or more relevant to contemporary human concerns).

In short, there seems to be little point in learning tonal harmony and counterpoint if the sole purpose were to compose in a contemporary tonal style. There may well still be some mileage in the Robbins doctrine that learning any one discipline with depth and rigour often provides skills transferrable to others, and this is amply echoed by the benchmark statement. But it is clearly impossible to affirm that skill in tonal techniques accords one some sort of mystical knowledge ('of the way that music correctly goes') that conditions one's judgment about any musical style or creative activity whatsoever.

So far, then, there is perhaps only a weak justification for continuing to include tonal skills in the music curriculum. Indeed, there is now also emerging the deeper issue of whether the classical tonal tradition still belongs to us', despite being historically completed (at least in terms of the trajectory of tonal development from say 1550–1950, beyond which the directions seem to multiply in ways that arguably preclude a sense of historical development). If it doesn't, then the techniques of harmony and musicianship are obviously the work only of the archaeologist. This is not the place to discuss this question in detail, but if there is a sense in which this tradition remains ours, then living within it, going through some of the same experiences and problematics as its original composers (and of course performers

26   John Butt

and listeners) must have some relevance, even if it is almost impossible to ascertain exactly what this might be. If, as I have argued elsewhere, the classical music tradition is of a piece with 'modernity' in the western world (and equivalent movements beyond it), then it must have some relevance if we are still concerned with the modern condition (Butt 2010). I relate modernity to a gradual progression from the era of Reformation and Renaissance, through the scientific revolution, the birth of the nation state, the Enlightenment, and into the capitalized and industrialized worlds of the nineteenth and twentieth centuries. This movement (by no means universal and often working side-by-side with many 'traditional' factors) engenders a particular range of individualities, empirical experimentation, methodology, division of labour and – most important – the acceptance of productive artificiality. The latter might range from forms of artificial polity based on democratic representation to useful virtual constructs (such as paper money, or indeed the financial system itself). All these issues (just like industrialization and capitalism) bring advantages and disadvantages, but quests for 'authenticity' or the 'natural state' (whether anti-technological or ethnocentric) tend to bring almost as many problems as they solve, particularly if we follow, for instance, Max Weber's (1958) stories of the development of 'instrumental reason' and 'disenchantment', and acknowledge the fact that much of our world and its concerns rest on 'necessary fictions'.

In short, the tonal classical tradition is of a piece with the origins and fibres of the world we have inherited, its arbitrary rules and forms of methodology engendering a sort of 'second nature' that may help exercise our broader cultural consciousness. Learning something of the rules of harmony and counterpoint may not necessarily make us more 'musical', but they will show how music of the utmost interest and beauty in the western tradition is the product of a complex, artificial practice, which itself has little directly to do with 'natural', unmediated musical urges. Perhaps western classical music should be considered a sort of 'fiction'; but if it is, it may remind us of how so many aspects of western culture have relied on necessary, useful fictions, ones which are hard won and which, if done well, can affect us to the core. Of course, abstract study of this sort of music is very much surplus to most utilitarian requirements we might have; indeed, the whole field of western art music is a costly art, one which has never securely yielded profits. But, in the spirit of the Robbins report, there is much to be gained from exercising a specialized discipline if this gives us the flexibility and adaptability to face unexpected challenges. The case for broadening the bounds of musical education to include any and every possible aspect of serious study is absolutely indisputable, but the retention of at least some aspects of the 'Kapellmeister' tradition has the potential to give us insight into the workings of a music that remains contemporary – through its fragile ubiquity – while also embodying something of our cultural roots and values. Universal ignorance of how composers in the classical tradition actually managed to compose could, at best, lead to a sense of mystical awe that entirely misses the very human struggle between creative urges and the historically evolving, arbitrary, rules, a struggle that makes this music valuable in the first place. If classical/art music does not become a narrow, isolated, quasi-religious practice in its own right, but one we recognise for the artifice it actually is, it might even help render us more resistant to the current culture of quantification, monetization and targeted production.

Notes

1 It is interesting to note that, as outlined below, performance was indeed a feature of the two Scottish universities teaching full degrees in music before the Second World War.

2 Johannes Mattheson (1681–1764) was an extraordinarily prolific German writer about music. His best-known work, *Der vollkommene Capellmeister* of 1739, outlines in the greatest detail the range of roles that a musical director would have to undertake (while 'Chapel Master' originally referred to a building, it came to relate to choirs and orchestras, in short any musical establishment – usually in a court – that required a musical director). The Chapel Master's skills would include the utmost versatility but also a rigorous and deep study of the theory and practice of music (Mattheson 1739).

3 Statistics for student graduations at universities in the UK show a growth from 17,300 in 1950 to 331,000 in 2010 (a rise from 3.4 per cent to over 33 per cent). Although a substantial part of this rise derives from the incorporation of polytechnics as universities, which took effect in 1994 and doubled the university population of around 100,000. But the growth accelerated dramatically from 2000 (Bolton 2010).

4 The announcement of the closure of the music department at Exeter University in 2004 hinged around its deficit rather than the specific content of the course, but there is no doubt that attracting a greater range of students, together with the consequent income, would have afforded it more protection (BBC 2004).

5 For a detailed study of the foundation of the Edinburgh Music Faculty, see Field 1994. Important primary documents include the *Edinburgh University Calendar*, 1900–1901. Tovey's comments on Niecks's pioneering work, together with a short essay by Niecks himself, are to be found in the *Souvenir of the Twenty-Fifth Concert of the Reid Orchestra* (McEwan Hall, Edinburgh, 4 March 1920, conducted by Professor D.F. Tovey. I am most grateful to Dr Christopher Field for providing access to these materials.

6 Glasgow's music degrees were also comprehensive 'Kapellmeister' courses. A remedial non-graduating course was set up for students who did not have the necessary school background in music in 1930 (University of Glasgow Library Special Collections, Court minutes: 9 October – 1930–1, p. 9) and the BMus was set up a few months later (Court minutes, 12 March 1931, p. 18). The BMus (University of Glasgow Library Special Collections, Senate minutes: 3 March 1932, p. 92) consisted of harmony, counterpoint, form and practical analysis, organology, history (this involved the works of just Handel, Bach, Haydn and Mozart), acoustics, performance and a further elective subject in performance. The specifications for the MA (Senate minutes, 24 May 1934, p. 104) were very similar (the main difference being that study of music would have been shared with that of other subjects), albeit with the addition of orchestration and a dissertation. I am most grateful to Prof. Marjorie Rycroft for providing access to these materials.

7 According to Picketty, in Continental Europe, the 'Trente Glorieuses', the thirty years spanning the late 1940s to the late 1970s was a period of unusual growth,

28   *John Butt*

but with low capital and high debt. Despite this being seen as the 'norm' from which they have deviated, Piketty notes that in historical terms, this era is the exception rather than the rule. He shows very clearly that both public assets and public debt peaked around 1950 while private and public capitals were simultaneously at their lowest level.

8 The Robbins report has continued to stimulate broad discussion, particularly when its central principles are perceived to be under threat. For a significant intervention along these lines, see Collini 2011.

9 I have very strong memories as a student in Cambridge 1979–82, when I would, in the morning, hear a distinguished lecturer scornfully dismiss what he saw as the lazy and conservative idiom of contemporary church music, and then, in the afternoon, accompany King's College choir in the selfsame repertory.

10 In this regard one might consider the respective influences and styles of approach of Milton Babbitt at Princeton (from 1948) and Allen Forte at Yale (from 1968).

11 Moreover, the most important structural factor in the demise of the university-conservatoire divide was the abolition of the division between universities and polytechnics (and thus, by extension, conservatories) in 1992 (QAA 2008: 9).

12 After all, the QAA (2016) describes its intentions for the Benchmark Statements on their website as follows:

> Subject Benchmark Statements set out expectations about standards of degrees in a range of subject areas. They describe what gives a discipline its coherence and identity, and define what can be expected of a graduate in terms of the abilities and skills needed to develop understanding or competence in the subject.

13 The Associated Board of the Royal Schools of Music (ABRSM) offers graded music exams, assessments and diplomas. The grade 4 exam in Music Theory tests basic rhythm; harmony is only introduced at grade 6. The syllabus for the grade 4 exam in piano includes J. S. Bach's two-par Invention in BWV 772 and Schumann's 'Jägerliedchen' from *Album für die Jugend*, Op. 68 (ABRSM 2016). Most established universities require grade 8 for entry into performance-focused music degrees.

Bibliography

ABRSM [Associated Boards of the Royal Schools of Music]. 2016. 'Our exams: Motivating students of all levels and ages'. http://gb.abrsm.org/en/our-exams/. Accessed 3 August 2016.

BBC [British Broadcasting Corporation]. 2004. 'University Confirms Subject Cuts'. *BBC News Channel*. 20 December. http://news.bbc.co.uk/1/hi/education/4105961.stm. Accessed 13 February 2016.

Bolton, Paul. 2010. *Education: Historical Statistics*. House of Commons Library: 4, 14. www.parliament.uk/briefing-papers/SN04252.pdf. Accessed 13 February 2016.

Breen, Edward. 2015. *Thurston Dart and the New Faculty of Music at King's College London*. King's College London. https://issuu.com/ahkcl/docs/thurston_dart_and_music_at_kcl?e=16507444/12965715.

Butt, John. 2010. *Bach's Dialogue with Modernity: Perspectives on the Passions*. Cambridge: Cambridge University Press.

Collini, Stefan. 2011. 'From Robbins to McKinsey'. *London Review of Books* 33(16): 9–14.

Cook, Nick and Mark Everist, eds. 1999. *Rethinking Music*. New York: Oxford University Press.

Cudworth, Charles and Richard M. Andrewes. No date. 'Cambridge'. *Grove Music Online. Oxford Music Online*. Oxford University Press. www.oxfordmusiconline. com/subscriber/article/grove/music/04642. Accessed 13 February 2016.

East, Leslie and Gordon Rumson. No date. 'Mellers, Wilfrid'. *Grove Music Online. Oxford Music Online*. Oxford University Press. www.oxfordmusiconline.com/ subscriber/article/grove/music/18340. Accessed 13 February 2016.

Education Act 1962. 1962. www.legislation.gov.uk/ukpga/1962/12/pdfs/ukpga_ 19620012_en.pdf. Accessed 13 February 2016.

Farmer, Henry George. 1947. *A History of Music in Scotland*. London: Hinrichsen.

Field, Christopher D. S. 1994. '100 Years On: The Genesis of Edinburgh's Faculty of Music', *Musical Praxis* 1: 1–8.

Griffiths, David and John Paynter. No date. 'York'. *Grove Music Online. Oxford Music Online*. Oxford University Press. www.oxfordmusiconline.com/subscriber/ article/grove/music/30706. Accessed 13 February 2016.

Grout, Donald J. 1960/2014. *A History of Western Music*. 9th international student edition, with J. Peter Burkholder. New York and London: W.W. Norton & Company.

Mattheson, Johannes. 1739/1981. *Der vollkommene Capellmeister*, Hamburg. Trans. by Ernest C. Harriss, as *Johann Mattheson's Der vollkommene Capellmeister: A Revised Translation with Critical Commentary*. Ann Arbor: UMI Research Press.

Kerman, Joseph. 1985. *Contemplating Music: Challenges to Musicology* [Alternative title in the UK: *Musicology*]. Cambridge, MA: Harvard University Press.

McCrea, Andrew. 1998. 'British Organ Music after 1800'. In *The Cambridge Companion to the Organ*, edited by Nicholas Thistlethwaite and Geoffrey Webber, 279–98. Cambridge: Cambridge University Press.

Piketty, Thomas. 2014. *Capital in the Twenty-First Century*. Trans. Arthur Goldhammer. Cambridge MA and London: Belknap Press of Harvard University Press.

QAA [The Quality Assurance Agency for Higher Education]. 2008. *Music 2008* (Subject Benchmark Statement). www.qaa.ac.uk/en/Publications/Documents/ Subject-benchmark-statement-Music-.pdf. Accessed 13 February 2016.

QAA. 2016. 'The UK Quality Code for Higher Education: Subject Benchmark Statements'. www.qaa.ac.uk/assuring-standards-and-quality/the-quality-code/ subject-benchmark-statements. Accessed 13 February 2016.

Robbins, Lord. 1963. *The Robbins Report: Higher Education*. Her Majesty's Stationery Office. www.educationengland.org.uk/documents/robbins/robbins1963.html. Accessed 13 February 2016.

SQA [Scottish Qualifications Authority]. 2014. 'Higher Music Course Support Notes', www.sqa.org.uk/files_ccc/CfE_CourseUnitSupportNotes_Higher_Expressive Arts_Music.pdf. Accessed 13 February 2013.

Thistlethwaite, Nicholas. 1990. *The Making of the Victorian Organ*. Cambridge: Cambridge University Press.

Weber, Max. 1958 [1921]. *The Rational and Social Foundations of Music*. Translated and edited by Don Martindale, Johannes Riedel and Gertrude Neuwirth. Carbondale: Southern Illinois University Press.

Wollenberg, Susan. No date. 'Oxford'. *Grove Music Online. Oxford Music Online*. Oxford University Press. www.oxfordmusiconline.com/subscriber/article/grove/ music/20620. Accessed 13 February 2016.

Workers' Music Association. 1945. *A Policy for Music in Post War Britain*. London: Workers' Music Association.

2 The learning community, a quodlibet

Martin Parker-Dixon

> I think it is very difficult to do philosophy if you do not have a kind of terminological certainty. Never tell yourself that you can do without it, but also never tell yourself that it is difficult to acquire. It is exactly the same as scales on the piano.
>
> −Gilles Deleuze (in Conway 2010, 134)

Quodlibet |ˈkwɒdlɪbɛt|
noun

1. Archaic: a topic for or exercise in philosophical or theological discussion.
2. Literary: a light-hearted medley of well-known tunes.

1. Preface

The 'quodlibet' was one of the ancient forms of disputation popular in the medieval university. It was a free-style, quick-fire form of questioning and answering that could take place during appointed feasts or seasons (like Lent), and could deal with less onerous, extracurricular problems. Something like the modern 'formative assessment', the quodlibet provided an opportunity for masters and scholars to try out what they had acquired in terms of skill in argumentation. I treat my task in this chapter as essaying an argued response to one such occasional, general question: the question I have in mind runs something along the lines of 'what, today, ought we to teach in university music departments?'

My short answer to this question is as follows: in parallel with everything else we traditionally teach (or might want to teach) in university music departments, we *ought*[1] to reacquaint ourselves with the techniques of rigorous argumentation; namely, with the *arts* of positing theses, explaining them, defending them from objections and counter-theses; with the arts of defining our terms, of using evidence, of evaluating other people's arguments, of producing novel ideas or theories and of examining their

The learning community, a quodlibet 31

consequences. Behind this call to a return to argumentation there is a reaffirmation of the principles that the art of music must be treated as an object of serious intellectual enquiry and that in universities our responsibility is to ask serious questions of music, and work through them with all the intellectual means at our disposal. We also have an obligation to set our thinking before others in our community so that it can be appraised, and so that others can learn from what we are doing. My basic point is that these ancient obligations, as well as making the study of music in the university distinct from study in the conservatoire sector, are worthy and eminently useful.

It seems to me, for example, that without explicit skills in argumentation we are failing to honour a core obligation of the modern university, that of being critical. For while we can talk about the importance of 'thinking critically', its application is not without its difficulties. Strictly speaking, being critical gets underway when we examine the propriety (the reasonableness) of certain assertions or beliefs (Brandom 2000, 193). Criticism does not simply declare a given assertion or belief wrong; being critical is more interested in the peculiar manifestation of inconsistencies or partialities in the way a belief is formed, and in the beliefs that might arise as a consequence of it. These factors can be obscured by the very workings of thinking and judgement, contradictions that consequently inhibit the development of new ideas and perspectives. Criticism produces a *crisis* in thought, a turning point and a change of mind. These changes of mind, these reappraisals of what we think we know, are celebrated as the decisive experiences of learning.[2]

However, what occasions and initiates critical examination might be something like a visceral reaction to an opposing view, an affront which is not itself reasoned through or understood. I am not in the least certain, however, that antagonism represents the ideal circumstances for the carrying through of a critical agenda. For examining propriety of an assertion requires one to treat it as a piece of reasoning, as worthy of time and attention, despite the fact that it might have frailties or deeply unpalatable consequences: criticism actually requires one to participate in and understand what others are trying to articulate despite what our personal reactions might direct us to do. For example, because racism is an affront to me, my inclination would be to denounce the racist, to silence him. But to be critical of racism requires me to hear him, engage with him and understand what is fuelling his hatred, and point out where, and why, his reasoning and analysis is faulty. In this case, critique treats racism as a form of incompetent or bad reasoning, one which can and must be corrected, not as an instance of irredeemable evil.[3]

If we are going, as I think we must in a university, to think critically about music and culture, it follows that we must treat everything about music and its associated discourses as material for reasoning, and not as a sphere to indulge personal prejudices, even if these are framed as oppositional 'debates'.

32   *Martin Parker-Dixon*

This calls us to learn and practice the fine-grained activities of analysis, discrimination, construction and re-construction, and to resist being dismissive or reactive.[4] If we extend this principle and think of music as a critical practice in its moment of production, we must similarly explore the argument that reasoning has a role to play in making music as such; that composition and performance can be subject to reasoned justification and intellectual enquiry. This is a view that might not sit well with the belief that music is all about gut feeling, or that instinctive, intuitive or unconscious processes are what count most when 'creating' music. It would be quite foolish to insist that there were *no* such processes at work in making music, all I would say is that we need to be vigilant that these more speculative kinds of theories do not prohibit or invalidate discourse and reflection on these processes by way of a kind of threat: 'you mustn't think too much about music or you will spoil its *magic*'.

More prosaically, in my way of thinking, in a university it is indeed a problem if something that is carried out under its auspices believes itself automatically exempt from being discussed in ways which satisfy normative criteria for evaluation and justification. While many worthy artistic products might indeed be appended with only one defiant remark, 'take it or leave it', in the university context, a posture which asserted 'I have nothing to answer for, and what is more, I have nothing to answer for because I am an artist' produces an unfortunate schism in the university community: one constituency must make and defend a case which stands up to close scrutiny, while another can present their work and let it 'speak for itself'.[5] While our evaluations can be extremely well rehearsed, and our preferences deeply ingrained, I do not think that it is possible that the value of artistic work is simply self-evident or obvious: there is always *something* that could be said about our evaluations. An interesting test for my approach would be to show that I can incorporate practical and creative working into the learning community. I will return to this in section 8 the Lemma on the performer and the composer in the learning community section.

So much for the short answer. The longer answer appears below. In it I am trying to practise what I preach and write self-consciously in a more rigorous manner than is usual for me. I try to set out ideas and their interrelationships using a style reminiscent of Spinoza's *geometrico tractatus*, his 'geometric handling', the expositional style evidenced in his *Ethics*. There are various reasons why I find this mode of writing attractive and worth experimenting with. Spinoza, as a rationalist, was attempting to strictly deduce defensible propositions – or in modern parlance 'theorems' – from something close to first principles. One appeal of this approach is that anything arrived at deductively really ought to be considered valid (supposing that the premises are also valid), and that such conclusions 'compel assent'. Which is to say, valid conclusions (i.e., as in the famous syllogism establishing the mortality of Socrates) are the kinds of things that all right-minded persons ought to agree over.

The learning community, a quodlibet 33

As in a legal dispute, coming up with a cogent route to a robust conclusion – informally, being 'right' – could be said to mean that the argument is over and the opposition silenced (Novaes 2005). A settled argument also looks very much like the discovery of a *truth*, a proposition that could be thought to have universal application and permanent validity. Examples of non-trivial truths would clearly be pearls of great price.[6] However, in the university context I am trying to model, the conclusion of a piece of reasoning is no more important than the sheer consideration shown to others by demonstrating one's working, the laborious business of spelling out what is being assumed, what is being challenged, and of showing how and why one idea leads to another. This demonstration is what admits others into my thinking and its methods; and, if there is anything of value in what I am doing, others can take hold of it relatively easily and make use of it for themselves. Demonstration removes that air of pronouncement and decree that turn academic authoritative 'opinion' into a parody of itself. By emphasising demonstration, the significance of 'truth' is being redistributed to the whole process of articulation, and is no longer concentrated in the outcomes – the terminal judgements – that are arrived at by reasoning. Instead, I would be inclined to say that it is the truth of a demonstration which is of interest, and this truth has conventional and ancient criteria: truth maintains a level of disclosure, it should not deviate from its task, and it is wary of complication for its own sake (cf. Foucault 2011, 218–9).

What I have taken from Spinoza – what I have found useful – are some of the various phases through which his argument proceeds: the prefaces, axioms, propositions, definitions, demonstrations, corollaries, scholia, explanations and lemmas which are the building blocks of the intellectual edifice which is the *Ethics*. These I treat as the equivalent of data types in programming languages: they stipulate and restrict the kinds of operation that one should expect to be performed on them.[7] An axiom is the kind of statement that will not have any particular need for further comment since it is obvious or a 'given'. While it may be a given, it is still worth declaring because the argument will rely upon it to some degree. A proposition is a statement which is not being treated as obvious, but is standing in need of some further elaboration or proof. A demonstration attempts to deliver the required support in terms which are logical and explicit. A scholium is a marginal note or comment, perhaps indicating a point of interest rather than anything which is absolutely vital to the progress of an argument (Deleuze 1988, 28–9). The reader can be made aware that this phase in my argument, the preface, is also another of Spinoza's discursive kinds.[8]

I have, though, taken the liberty of including an additional discursive type which I am calling objection, a peremptory, contradicting voice which moves this paper away from a closed scheme of deduction into the genre of dialogue. In this I am following another great model of scholastic thinking, the *Summa Theologica* of Thomas Aquinas, which proceeds with almost painful deliberateness through a series of 'articles', questions and

34   *Martin Parker-Dixon*

objections. Each set of questions is furnished with an initial and predictably inadequate set of answers which are promptly overturned by vastly superior interpretations given by Aristotle (whom Aquinas calls, simply, 'The Philosopher') and Holy Scripture. This manner of proceeding resembles a rather staged encounter between hapless students (whose ideas are not fully worked out) and the authoritative corrections of their theological Masters. Though formulaic, the dialogical presentation of arguments is compelling, and it is a good reflection of the pedagogical practices of the time.

2. The argument

Below is set out the outline of the first part of my argument. It will be followed by short digressions (I term these lemmas) exploring issues that arise from this argument. Point (δ) can be called the main contention of the argument, a claim which, if taken to be reasonable, can be used to generate some insights into the priorities of music education today:

(α) [*Axiom*]: A university is a *community* of scholars.
(β) [*Proposition*]: Scholars are committed to *studying*.
(γ) [*Proposition*]: Study is the dedication to the improvement of one's *understanding*.
(δ) [*Proposition*]: Scholars have an *obligation to make available* to the university community their understanding of a particular subject.
(ε) [*Theorem*]: Scholars ought, therefore, to practise writing and speaking in discursive modes which facilitate the distribution of ideas and methods, and provide opportunities for constructive engagement.

2.1. [Comment]

Statement (α) can be treated as *axiomatic*, that is to say, it is tantamount to being self-evidently true since it adapts the Latin *universitas magistrorum et scholariam*, meaning a 'community of masters and scholars' and it is from this phrase that the modern word 'university' is derived. By definition, a university is always already a community. It can be noted that in my analysis, however, I have not found it necessary to inscribe the role of 'master' (or teacher) as a distinct category over and above the student or scholar, and in the interests of simplicity I have omitted the term.[9] In my account, the community I envisage contains only *one* category, the scholar.

2.2. [Objection]

It might be objected that you have taken a liberty here by eliminating the ancient role of 'master'. After all, is not the reputation of a university based on the standing and fame of its professors?

2.3. [Sed contra]

To begin with, admission to, and remaining a member of, the university community as a student is conditional on demonstration of a sincere interest in studying and the continued commitment to learn. A student who takes no interest in learning would not be admitted in the first place, and should they give up any ambition to learn, and thence decline to attend lectures or submit assignments, they will, in any case, be suspended from university. And similar conditions apply to academic staff as well, since they themselves are enjoined to continue learning, though in their case their learning is called *research*: they must be 'research-active'. All I am suggesting is that while some members of the university community might be more advanced than others in terms of the depth, extent or sophistication of their learning (or research), they can all be located on a continuum by which there is no essential difference between their activities or responsibilities; there is absolutely nothing in principle to prevent a student from being well ahead of their 'masters' in some aspects of music. Setting aside cynicism, in my view, for any university that is attempting to honour its basic constitution, *all* members of the community are *always learning*. Further to that, it is worth mentioning that in its modern incarnation, any teaching that takes place in the university is, or ought to be, 'research-led'. I take seriously the statement set out in clause 2 of the *Fundamental Principles* of the *Magna Charta Universitatum* (1988) which states: 'Teaching and research in universities must be *inseparable* [my emphasis] if their tuition is not to lag behind changing needs, the demands of society, and advances in scientific knowledge.' I will endeavour to sustain this principle in my interpretation.

2.4. [Demonstration]

With regard to proposition (β), before addressing my definition of study, I will defend the claim that scholars are *committed* to studying. Or, in terms which amount to the same, they are *dedicated to a field* of study. For it can be noted that dedication and commitment are transitive: we are dedicated or committed *to something*. Generally, in universities we can say this is a field of study, or a particular historical period and such like. So if scholars have a disposition to study, they will tend to be drawn into attending closely to an object of study, they will prioritise that object, and concentrate their powers upon that object. The verb 'study' comes from the Latin *studium*, meaning zeal, eagerness, keenness and painstaking application – as in Hildegard von Bingen's hymn 'Studium divinitatis in laudibus excelsis osculum pacis Ursulae virgini cum turba sua in omnibus populis dedit.' Scholars study because they are devoted.

2.5. [Objection]

In fact, is not proposition (β) effectively a pleonasm, a kind of logical redundancy?

36   *Martin Parker-Dixon*

2.6. *[Sed contra]*

The point is well made. However, the modern English usage of 'study' might not immediately connote that sense of devotion or commitment; today we might hear in the word something more like toil and drudgery, with the goal of getting through some exams.

2.7. *[Scholium]*

In Spinoza's understanding, an object which strikes one as being *singular* will stimulate devotion (along with other related affects, like wonder and veneration (see *Ethics* III, 52, 97)). What is *singular* has little or nothing in common with other things; nothing that is singular can be subsumed under a common term and grouped with other things. If, in the mind of a music scholar, one composer is much like another, then she has no inclination to consider one particular composer for any longer, or with any more intensity, than any other.[10] In such cases, her attention can drift from this to that music with alacrity, and whatever can be said of one thing can be said of another.[11] Without saying *why it is* a scholar should have become so devoted,[12] we can acknowledge that devotion will entail an attachment to, and a concern with, a *particular* object or objective. Logically, the narrower the concern, the stronger the devotion. Academic specialisms can arise very naturally from this pattern.

2.8. *[Corollary]*

The relationship between a scholar and his or her subject is very special. A scholar must be studying the right kind of subject for them: and the right kind of subject is one that they can genuinely be devoted to. There is a reflective question for the scholar here: where does the focus of one's genuine interests lie? It is also possible to consider the possibility that whatever a scholar devotes themselves to become a subject; a scholar creates for themselves an object of study by their work and investment by creating new concepts. This inverts the view that a subject or discipline comes first and that scholars are conditioned to serve and obediently extend certain principles or paradigms that are at the core of the discipline.

2.9. *[Theorem]*

Another aspect that justifies calling the university a *community* is that scholars have this sense of devotion (or a capacity to be devoted to something) in common, they recognise and respect it in each other. Those that progress in the university system are those that uphold this dedication to learning throughout their careers.

The learning community, a quodlibet 37

2.10. [Objection]

That might be true, but while scholars do not have the *object* of their devotion in common, surely the consistency of the community will be in jeopardy. Will not each scholar retreat into their own private specialism and find themselves increasingly unable to engage others? Worse still, perhaps this suits the interests of the scholar who would prefer to guard their personal fascinations from the interference of others.

2.11. [Sed contra]

I agree that this is a danger, which is why I am advocating that thought be given to the arts (and culture) of argumentation and disputation, since these are useful means for opening out our thinking and encouraging participation from others in ways which remain faithful to the constructive purposes of learning, and are not simply disruptive or injurious. In addition to the private specialisms and disciplines of modern academia, I am wondering if there is not good reason to insist that they give over at least some of their time to one meta-discipline of argumentation with a view to honouring their relationship with their community.

3. Lemma on learning and desire

3.1. [Definition]

In the following, *learning* is understood as increasing or enhancing the capacity to *act* in various ways.[13]

3.2. [Postulate]

The learner learns most effectively if they have a *genuine interest* in increasing or enhancing their capacities: that is to say, if they identify something that they would very much like to be able to do and are prepared to work at achieving it. Put in psychoanalytic terms, learning is advantaged (rendered more focused, concentrated and energetic) if it is mobilised by *desire*.

3.3. [Example]

The phenomenon of curiosity, the determination to solve problems and wanting to find out how something is done – or what something means – all share a moment of desire.[14]

3.4. [Corollary]

Further to §3.2, one can envisage a case whereby an able and talented person is in a position to enhance their capacity to act in some respect but for one

38   Martin Parker-Dixon

reason or another does not wish to do so, and is not prepared to invest their energies in that way, i.e., not everyone who has the potential to sing very well will want to sing very well. Various scenarios can be drawn in which learning is complicated or disrupted because desire is not intrinsically well mobilised in the act of studying: think of covert means of distraction using technology, self-doubt and self-sabotage, or the positing of rewards or incentives which lay *outside* the sphere of study (if I study hard I will get a good job). This can be read in connection with the definition set out in §3.5.

3.5. [Definition]

With reference to the concept of desire, two Lacanian formulae will apply: (i) *Desire desires desire*; and (ii) desire is the *desire of the Other*. These formulae are useful in that they invite us to consider that desire is not subject to an economy of satisfaction which would entail the extinction of a given desire as such; rather, desire seeks to be renewed and revivified without cease. And secondly, it is not necessarily the case that *our* desires are phenomena of a putative and private inner life; we need not refer to our desires as to obscure innate drives and forces. Rather, our own desires and enthusiasms can be stirred by and modelled on the desires and enthusiasms of *others*. We desire by way of a supposition regarding what (and how) others seem to desire. Our desires are thoroughly socialised.

3.6. [Example]

Today, it is not uncommon for composers to be photographed in remote locations, wearing serious expressions and looking moodily into the middle distance.[15] Such pictures furnish a succinct *imago* of the activity that these composers are *supposedly* engaged in: their artistic struggles bring them to spiritually and intellectually isolated states; their work is deep and serious, and they regard things far beyond the purview of ordinary people. These images and their interpretations are not necessarily any direct reflection of what composers actually do or how they themselves might wish to be presented.[16] These suppositions are the anonymous discourse of the Other, it can be taken without comment that this extremely limited repertory of postures encapsulates 'what everyone knows' with regard to composers and their work. Nevertheless, the *imago* of what it is to *be a composer* might, for some, present appealing ways of being: as a composer one can mark oneself off from the herd; one is left alone to explore one's ideas, technical and expressive problems; and these misunderstood endeavours could be greeted with a certain admiration by the public and critics, or, indeed, considerable resentment.

Consider also how the judgement 'cool' is used in everyday discourse. If *x* is judged to be *cool*, the implication is that other people will also desire and esteem (and perhaps envy) x. 'Cool' is often used to register esteem for the latest consumer gadget, and indexes covetousness.

3.7. [Theorem]

We can conclude that in some cases, wanting to *be* a *musician per se* precedes and motivates the arduous task of learning the art of music. Certain key figures or roles within the industry ('I want to be a film composer') hold together, unify and stabilise the very disparate and mundane tasks relating to what it is to be a musician.

3.8. [Theorem]

From §3.2. and §3.5 (ii), in principle, learning can continue indefinitely.[17]

3.9. [Objection]

If there is any truth to the theorem at §3.7, then it might be that the university is unable to support the learning of a student because the institution cannot share the desire of the learner. This will result in the alienation of the desire and the subsequent disillusionment of the student.

3.10. [Sed contra]

I can only concur while emphasising that this is the positive function of critical thinking: university education shatters the *imago* of the musician (by arguing that 'thou art *not* that'), and questions those rather illusory patterns that hold together music and musicians in wider culture.

4. Lemma on understanding

With regard to proposition (γ), the word 'understanding' requires some attention. So:

4.1. [Definition]

Study results in a better understanding of something. In my interpretation, 'better understanding' amounts to *concept acquisition*. At the risk of circularity, to understand understanding I have to acquire a conceptual grasp of understanding. If I have a conceptual grasp of understanding, I will be able to *explain* (which is simply to talk about or show by means of illustrations) how certain words can be used, what certain sentences or judgements can be applied to someone else and in such a way that they might 'get' what understanding means. If they get understanding, there is a chance that they might

40   *Martin Parker-Dixon*

be able to explain it as well. Explanation is a means of distribution; what is being distributed is the ability to *use* certain concepts.

4.2. [Scholium]

Here I will follow the philosopher Robert Brandom's inferentialist explanation. To begin with: 'An assertion, even if true, is not taken to express knowledge unless the one making it *understands* the claim being made' (Brandom 2000, 214). In this statement, assertion (or claiming), truth, knowledge and understanding are all coordinated. Let it be noted that in the first instance, the uttering of statements that happen to be 'true' does not make such statements 'knowledge', and neither does it make those that utter them *bearers* of 'knowledge'.

4.3. [Demonstration]

A boy is given a simple addition to carry out: 'what is 7+5?' If the boy, by way of response, merely suggests numbers off the top of his head until he hits upon an answer his teacher accepts as correct, he could not be said to fully *understand the concept* of addition (any more than a hat understood the concept of addition because numbers were being pulled out of it). To begin with, he will be entirely reliant on someone else to confirm or disconfirm the success of his guessing (without whom he would be proposing candidate answers indefinitely without ever knowing whether or not he had fortuitously uttered the 'right' one); but more importantly, a number of auxiliary practices would be impossible for him: there is a no chance that he would be able to add other pairs of numbers together, and he would be unable to *explain* how a correct answer could be arrived at to anyone else. What is philosophically interesting about our incompetent mathematician is that, in Brandom's terms, he is not and cannot be *committed* to any of his arbitrary attempts at an answer, none of them is advanced with confidence or in such a way that he could *insist* or *show* or *defend* that he was indeed *correct*. In short, he could not be *claiming* that 7 + 5 = 12, he was only *hoping* that it was.

Making a claim is a peculiar activity which implies that we are prepared to *reason* about our claim, even if this is only to a very limited extent.[18] Claiming means that we should be prepared to stick up for our claim by giving more information in response to queries such as 'what do you mean by...?' In Brandom's terms, a claim constitutes a move in an interpersonal *game* of reasoning:

> A practical grasp of the significance of making the claim is inseparable from an appreciation of its role as possible reason for other claims, and as something that reasons can in turn be offered for. It is being caught up in this way in the game of giving and asking for reasons that makes a performance the undertaking of a commitment (the making of a claim)

The learning community, a quodlibet 41

in the first place. Unless one accords one's own performance such a significance (treats it as a move in that game), one is not making a claim, not undertaking a commitment that is eligible for the status of knowledge.

(Ibid., 214)

As a pragmatist, Brandom is happy to emphasise that claiming, reason-giving and reason-asking are in no way *mysterious* mental activities that take place unseen and unaccounted for, they are practices and activities that can be rehearsed, improved, discussed and philosophised about.

4.4. [Theorem]

Knowing something is *being able to do* something, namely maintain ourselves in a game of reason-giving such that we can demonstrate, to the satisfaction of others, our knowledge.

4.5. [Demonstration]

Understanding, because it is caught up in a practice of reason-giving and asking, can dovetail with a myriad of other claims and reasonings. If $7 + 5 = 12$ is properly understood then we will know with confidence, and be able to commit to, the fact that $5 + 7$ yields the same answer. We can conclude that the order in which numbers are added together does not affect the result, and I can provide examples to prove it.

At some later stage I can learn that this property has a name, 'commutativity'. Someone asks, 'if addition is commutative, presumably subtraction is also?' Someone who understands these matters says, 'Actually no, subtraction is non-commutative. Here is an example: $7 - 5 \neq 5 - 7$.' The questions continue: 'I don't understand, what does that peculiar sign "$\neq$" mean? All this seems to rely on certain conventions. When and how was the manner in which these calculations are notated and processed agreed?' Someone who has a competent understanding of addition (this knowledge has an historical aspect also) will be able to deal with questions like this. Learning deeply about these concepts will be a process of learning to make, commit to and defend claims such as 'subtraction is non-commutative'.

4.6. [Proposition]

The game of asking for and giving reasons is the *sine qua non* of university discourse.

4.7. [Demonstration]

Brandom is making a general point about asserting and understanding one another; it is a point which is to be applied to all meaningful discourse.

42 *Martin Parker-Dixon*

Whatever one might think about these ideas, at the very least, I think Brandom describes very precisely the nature of *university* discourse. These commitments to practice participation in a game of asking for and giving reasons are generally more closely and scrupulously observed by members of a university and are evidenced throughout all the set pieces of academic performance: seminars, lectures, books, essays and papers. Outside the university (in that strange place called the 'real world') we also assert things, but on the whole, we might not expect or tolerate provocative and searching questioning about our assertions, and neither are we placed in *formal* relations with one another whereby one party explains in well-referenced detail some feature of the world to others. Indeed, speaking to each other like that might seem very unusual or misplaced, and we would rightly be told to 'stop lecturing'.

No, in the real world, what we say, believe or value is not generally 'up for discussion', it is our *right* to say, believe or value as we do. It is sufficient that we should aspire to have a forum to voice our thoughts.

4.8. [Proposition]

What is special about the assertions and claims that take place in universities is that we all, as members of a learning community, have a *duty* to answer as best we can *any* question that is asked of us in connection with our claims. By the same token, we are free to enquire into any problem that interests us.

4.9. [Demonstration]

Can one countenance a university in which certain questions or approaches were not permitted? Where someone was told not to 'rock the boat'? Or some of its members felt that they were free to ignore certain difficult questions and their implications? This would be a university that was organised around the privileges of power and status, and believes that it did not need to listen to reason.

5. Lemma on university hierarchy

5.1. [Proposition]

Further to §2.1., the difference between a junior member and a senior member of a university is the degree to which they can be held responsible for what they claim.

5.2. [Demonstration]

In practice, a senior member *might* be able to hold their own in a game of reasoning for a great deal longer than a junior member. They make claims that are more robust, more useful, more far-reaching, etc., and they can withstand the pressure of cross-examination much better. Senior members can draw upon more experience, and have more command of the implicit knowledge that can inform their claims. Such would justify their status and 'authority'. Equally, searching questions from 'junior' members could make a real impact on the arguments of a more senior member, especially if something crucial had been missed. There ought to be nothing in the organisation of the community that would prevent such an eventuality.

5.3. [Corollary]

Advancement in the community of learning, and passing thresholds such as graduation, are an intrinsically community matter; it is a matter for the community to decide when (and to what extent) a person has gained sufficient performative authority in a certain field.

6. Lemma on authoritative judgement

6.1. [Proposition]

Musicological writing is primarily composed of judgements.

6.2. [Demonstration]

Let us consider a piece of prose from a highly distinguished musicologist, Joseph Kerman:

> Like *Haec dicit Dominus*, *Circumdederunt me* stands out as one of Byrd's greatest works in the mournful vein. If it is less austere in mood and less extreme in technique, that may in the last analysis reflect Byrd's mature response to the two main types of text which called for this kind of expression, one political, one personal. Though both motets count technically as Dorian *Circumdederunt me* employs a more limited harmonic range, never extending to the Phrygian Eb that colours *Haec dicit Dominus* (and *Vide Domine*) so vividly. The music is almost programmatically Dorian.
>
> (Kerman 1981, 173)

This text presents a series of strongly worded *judgements*. A judgement (which takes the form 'an *a* is *b*') draws concepts together into cogent and meaningful relationships. Because the concepts that are drawn together are not intrinsically associated by virtue of their meaning, they can be termed *synthetic* judgements.[19]

In this passage, Kerman is making a string of comparative assertions which bind, via a copula, a work (a Motet) to certain evaluations or qualities.

44   Martin Parker-Dixon

i   *Circumdederunt me* is in the mournful vein.
ii   *Circumdederunt me* is one of Byrd's greatest works (in the mournful vein).
iii   *Circumdederunt me* is less austere in mood (than *Haec dicit Dominus*).
iv   *Circumdederunt me* is less extreme in technique (than *Haec dicit Dominus*).
v   *Circumdederunt me* is in the Dorian.
vi   *Circumdederunt me* is more harmonically limited (than *Haec dicit Dominus*).
vii   *Circumdederunt me* is almost programmatically Dorian.

Which bracket a more speculative assertion:

viii   Judgements (iii) and (iv) may reflect Byrd's mature response to the two main types of text which called for this kind of expression.

Given an understanding of technical vocabulary ('Dorian', 'harmonically') there is nothing intrinsically difficult in these statements, and most competent essay writers would be able to cite, perhaps via techniques of precis, these authoritative judgements in their own work, i.e., 'Kerman takes *Circumdederunt me* to be an interesting example of a motet in the Dorian mode.' Or, 'For a good example of a Tudor motet which is somewhat austere and mournful, Kerman suggests *Circumdederunt me*.'

Now, knowing that Kerman made a certain judgement (the consequence of doing some reading) is advantageous for someone wanting a foothold in musicological writing relating to Tudor motets; *understanding* what he means (comprehending), and *being able* to redeploy them in one's own prose (writing) are similarly useful for those needing to produce essays and assignments of their own. However, there is a sense in which a manner of writing that *only* transposed the judgements of other (worthier) people from published books into one's essays would be as odd as writing things like 'Kant states that 7+5=12' in place of actually doing some addition for oneself.

6.3. *[Proposition]*

It is not just the content of judgements themselves that matters to the learning community, it is the distribution of the *capacity to make judgements* that is important.

6.4. *[Demonstration]*

I would suggest that what the novice reader of musicology lacks is an appreciation of *how* Kerman managed to formulate these sophisticated judgements in the first place, why they might be plausible, or how (if at all) they might be opened up to query. Kerman states that *Circumdederunt me* is less 'austere' than *Haec dicit Dominus*: how does the concept of *austerity* play into the appreciation of these motets? It can only really be the outcome of some form of material quantification, the comparison of a meaningfully large set of works from a certain genre, across which (it can be argued) Byrd demonstrates technical 'generosity' (presumably meaning more intricate counterpoint, more voices, more melisma) in response to some texts, and 'austerity' for some others. Of course, in a more interactive environment this line of thinking could be verified with a direct intervention along the lines of 'is this what you mean by austerity'? But in any case, what is decisive here is that we actually go through for ourselves the procedures – the leg work – that might have led to this judgement.

We can add that the *truth* of such judgements (in the sense of it 'really being the case that' *Circumdederunt me* is mournful and great), if treated as a stand-alone characteristic, or indeed a verdict, is something of a distraction. What matters is going through the transitions and phases of a process of reasoning, weighing up evidence and considering the consequences of various assertions. If I, as a scholar, participate in such processes and practise my reasoning, my judgement-making can develop similar levels of authority. In terms of the operation of a learning community, the pronouncements of an authority are motivational: they provide ideas that are, on balance, worth working with and following up, and should not be treated as Holy Writ.

7. Lemma on taste

7.1. [Objection]

This is all very well, but you were speaking earlier of mathematics, a discipline which enjoys enormous conceptual clarity from the outset. Yet didn't your favourite musical thinker, Adorno, say that musicians were truants from the maths class? What, then, of music? For was it not well said, *de gustibus non est disputandum*, 'matters of taste cannot be disputed', and is not music controlled by personal taste? Neither do we have to account for and explain our private pleasures and enjoyments, our recreation. Does not cold analysis and hair-splitting conceptual wrangling simply ruin the simple pleasure of musical experience? Does not art – and especially music – bypass reason all together? And while I'm about it, what has music to do with *linguistic* performance? If it has any dealings with language, is it not as a language of emotion? Of mute, internal communication of soul to soul? If we want to speak of two cultures, an ancient and venerable culture of disciplined, discursive reasoning, and a culture of sensibility and feeling, music belongs to the latter. And what is more, this is the 'real world', a world which lives and dies with the passions of real people.

7.2. [Response]

Indeed, in my own experience, I've heard it said often enough that study actually spoils one's affection for music. For a minority of its members, university study seems to ruin whatever interest they may have had for music, and they abandon it as a field of formal study altogether. And even if a scholar could maintain their affection for music while studying it, it is not yet clear that studying (formal study, learning to reason about music) would benefit them as musicians since they, *qua* musicians, are in communication with an audience, and what interest would the audience have in taking up the cause of reasoned argumentation, especially when the forceful mobilisation of partial interests, identifications and emotional needs seems much more urgent and frankly more enjoyable?

However, I make the following point:

7.3. [Proposition]

The obligations inherent in a community of learning, and the operations of the socio-economic sphere of consumption are simply *incompatible*. Therefore, to think of one in terms of the other is a *category mistake*.

7.4. [Proof]

Let us consider two existential categories (ways of being in the world), one relating to *striving* and one to *recreation*. As was set out earlier (γ), the scholar strives to *understand*, such is their devotion. This is mentally effortful, requiring enormous concentration and resilience. However, human energy is a finite resource: one cannot strive indefinitely without resorting to some form of *recreation*. By definition, the sphere of recreation occasions no striving (the pleasures of recreation should come easily and unbidden). Neither should we be concerned with our duties, in recreation we are not *obliged* to anyone else for this enjoyment is a private matter. Any requirement to justify, defend or account for our personal pleasures draws us into interpersonal entanglements and obligations which are anathema to recreation.

We can conclude that music – like other arts subjects – is ambiguous as it is both an object of serious study and application (and therefore of striving), and it has a very well-established role in providing for recreation and enjoyment. These roles are, though, conceptually and practically distinct.

7.5. [Corollary]

One could also suppose that a relationship pertained between the two categories: the restorative effects of recreation enable us to return to effortful working. If we follow the suggestion of Spinoza and agree that the 'human body can be affected in many ways in which its power of acting is increased or diminished' (Spinoza 1994, 70), the act of listening to music designates a private, well-ordered sphere of repose (the formula is 'sit back and relax') in which our requirement and opportunity to *act* is suspended. Any responses to the music are not categorised as actions (defined as the constructive realisation of an intention), they are *reactions* or 'passions', and as such are not

The learning community, a quodlibet 47

subject to any accounting or justification, but instead arise 'naturally'. The effects of recreation temporarily diminish our power of action but when we are returned to our actual responsibilities, we are better able to face them because we have enjoyed a period of respite (hence the Marxist's usual reproach that the culture industry is complicit in the operation of capital).

8. Lemma on the performer and the composer in the learning community

8.1. [Objection]

There is an acute point of tension here that you have missed: those engaged with the serious study of music (like performers and composers) are called upon to provide recreation for those that are not (I refer to the listening public). The interests – or even rights – of the audience to be entertained and amused continually encroach on the interests of those that are striving for ever-greater excellence in their art. Surely there must come a point when all such striving becomes redundant (merely 'academic' in the pejorative sense) because no 'ordinary listener' could possibly have the discrimination to enjoy high levels of sophistication, or have the time to learn about new repertories, or have the patience to have their preferences and inclinations 'challenged' by difficult music. Without some sort of equalisation in the interests of these factions, the result is confusion, miscommunication and alienation. I'll quote Spinoza back at you: 'The idea of any thing that increases or diminishes, aids or restrains, our body's power of acting, increases or diminishes, aids or restrains, our mind's power of thinking' (1994, 76).[20] Might not the audience (or suppositions regarding the audience formulated by artistic directors and other cultural gatekeepers) haunt and inhibit the musician's actions (simply, the sounds they are prepared to make in the presence of others) and consequently the ideas they are prepared to entertain. The 'audience' or the market exerts an inertial and moderating force in the strivings of the artist.

8.2. [Response]

The analysis is correct. And because nothing in culture is made in a vacuum, it is of the utmost importance to sort out one's alliances and state them clearly. For it is quite legitimate that an artist should propose to work moderately and conservatively with genres that the public might tolerate and even take pleasure in (the music of the young American composer Timo Andres fits this brief rather well): as far as the learning community is concerned there will still be plenty to talk about, discover, assert and argue. Likewise, it is quite legitimate for an artist to pursue a line of enquiry as far as it will go without considering the interests of the potential audience, for they will not need to fear complete isolation: they are always in a position to talk about, explain and ask for help and encouragement from within their

48 *Martin Parker-Dixon*

community. My only concern would be if one interest group took it upon themselves to annihilate what they saw as a competing position by settling once and for all the illegitimacy of a certain way of making music.[21] In as much as musicology is also *for* a readership, the same considerations apply to the writing of musicology.

8.3. [Proposition]

The model of understanding set in section 4 represents a counterposition (or, if you like, an antidote) to the 'slave' interpretation of musical performance (Nichols 2011, 321).

8.4. [Demonstration]

Generally, for good or for ill, I would suggest that classical performing musicians are, at the outset of their learning, more preoccupied with proper conduct, discipline, formality, of 'right and wrong', of not making mistakes and so forth, than performers working in other art forms. Musical performance seems to have a rigorously *executive* function: this interpretation could conceive of a musical score as embodying a set of more or less explicit instructions which are simply to be *obeyed* by the performer and in such a way that the *self* of the musician is not put at stake. There might be much to respect aesthetically in the fact that the musician is not personally invested in the music they are playing, and is instead working in a detached, precise or abstract way with their performative 'duties'.

However, introducing a deontic inflection into this description, it could also be suggested that the score asserts an implicit imperative, an intricate *thou shalt*, i.e., 'thou shalt play *these* notes, and only these notes, as accurately as possible'. All too familiar ideological patterns emerge: scores mediate composers' intentions, performers do what composers tell them to do, musical works demand (and get) *absolute respect* from all concerned, be they performers, musicologists, consumers or record companies.

Is there a problem with these patterns? Perhaps there is if, for example, the virtue of respect precipitates less attractive phenomena such as intimidation, anxiety, or a sense of personal inadequacy in the face of the towering masterpiece. And worst of all, what if a sense of duty suppresses dimensions of conduct that could be vital to art, such those of *irresponsibility, freedom* and *play*. Such would be Nietzsche's view:

> [N]othing does us as much good as a *fool's cap*: we need it in relation to ourselves – we need all exuberant, floating, dancing, mocking, childish and blissful art lest we lose the *freedom above things* that our ideal demands of us. It would mean a relapse for us, with our irritable honesty, to get involved entirely in morality and, for the sake of the over-severe demands that we make on ourselves in these matters, to become virtuous monsters and scarecrows. We should be *able* also to stand *above* morality – and not only

to stand with the anxious stiffness of a man who is afraid of slipping and falling at any moment, but also to *float* about it and *play*. How then could we possibly dispense with art – and with the fool? – and as long as you are in any way *ashamed* before yourselves, you do not yet belong with us.

(Nietzsche 1974, 164)

If musical culture has produced its fair share of 'virtuous monsters and scarecrows' this might be because a performative obedience (not 'slipping and falling') and indeed an *affective* obedience, being in the thrall of the music and striving to establish in oneself an affective disposition that is adequate to the music, can be too easily *substituted* for understanding and reasoning. As Deleuze puts it, 'all that one needs in order to moralize is to fail to understand. It is clear that we have only to misunderstand a law for it to appear to us in the form of a moral "You must"' (Deleuze 1988, 23).

8.5. *[Theorem]*

If a performer *gives reasons* for what they do – if they can respond to reasonable enquiries about what they are doing and why – then they have a legitimate and constructive role in a learning community.

8.6. *[Scholium]*

Furthermore, performers also change their relationship to what they do: performance becomes an action, an activity carried out under a description. If a performer analyses[22] the piece they are intending to play, performance takes place under the aspect of interpretation, and the interpretative process shifts performance into a *space of reasons* (cf. Sellars 1963, 169). By virtue of this investment, the performance becomes an action. Put another way, the performer *qua* interpreter is then in the position of making a *claim* about the music they are playing as they are playing it. Here, the claim amounts to proposing that the manner in which the music is being performed has certain virtues or merits that could be discussed and endorsed. An interpreter is responsible for the music in a way which transcends mere obedience. In inferentialist terms, the performer thus becomes *committed* to what they perform (they are in a position to state and defend their interpretative decisions) and are therefore *entitled* to their performance (they are answerable for it, implying that the interesting aspects of the performance don't just unaccountably happen as a kind of brilliant accident).

8.7. *[Proposition]*

The meaning and intelligibility of everyday, reasonable *linguistic* performances, and the meaning and intelligibility of *musical* performances are subject to the *same description*, and both demonstrate the virtues of commitment and entitlement.

50 *Martin Parker-Dixon*

8.8. *[Demonstration]*

A performer is not *entitled* to her performance if she merely goes through the motions and plays the score accurately and obediently. However, understanding the music is just like understanding reasonable linguistic utterances: she could formulate reasons why the music is the way it is and satisfy herself that those notes are the 'right' notes and therefore *commit* to playing *those* notes. A committed performance is one that *implicitly* defends the belief that the work *is* as it *arguably ought to be*. This can only be achieved if we *reason* about the work.

8.9. *[Scholium]*

§8.8. is a general description of how analysis can be useful to the performer. Talking about the work in terms of an analytical reasoning (this can include prolongation graphs, set theories, or informal discourse) makes that defence *explicit*, but it does not make the defence perfect, final or absolutely 'correct'. Rather, reasoning about the work makes performance *corrigible*, capable of correction and development in such a way that, in Nietzsche's terms, we can 'float' above it; we are more able to generate additional strategies of reasoning about the work and thus keep the work and our relationship to it alive. Furthermore, if interpretative reasoning goes one step further (and perhaps presents ideas using very general schema), then we arrive at a kind of formalism or musical logic, a new level of explicitness, but one that is entirely dependent on the prior effort to establish the cohesion of the music as such as a lived or performed activity. The danger here is that rigour and explicitness are mistaken for finality, or for justification, or close off the possibilities for alternatives, for *play*. Musical formalism or logic is only a pragmatic metalanguage, a way of talking usefully about what we were already trying to do. The metalanguage can have the advantage of multiplying creative possibilities if we are challenged by a tendency to become fixated on narrow range of options.

8.10. *[Theorem]*

Everything that has been said with regard to the performer can also be said of the composer who works in the university.

9. In summary

My argument in this essay places a premium on the university musician striving to continually enhance their *conceptual* understanding of music. To demonstrate such an understanding requires musicians to participate in a language game of reasonable and dialogic elaboration on the aspects of the art of music that interest them. It seems to me that all the practical arts of music making can be fully and usefully integrated in this model.

The learning community, a quodlibet   51

I hope that what I have set out will not be read as a celebration of merely talking about music: reasonable talk is not 'mere' talk, talk which is vague, inconsequential or open-ended. Reasoned, dialogical talking is *worked through*, it can hold its own and it can make a genuine difference to the way we think and what we do. Because in the inferentialist account of understanding, knowing something is being able to do something, and because reasoning intersects language-use and action, it is very difficult to entertain a fundamental split of theory from practice, or assign theory and practice to different types of experience, or place them in some kind of hierarchy. Thinking rigorously about music is a genuinely creative thing to do, and making music can be genuinely thoughtful.

Bernard Shaw's quip 'Those that can, do; those that can't, teach' is in this light a false dichotomy. I would be more inclined to say that those that can't 'do' don't have anything to teach (and if such people happen to be teachers, they are, regrettably, bad teachers) and might be best deployed in trying to inculcate the basic 'knowledge' that was once passed to them in those who aren't really interested in learning anything for themselves. The situation I have been trying to describe is one in which those that *can* really do something well are trying to explain, hint, show, tell, challenge, upbraid, praise, draw out, motivate ... in short, *teach* those that are *also* striving to do something well. Importantly, at no point in this discussion have I invoked the principle that a learning community must be consensual or strive for agreement. The minimal condition for a learning community is that from time to time we listen respectfully to what others have to say, and try and understand them on their own terms.

Notes

1 I am using the modal verb 'ought' with a certain amount of moral intent, namely to signal the fact that I am stipulating an obligation.
2 To take one very striking example, the classical law of thought known as the 'law of the excluded middle' which states that either a proposition is true *or* its negation is true (i.e., $\vdash (A \lor \neg A)$), and that there is no middle way between these options, had currency for well over 2000 years. However, in the early twentieth century, the Dutch mathematician L.E.J. Brouwer argued that there were circumstances in which the law was not in fact valid, and a new branch of mathematics known as 'intuitionism' came into being as a result.
3 Here I am following Deleuze's (1988, 22) endorsement of Spinoza's ethical interpretation of the bad versus the evil.
4 Anecdotally, my undergraduate years were spent in an atmosphere in which modernism and the avant-garde were variously demonised, mocked or ignored. Serious and sustained access to the work of, say, the New York School, Boulez or Stockhausen was effectively barred for me because one set of dogmatic certainties (grouped under the rubric of modernism) had been rapidly replaced with another which valued representations of place, nation and personal feeling. On the whole, I would say that this change of perspective, while exciting, was, from an educational point of view, deleterious because a great many useful technical resources and aesthetic stances were simply abandoned, or reintroduced

52 *Martin Parker-Dixon*

incompetently under the new management of localised and rather arbitrary expressive intents and purposes.

5 One way to tolerate this position would be to accept that universities offer *de facto* patronage to composers, writers and artists-in-residence, for which they recoup publicity, impact and esteem. It might be artists need not be considered as part of the learning community at all, but are part of the economy of reputation that also preoccupies universities today. The current debate relating to practice-as-research and the composer's contribution to the REF process is in the background to this paper. I clearly believe that the composer can make a contribution to the learning community of the university, but institutionally, the patronage model also has its merits.

6 Consider Thomas Jefferson's assertion in the U.S. Declaration of Independence: 'We hold these truths to be self-evident, that all men are created equal, that they are endowed by their Creator with certain unalienable Rights, that among these are Life, Liberty and the Pursuit of Happiness.'

7 Programmers had to be wary of the fact that certain symbols could be subject to inappropriate and meaningless operations. In the C programming language it was possible to *multiply the character 'T' by the character '&' and get a numerical result. This makes no logical sense and produces chaos at runtime. The data-type CHAR can be introduced to indicate that what we are dealing with is indeed a character and not a number.*

8 An autobiographical note can also be posited. I suffer from chronic fatigue following chemotherapy treatment and one of the consequences of this is a degree of cognitive impairment: I have highly variable levels of concentration, attention and memory. What frustrates me more than usual is digression, revision and all the inefficiencies associated with my poorly structured writing practices. I have found these discursive 'types' or categories useful because they can define for me an economy of attention: at any stage of writing I have a fairly secure notion of where my efforts should be concentrated. The task of writing becomes distributed through a finite set of subsidiary activities: defining, stating, commenting, proving, inferring and so forth. In short, the little mental and physical energy I have *must* be well-directed if I am to produce anything. Such is the *causa efficiens* of this aspect of the paper. So, at the risk of opening another can of worms, as well as attempting to argue the case for argument, this chapter is also an experiment that arises in part from learning to live with a disability.

9 I will refer to scholars rather than students throughout, largely in deference to the ancient terminology. Aside from the question of simplicity, I also have in mind Lacan's (2013, 55) assertion that the role of the teacher in our social order is 'untenable'. He writes also: 'But, frankly, it isn't necessary to educate man. He gets his education all by himself. In one way or another, he educates himself. He must learn something, and that requires a little elbow grease. Educators are people who think they can help him.' (Ibid., 56–7.) I am more inclined to try and proceed in such a way that my argument does not divide the university constituency also these lines. I have no doubt that this approach betrays a political prejudice, a preference for non-authoritarian and horizontal styles of organisation mediated by the collective application of reasoning.

10 Just as a football fan cannot transfer his or her alliances arbitrarily (fandom necessarily entails loyalty), devotion can also entail hostility towards those who are differently devoted.

11 For an applicant seeking a place on an undergraduate programme in music, the declaration 'I like all sorts of music' is not, on the face of it, the talk of a scholar, only that of the average music listener. A well-focussed interest in a narrow area of music appears at once more promising.

The learning community, a quodlibet 53

12 Unfortunately this issue will be too distracting for my current argument. Folk psychological notions such as 'gifts' or 'vocation' will have to suffice.

13 Throughout I take the classical pragmatic position of prioritising *action* and echo the prejudice that 'in the beginning was the *deed.*' This expression, taken from Goethe's *Faust*, was also endorsed by Wittgenstein.

14 For myself, as an undergraduate I came to very much admire the intellectual depth and sophistication of T.W. Adorno's writing – and the Frankfurt school – especially in comparison to musicological writing that I was obliged to read for my music history studies. This admiration occasioned the desire to emulate this writing, an interest sustained me for 10 years or more, up to and beyond my doctoral thesis. In the current paper I am clearly emulating the Geometric Method.

15 A photograph on *The Herald* newspaper website on the happy occasion of James MacMillan's knighthood depicts the composer standing alone on a rocky, post-industrial wasteland, the ironwork of a pithead winding gear looming in the background. He stares contemplatively into the distance. The image drops a large hint that the dignity of artistic vocation is not assimilable to such courtly, 'establishment' rituals as being knighted.

16 We could, for example, imagine that in all likelihood they spend hours sitting in front of computers drinking coffee and making some rather finicky decisions about irrelevant details like most educated people in the Western world.

17 'Nothing other than the eternal entity of desire seems suitable for designating the variations that clinical experience uncovers in the interest that the subject takes in reality, and in the *élan* that sustains his conquest or his creativity.'

18 For instance, if this child said something along the lines of 'I split the number 5 into two parts, 3 and 2; I added the 3 to the 7 to make 10, then added on the 2', he would have impressed upon us his capacity to reason about the nature of numbers and the efficacy of staging mental calculations around multiples of 10. He would also have a reflective awareness of what he was *doing*.

19 The statement 'a bachelor is an unmarried man' is an analytical judgement because the subject contains the predicate. This is not true of any of Kerman's judgements.

20 It is worth mentioning that this statement is an instance of Spinoza's doctrine of parallelism, the idea that the 'mind's striving, or power of thinking, is equal to and at one in nature with the body's striving, or power of acting.' (Ibid., 85) In other words, Spinoza does not subscribe to the Cartesian dualism of mind and body. The doctrine of parallelism could be of the utmost importance to the musician who might find herself torn, as Schoenberg put it, between the 'heart and the head'.

21 This could be thought of as a language game that was played once only, and to the death.

22 In this context I conceive of an analysis as being occasioned by *questions* relating to the piece – e.g., how is the form of this piece articulated? What musical ideas are at play in this piece? – not as an exclusive commitment to an analytical methodology.

Bibliography

Brandom, Robert. 2000. *Articulating Reasons: An Introduction to Inferentialism.* Harvard University Press.

Conway, Jay. 2010. *Gilles Deleuze: Affirmation in Philosophy.* Palgrave Macmillan.

Deleuze, Gilles. 1988. *Spinoza, Practical Philosophy.* City Lights Books.

54   *Martin Parker-Dixon*

Foucault, Michel. 2011. *The Courage of Truth (the Government of Self and Others II): Lectures at the Collège de France, 1983–1984*. Palgrave Macmillan.

Kerman, Joseph. 1981. *The Masses and Motets of William Byrd*. University of California Press.

Lacan, Jacques. 2013. Translated by Bruce Fink. *The Triumph of Religion: Preceded by Discourse to Catholics*. Polity Press.

Nichols, Roger. 2011. *Ravel*. Yale University Press.

Nietzsche, Friedrich. 1974. Translated by Walter Kaufmann. *The Gay Science*. Vintage.

Novaes, C. Dutilgh. 2005. 'Medieval 'Obligationes' as Logical Games of Consistency Maintenance'. *Synthese*, 145/3: 371–395.

Observatory of the Magna Charta Universitatum. 1988. *The Magna Charta Universitatum*. [Last accessed: October 2016].

Sellars, Wilfrid. 1963. *Science, Perception and Reality*. Routledge.

Spinoza, Benedict de. 1994. *Ethics*. Penguin Books.

3 Integrative music history
Rethinking music since 1900[1]

Björn Heile

Some years have passed since David Clarke (2007) envisaged a historiography of music that would, in his words, narrate 'Elvis and Darmstadt' together.[2] As Clarke would be the first to admit, his call was not entirely novel even then. He cites a number of precursors (although, possibly because it typically doesn't 'narrate' music history, he neglects to mention cultural studies, an entire field for which the switching between and comparative study of high art and popular culture is arguably constitutive). Since then or concurrently, there have been many related projects, some of the most prominent of which are Nicholas Cook and Anthony Pople's multi-stranded *Cambridge History of Twentieth-Century Music* (2004) and Georgina Born's idea of 'relational musicology' (2010); many others have similarly combined investigation of classical and popular traditions without much explicit methodological argument (see, for example, Metzer 2003; Katz 2010; Piekut 2011; Kutschke and Norton 2013). If my idea of an integrative music history seems therefore to follow a well-trodden path, there are several reasons why I think it is worth pursuing that path further. One is that, despite our best methodological intentions and some laudable counterexamples, we seem to mostly continue to neatly compartmentalise music in our daily practice, whether in teaching or research. Most courses on twentieth-century music at UK universities or conservatoires are really about western classical music, and they may or may not be complemented by similar courses in popular, jazz, traditional or non-western music. Similarly, most music histories are scrupulously single-stranded: Richard Taruskin's monumental *Oxford History of Western Music* (2010) is a prominent case in point. Taruskin's (2010, xii–xiii) rationale is that he is focusing on the 'literate tradition', yet that doesn't stop him from devoting a chapter to Rock 'n' roll/Rock, which really is non-literate, whereas he fails to do so for earlier, notated, traditions of popular music, such as the popular song traditions discussed by Scott (2008), Tin Pan Alley or Big Band Swing. While literateness means more than the use of notation, there remains an inconsistency which can only really be explained by the impact 1960s youth culture had on the author himself. This is perhaps understandable but not a sufficient rationale for a historian, considering too that the effect of earlier forms of popular music was every

56   Björn Heile

bit as strongly felt as that of post-1950s ones. Even Cook and Pople's afore-mentioned *Cambridge History* (2004) serves as a counterexample in only a limited sense, since the different strands remain largely separate, presenting several parallel histories, rather than one interconnected one.

Another reason to pursue this path is that my approach is informed by teaching an integrative advanced-level undergraduate course on music since 1900 at the University of Glasgow, titled 'Aspects of Modernity'. This experience has taught me that, whatever role historiographical and methodological literature may have played in persuading me of the value of such an endeavour, it doesn't really address the practical difficulties, such as – pace Taruskin et al. – finding appropriate teaching materials. Although a level of methodological and historiographical reflection is appropriate at this level, students have the right to expect some taught content involving discussion of actual music. Here, suitable examples are surprisingly thin on the ground.

In the following, then, I want to not only present further reasons why we should seek to study musical styles, genres and traditions in relation to, rather than in isolation from, one another, but also provide examples of how this can be done. I will focus on the relationship between classical or 'art' and popular traditions within the western world.[3] A similar argument can be made about the binary between western and non-western music, but I cannot pursue this here.

Since I don't share Clarke's enthusiasm for postmodernist pluralism, I don't wish to recite the familiar litany of genre-busting, crossovers, iPod shuffle and BBC Radio 3 Late Junction culture (cf. also Gloag 2012). On the contrary, when it comes to questions of style and tradition, I often wish that differences were respected more, and I also believe that we owe it to our students to alert them to the specificities and subtleties of each style and tradition instead of emphasising often superficial similarities. To avoid mis-understanding, then, I am not primarily interested in the mutual influences between essentially separate traditions: as interesting and revealing the boundary-crossings of Debussy, Stravinsky, Charlie Parker, Frank Zappa, Sonic Youth, Brian Eno, Aphex Twin, Uri Caine or Bernard Lang (to name just some) may be, they typically confirm the existence of boundaries rather than negating them. Nor do I wish to argue, as Peter van der Merwe (2004) does with an earlier period, that at some deep-structural level, western music since 1900 is really much more homogeneous than it seems on the surface.

Instead, I wish to suggest that different musical traditions are intercon-nected *by virtue of* their stylistic differences. If we follow Andreas Huyssen's (1986) argument that modernism is a defensive reaction against the emascu-lating encroachments of mass culture, a contention that provided much of the impetus for Georgina Born's (1995) study of IRCAM, different musical traditions may implicate one another the more profoundly the more dis-tinct they are stylistically. Despite my reservations against both Huyssen's and Born's work, the general contention that certain but by no means all forms of modernist and popular music respectively are united by a mutual

Integrative music history   57

repulsion is well-founded and deserving of the same attention as is lavished on supposed mutual influence and boundary-crossings.[4] In this context, Adorno (2002, 292–93) spoke of the 'flight from the banal [whereby] serious music reflects in reverse [*als Negativ*] the outlines of light music', adding that:

> the unity of the two [serious and light] spheres of music is ... that of an unresolved contradiction. They do not hang together in such a way that the lower could serve as a port of popular introduction to the higher, or that the higher could renew its lost collective strength by borrowing from the lower [which, *in nuce*, is van der Merwe's argument]. The whole cannot be put together by adding the separated halves, but in both there appear, however distantly, the changes of the whole, which only moves in contradiction.[5]

An important aspect of my argument concerns the development of listening habits. Here, recent years have seen significant changes, even in our immediate environment: while among older generations of academics, the exclusive or near-exclusive commitment to only one type of music is still common, this is highly exceptional in my own generation. All the indications are that it is nearly unheard of among students (among whom, additionally, classical music is very much a minority concern). These admittedly informal and anecdotal observations are backed up by a wealth of sociological studies on musical taste (which are rarely cited in musicology, as if it didn't matter what people actually listen to). One of the most hotly debated issues in this field is the theory of 'omnivorousness', proposed originally by Richard A. Peterson and Albert Simkus (1992). Where earlier research, such as Pierre Bourdieu's (2013) classic study had suggested that high status is expressed in a preference for supposedly prestigious genres such as opera and classical music, Peterson and Simkus found that what they, somewhat contentiously, call 'high-brows' demonstrate their status by their omnivorous appreciation of a wide range of genres (cf. also Warde, Tomlinson, and McKeekin 2000).[6] Although 'experts' are a special category, it is fair to say that the general thrust of the theory chimes in with informal observations of the musical tastes of music students and lecturers.

What this illustrates is the need to remain alert to the specificities of each style and genre, which, given such listening habits, could otherwise too easily disappear in an undifferentiated cultural mélange. Nevertheless, what is demonstrated even more clearly is that the neatly compartmentalised musical culture depicted in traditional courses and textbooks is far from the reality most of us experience in our daily lives. While these two insights may occasionally be at cross-purposes, they do not necessarily contradict one another: the understanding that various styles, genres and traditions inhabit the same universe, variously attracting, repelling and interacting with one another can make us more rather than less aware of their differences.

What I am concerned with, then, is a social history of music, one that is interested in patterns of consumption as much as production, performance as much as composition, social functions as much as works. What I am

58   *Björn Heile*

arguing is that classical and popular traditions respond to the same underlying technological, political, economic and social developments, although they often do so in diametrically opposed ways. A comparative study of how different styles and traditions respond to such changes not only provides us with a bigger picture, but also reveals more clearly what is specific to each of them. I will present two such studies, one focusing on the impact of the incipient record industry on jazz and classical performance and one on the responses to and potentially involvement with the events of 1968 by classical, jazz and rock musicians. The first of these illustrates a divergence of musical developments, driven seemingly by mutual antagonism, the second if not a convergence, a certain parallelism between them.

Economy and technology: the impact of recording on jazz and classical music performance

It goes without saying that the impact of recording and, to a lesser extent, broadcasting on popular music was profound: the triumph of popular music in the twentieth century rested on the use of recording as the primary mode of dissemination. The same cannot be said about classical music, which by that time already had a long history behind it. Indeed, it is perhaps no coincidence that its entire canon is, if not pre-Edisonian, pre-recording in its fully commercial form.

Recording's impact on classical composition in particular is hard to gauge, but what is perhaps most remarkable is how stubbornly most composers have stuck to a model of dissemination that, in terms of media technology, has long been obsolete. With some notable exceptions, instrumental composers in the classical tradition produce works or pieces in the form of scores for live performance, which may or may not be recorded or broadcast.[7] Similarly, although its history aligns it closely with the radio, radiophonic and electronic composition are now largely separate, if closely aligned fields. Furthermore, electronic composers in the classical tradition have largely been resistant to associate their work too closely with a dissemination medium. By and large, they produce 'works', not tracks, albums or CDs. Only the increasing dematerialisation of music as sound files distributed over the internet may have brought about a closer alignment of classical and popular traditions in this respect (in general, it is in electronic music that distinctions between popular and classical traditions are most difficult to undertake). That said, the extent to which the wider aesthetics of classical music since 1900 and the musical imagination of composers have been affected by the development of recording and related technologies is impossible to gauge. The widely observed impact of electronic music on instrumental composition would suggest that this effect has been profound albeit often indirect.

When it comes to performance and consumption, however, the impact of recording and broadcasting has been felt every bit as profoundly in classical as in popular music. Most commentators agree that performance practice of classical music changed radically at around the time that recording became

Integrative music history 59

an economically significant activity (the 1910s–1920s) and, although it can be difficult to isolate it from other factors, most regard recording as one of the catalysts for those changes (Day 2000; Philip 2004; Katz 2010; Cottrell 2012). Generally speaking, this period saw a homogenisation of performance practice and a move towards fidelity to the written text. Informal practices, such as non-synchronised rubato, portamento, variant articulation and often extreme tempi were driven out in favour of a comparatively streamlined international style. Although the ideas of *urtext* and *werktreue* are of earlier origin, they came of age during this period (cf. Stephan 1994). According to Philip (2004), not only can the drastic changes in recorded performances be largely explained with the introduction of recording, but the latter also impacted significantly on concert culture. Up to the 1920s and 1930s, it was still common to play encores of individual movements, make significant cuts and so forth. A famous virtuoso such as Fritz Kreisler deliberately eschewed detailed preparation and rehearsal since he valued spontaneity more highly than polished, flawless execution (Philip 2004, 22). The availability of supposedly authoritative recordings and audiences' ability to compare what they heard with existing records soon put a stop to such practices. Similarly, the influential magazine *Gramophone*, founded in 1923, railed against cuts from the start, at a time when the playing time on 10 inch records effectively made this a technical necessity (Philip 2004, 30).

The recorded history of performance practices in popular traditions reveals the flipside of this story. The first form of popular music to fully embrace recording was arguably jazz. What distinguishes jazz from its precursors, such as blues, ragtime and marching band music, which largely stuck to notation or oral transmission, is that it adopted recording as its dissemination medium of choice. But this was far from a straightforward process: the cornettist Freddie Keppard, for instance, whom contemporaries regarded as Louis Armstrong's equal, was said to have refused a recording date since he feared that other players might steal his music (Souchon 1957, 45; see also Berliner 1994, 55); others, such as the legendary Buddy Bolden, never had the chance. Armstrong, by contrast, who, at this time, earned his bread in Fletcher Henderson's band, put all his faith in the still fledgling medium when he made his famous 1926–27 recordings with his Hot Five and Hot Seven, pure studio bands that did not play together live (Horn 2003, 13). In retrospect, it seems obvious to us why Armstrong is still a household name, whereas Keppard and Bolden are known only to specialists, but at the time Keppard's stance would have made good business sense to most. From then on, jazz's history is intimately connected with recording. It is the mobility of recordings that allowed performers from all over the world to pick up what used to be one of many local styles practised in the South-East of the United States and catapult it to global prominence with astonishing speed (Chanan 1995, 18–19), and it is its ability to capture the individual nuances of the playing of admired masters that enabled others to follow in their footsteps (Berliner 1994, 23–24; Rasula 1995, 141–42). As Frederick Garber (1995, 74), citing James Lincoln Collier, has put it: 'jazz

60   *Björn Heile*

would not have developed as it did, perhaps would not have developed at all, were it not for the phonograph'. Not only players relied on recordings, so did historians: what we know of the history of jazz, its genealogy of styles – New Orleans, Chicago, swing, bebop etc. – recited in textbook after textbook is based on recording. In this case, exceptions really do prove the rule: consider the importance of the recording ban between 1942 and 1944 in the history of bebop (DeVeaux 1988). An 18-month delay between a stylistic innovation and its global dissemination had already become exceptional.

As I see it, jazz's reliance on recording had a seemingly paradoxical consequence: the primacy of live performance in jazz myth. There are countless examples in jazz lore, attributed to this famous musician or that influential critic – the wording changes, but the essence is the same: in Rasula's (1995, 135) formulation, recording is 'a secondary substitute for the "living presence" of actual performance'. The reason for this rhetorical emphasis has to be found in the fact that live performance's status can no longer be taken for granted. This may also explain another rhetorical trope within jazz, namely the importance of improvisation. Jazz isn't the first and not the last form of music that makes use of improvisation, but, as far as I know, it is the only one to have elevated improvisation to the status of an ideology. This exalted status can only be understood through the fraught dynamics of recording and live performance in jazz: it is improvisation that guarantees the uniqueness of live performance. In a further twist, many famous improvisations have of course been recorded – and only that made them famous. In other words, although, as Walter Benjamin (1999) famously observed, recordings are subject to mechanical reproduction, what is captured on them is a unique unrepeatable moment – or that at least is jazz's promise, a promise underwritten by the ideology of improvisation (cf. Heile forthcoming). In actual fact, as Katz (2010, 83–85) has pointed out, during the 1920s and 1930s influential jazz recordings by the likes of Louise Armstrong, Duke Ellington, Jelly Roll Morton or Fletcher Henderson, contained much less improvisation than is typically assumed – indeed in many cases none at all – and were typically much shorter than live performances, which probably involved more improvisation. So, in that sense, the introduction of recording had a similar levelling and standardising effect on jazz as it did on classical music. However, in terms of the *values* associated with both musical traditions, recording had diametrically opposed effects on the worlds of jazz and classical performance respectively, the former leading to a celebration of spontaneity as embodied in improvisation, the latter to the hardening of *werktreue* ideals and the streamlining of performance practice and concert culture.

This comparison is instructive in itself, but there is also evidence that both cultures affected one another, essentially by depicting themselves as one another's opposite. Consider the relation between notation and improvisation. From around the 1920s onwards, the two appear as polar opposites, something we are still familiar with, although attitudes have softened in recent years. This dichotomy is a historical anomaly, however. Well into the nineteenth century and beyond, the two were part of a continuum. Even in classical performance, notation was rarely afforded absolute authority and forms of improvisation, notably by virtuosos, persisted (remnants of that practice, such as organ improvisation, have survived much longer, although that is arguably a special case) (Moore 1992). Similarly, the popular notion that jazz performers spontaneously pluck notes out of thin air is wide off the mark for most forms of jazz. In the 1920s and 1930s, there were probably fewer jazz musicians who were unable to read music than who were unable to improvise; Bix Beiderbecke's troubled career is an indication. Nicholas Cook (Cook and Pople 2014, 224–47) has compared Corelli's Op. 5 with a lead sheet for a jazz standard, arguing that, particularly in the slow movements of the Corelli, performers were expected to richly ornament the skeletal notation. A similar comparison can be undertaken between how a nineteenth-century opera singer would treat an aria and how a performer in an oral tradition renders a tune. There is no unbridgeable gap between these traditions.

My contention is that, concurrent with the development of the recording industry, practitioners in each genre, jazz and classical music, increasingly emphasised what they regarded as distinctive about their art. It is admittedly difficult to find unequivocal proof for this hypothesis, but it is instructive that many scholars have voiced similar ideas. For instance, Philip (2004, 180–81) has argued that:

> one of the points that recordings make is that performance of classical music used to have rather more of the free elements of jazz performance.... In the early twentieth century some of the freedoms we now associate with jazz were still allowed in classical music. The old rubato in which the melody frees itself from the accompaniment – a practice for which there is evidence as far back as the seventeenth century – is the essence of jazz performance but is now frowned upon in performance of classical music. Indeed, it is possible that its adoption and exaggeration in jazz and other popular genres is one of the reasons that classical performers began to adopt a more literal interpretation of the composer's notation.

Note that Philip is discussing a specific field, rubato, rather than general principles like the practice of improvisation, yet he clearly regards rubato as symptomatic of wider notions of freedom and spontaneity, even though he does not pursue these ideas further. If anything, Timothy Day (2000) is even more cautious, only mentioning jazz on a few occasions in very specific contexts. Like Philip, however, he describes its influence in negative terms, as providing an example that classical performers would strive very hard to avoid. For example, writing about the curious avoidance of vibrato among classical clarinet players, Day (2000, 167) suggests that they wished to distance themselves from a tonal quality associated with jazz (or related styles).

At this point I don't need to recount the often hysterical, and not least racially motivated, responses to jazz during the 1920s and 1930s; maybe Alfred

62   *Björn Heile*

Einstein's description of it as 'the most abominable treason against all the music of Western civilization' (quoted from Day 2000, 207) would suffice. In such a climate, is it any wonder that classical musicians would go out of their way to avoid any association with this threat to civilisation, notably when, through the changes brought about by recording and broadcasting, popular music had become a much more potent force and competitor than ever before? On the other side of the divide one doesn't have to look long and hard to find examples of jazz musicians or critics disparaging classical performers for their conservatoire training and alleged lack of creativity and spontaneity. Thus, what is behind the seemingly innocuous questions of performance practice is the fraught cultural dynamic of the inter-war years, characterised as it is by such dichotomies as black/white, America/Europe, popular culture/high art, spontaneity/formal rigour. Both jazz and classical performance formed parts of this dynamic, being shaped by it, while simultaneously contributing to its formation. Neither can be understood autonomously, without also considering its counterpart.

Politics and society: 1968 and its immediate aftermath

The repercussions of the student revolts of 1968 were felt throughout the world of music. Although their impact on popular music is more widely known, classical music and jazz have by no means remained unaffected. Musicians' involvement with and responses to the events were as diverse as those of the wider population of which they formed a subset, so the rationale for this section is not to present a representative cross-section. Rather, I will discuss three examples from the areas of classical composition, jazz and rock, illustrating parallels between different artistic domains which throw light on all of them. In this, I will be guided by similar approaches as those adopted in a recent collection on the topic (Kutschke and Norton 2013).[8]

My examples, Mauricio Kagel's *Ludwig van* (specifically the record version), the Art Ensemble of Chicago's *Live in Paris* (The Art Ensemble of Chicago 2008) and Jimi Hendrix's performance of 'Star-Spangled Banner' at the Woodstock Festival (Wadleigh 1970), all date from 1969, the immediate aftermath of the events of 1968. Hendrix's performance is arguably the most 'iconic' and has been widely regarded as epitomising the zeitgeist. As will be seen, however, it is in some ways further from the spirit of the times than the others.

Depending on one's viewpoint, Kagel's composition exists in two or three versions (he himself spoke of it as a 'concept'):[9] a film for Beethoven's bicentenary in 1970, entitled *Ludwig van: Ein Bericht* ('A Report', Kagel 2008); a score, entitled *Ludwig van: Hommage von Beethoven* ('Homage by Beethoven', Kagel 1970a) based on still shots from the film's 'music room' scene (or, more likely, photos taken on the set), in which all surfaces are plastered with scraps of Beethoven's compositions and which can be performed in almost any conceivable way; and a record (Kagel 1970a) consisting of another collage of Beethoven's music, carried out live (by musicians performing different

Integrative music history   63

snippets simultaneously in the studio) and edited by the composer.[10] The record version uses different, and generally longer and more easily identifiable, fragments from the ones used in the score. This too can be justified with a performance option called 'Montage' given in the Preface to the score, according to which performers would play from an original part for their instrument or different passages from various Beethoven works. Indeed, a footnote states that these options have been chosen for the record version. Ignoring the actual notes but following a basic instruction seems to reduce the notion of 'score' ad absurdum, however. The question then becomes why we need another composer's authority to perform Beethoven's works in unusual ways and why Kagel's name and work title appear on programmes and record sleeves. Furthermore, it is noteworthy that, although he worked with regular collaborators on both occasions, the record version has been performed with a completely different set of musicians from the live premiere of the score version, as if Kagel wanted to ensure that the two are separate and that musicians would not be guided by their experience with one in their interpretation of the other.[11] It is perhaps best to regard the score and record as parallel realisations of the same underlying idea. Although all versions were premiered or released in 1970, 'the composition' was completed in 1969.[12]

I am focusing on the record version since that allows concentration on music *qua* sound and comparison with Hendrix and the AEC. As already pointed out, the piece is a collage, or as Kagel insisted a 'meta-collage', consisting entirely of fragments from Beethoven's compositions, combined vertically (played simultaneously) as well as horizontally (in succession). Some of these are quite extended. For instance, in the liner notes Kagel (1970a) explained that he remedied the absence of a viola sonata in Beethoven's oeuvre by combining the fourth movement of the String Quartet op. 131 with the Largo of the *Hammerklavier* Sonata Op. 106, since both are in A Major. He also draws attention to a long-fragmented treatment of the largo from the 'ghost trio' Op. 70 No. 1, which he calls a 'potentiated ghost trio' (side 1, 11'35" – 15'40"). On other occasions, the music consists of short segments, such as repeated cadences (side 1, 1'25"–1'35"), countering the overexposure of characteristic themes and hummable tunes notably during an anniversary – all the 'Freude, schöner Götterfunken' and rumpumpumtum fate motifs – with a preference for the anonymous nuts and bolts of the music. Likewise, recognisable elements can be fleetingly glimpsed among a stream of musical material whose provenance may be detectable but whose identification is frustratingly just beyond reach. Despite Kagel's (1970a) protestations against 'anecdotal identification', like many quotation and collage-based works from the period, *Ludwig van* plays with memory, identity (and non-identity), recontextualisation and defamiliarisation.

Kagel explained some of his intentions in two widely publicised interviews, one (Kagel 1970a) published on the record sleeve and reprinted in the Preface to the score, the other (Kagel and Schmidt 1970) in the widely read weekly *Der Spiegel* and reprinted in a collection of his writings and interviews (Kagel 1975). In both, he seems at pains to contradict the popular

64   *Björn Heile*

image of the *enfant terrible* of the avant-garde who is intent only on shocking his audiences and profaning the most holy of art, that of Beethoven, which is how most reviewers understood the film version in particular.[13] Rather, his stance can be characterised as 'enlightened historicism': the declared aim is to reclaim Beethoven, to reveal the radicalism of his music, which had been stifled by bourgeois culture with its mixture of conventionality, habituation, reverence and commerce, and to show the way towards a creative engagement with it. In other words, if we are to believe Kagel, his critique is not directed at Beethoven, for whom he professes great respect, but at Beethoven's co-optation, arguing for instance, that one shouldn't perform individual works by 'the masters' over and over but instead interpret 'their essence', something for which he explicitly claims the idea of *Werktreue* (Kagel 1970a) – alternatively, it could be considered to stop performing canonic composers altogether for a while, as he also suggests (Kagel and Schmidt 1970, 196). Characteristically, the seriousness of his arguments is enlivened (or undermined) by quips, as when, for instance, he appears to caricature the idea of historical authenticity by arguing that Beethoven's music should be performed the way he himself heard it: badly (Kagel and Schmidt 1970, 196).

What is interesting to see, though, is that, however anti-bourgeois Kagel's work often appeared, in his own working practices he found it hard to relinquish conventional hierarchies. As pointed out above, as a piece, *Ludwig van* arguably liberates performers, and Kagel's own authorial signature on it is of questionable legitimacy. Like most of his work from the 1960s and early 1970s it is the result of collaborative processes, involving the musicians from the Kölner Ensemble für Neue Musik or the fellow artists of the Labor zur Erforschung akustischer und visueller Ereignisse e. V. ('Laboratory for Research on Acoustic and Visual Events, registered association'), a kind of artists' collective. His working method for the record and, it would appear, live performances, was different though: it was he who told the musicians what to play (although he responded to their wishes) and it was he, too, who edited the recording. This is symptomatic: Kagel seemed to have been unwilling to or incapable of giving up artistic control and authorship, which often led to tensions with his collaborators (Kunkel 2011).

One aspect of the record is of particular importance here: the frequent use of unusual or extended playing techniques (also suggested in the Preface to the score). The strings make frequent use of unconventional techniques and unusual mutes, and one of the pianos is prepared. Also noteworthy are Kagel's editing and production techniques. Not content with the naturalism of traditional classical record production, he has included bewildering panning and other spatial effects, distorted some of the signal and also run it through a chopper. These techniques are used sparingly, though, so the experience is of a naturalistic space and signal to be occasionally transformed into a surreal and nightmarish aural space, in which instruments move around or suddenly change place irrationally and sounds appear

Integrative music history 65

defamiliarised. It is difficult to convey what makes this DIY Beethoven so special, even revelatory: it often sounds scratchy and unbalanced, even amateurish, but also joyful, fresh and radical.

Much the same can be said of Jimi Hendrix's famous performance of the 'Star-Spangled Banner' at the Woodstock Festival. There are a number of recurring claims about this performance: that the downward glissandi, followed by erupting noise clusters in the low register depict the rockets and bombs mentioned in the lyrics at this point (which is convincing) and that this acted as a sonic representation of the Vietnam War, thus galvanising the peaceful atmosphere at the Festival and making Hendrix a spokesperson for his generation (which is debatable).[14] As Murray (quoted from Daley 2006, 57) put it:

> [T]he 'Star-Spangled Banner' is probably the most complex and powerful work of American art to deal with the Vietnam War and its corrupting, distorting effect on successive generations of the American psyche. One man with one guitar said more in three and a half minutes about that peculiarly disgusting war and its reverberations than all the novels, memoirs and movies put together.

The reality is somewhat more prosaic. As Shapiro (in Daley 2006, 56–57) has shown, Hendrix, a former paratrooper with the 101st Airborne Division, actually supported the Vietnam War (however cautiously), and, in a televised interview on the Dick Cavett Show (*The Dick Cavett Show, Sept. 9, 1969- Jimi Hendrix* 2013), he played down the host's suggestion of a 'controversy' surrounding the performance and rejected his characterisation of it as 'unorthodox', saying instead that he 'thought it was beautiful'. At the Isle of Wight Festival, he opened his set with 'God Save the Queen', and, although this performance seems a pale shadow of 'The Star-Spangled Banner' at Woodstock, it does indicate that Hendrix was quite relaxed about national anthems and their various meanings and associations.

Overall the evidence suggests that any connection with the Vietnam War is a matter of reception not production (although that is by no means illegitimate). Moreover, as Daley (2006, 55) has demonstrated, the significance of Hendrix's performance itself is a largely retrospective construction: by the time of his set, the last, most of the audience of originally around 400,000 had left and many of the remaining around 30,000 were in the course of leaving. Early reviewers of the event typically mentioned Hendrix only fleetingly or not at all. Only by the late 1980s and based on compilations of the event, does the current interpretation of the performance take hold (Daley 2006, 56). That the black Hendrix could ever have acted as a spokesperson for the largely white, middle-class hippies is probably a romantic assumption to start with.

Even if the authenticity of Hendrix's performance as the embodiment of the 1968 spirit is in doubt, there are good reasons why it is commonly understood in this way. Without wanting to minimise the differences, there are some parallels with Kagel. Both were associated with the social movements

66 *Björn Heile*

of 1968, although in neither case unproblematically so (for Kagel's relation to the new social movements, see Heile 2007). Both chose an iconic model as the basis for their work, whose performance or alleged desecration tend to evoke strong emotions (if for slightly different reasons). Both defamiliarised this model with critical intent, particularly through the use of extreme instrumental timbres and noise. Although any metaphorical connection between political and musical authority can be taken only so far, both also seem to claim to respect their respective models and to protest primarily against what they regard as their misuse.

Although, like the other artists discussed here, the Art Ensemble of Chicago were reticent about describing their work as explicitly political, Paul Steinbeck (2013) has subtly argued that there are good reasons to view them as politically committed, and Robin Kelley (1997), for one, has established an explicit link with 1968. The group grew out of Chicago's Association for the Advancement of Creative Musicians in the late 1960s and embodied the AACM's revolutionary political and artistic ideas. On their website, the AACM (2013) describes itself in the following terms:

> [The AACM is a] non-profit organization ... [and] a collective of musicians and composers dedicated to nurturing, performing, and recording serious, original music. ... The AACM first coined the phrase Great Black Music to describe its unique direction in music ... [and it] pays homage to the diverse styles of expression within the body of Black Music in the USA, Africa and throughout the world. This experience extends from the ancient musics of Africa to the music of the future. ... Another equally important aspect of AACM's mission is the high moral standard members seek to provide in their capacities as performers, artists, teachers and role models.[15]

The Art Ensemble of Chicago was founded at the end of the 1960s in Paris, where many of the AACM's members were then staying. Like so many African-American musicians before them, they relished the attention and respect with which they were greeted, and the AEC's first concert at the Théâtre du Lucernaire in Montparnasse, on 12 June 1969, was an immediate sensation, something Edwin Pouncey, in his liner notes to *Live in Paris*, relates to the 'new sense of political and artistic liberation ... during the aftermath of [the] social and cultural upheaval [of the student riots]'. However, as Lewis (2009, 222–23) points out, their success also had a lot to do with continuing racial and exoticist stereotypes, leading him to a comparison with the use of the 'jungle' trope during the Parisian reception of Josephine Baker.

Although their music is typically described as 'free jazz', the AEC, following the AACM, preferred to speak of 'Great Black Music – Ancient to the Future' (for a critique of this notion see Berry 1997).[16] What arguably set them apart is the isomorphism between their form of organisation and their music. As Lewis (2009, 227) has put it, the AEC was 'one of the AACM ensembles

Integrative music history 67

that most radically exemplified the collective conception of the AACM as a whole', taking all decisions as a collective. Likewise, in their music, there is no clear leader or hierarchy and there don't appear to be any pre-established rules; instead the flow of the music emerges out of the negotiation between the performers. As we have seen, these ideals were shared with Kagel in principle, although the latter found it harder to actually realise them. It is worth noting, though, that the same could be said about other AACM groups, notably those headed by Anthony Braxton (Lewis 2009, 227–28).

'Oh strange – part one', the first track on *Live in Paris*,[17] starts innocently enough with a lyrical and tuneful saxophone melody which could well qualify as a 'tune' in jazz parlance, not unlike a standard. Other instruments – some identifiable, others not – join in, hesitantly and tenderly at first, but increasingly assertive. Although, at this point, the saxophone's lead is unchallenged, resulting in a more or less conventional melody-and-accompaniment texture, the harmonies created by the musicians can't be found in any textbook and seem to be freely emerging from the player's linear statements. This incongruence between the recognisable, largely jazz-derived idioms (in however radical form) on the level of individual instrumental line and gesture on one hand and the resulting totality in terms of harmony and form, for which no such model is perceptible, on the other, is noticeable throughout the double-CD. As Tucker (1997, 34) points out, the AEC's eschewal of a piano (or, as he could have added, other harmony-bearing instruments used in jazz such as guitar or vibraphone) can be seen 'to signal freedom from the tyranny of pianism and harmony' – and a similar point can be made about the liberation from pulsed rhythm and metre which is facilitated by sidestepping the conventional drum kit, although not percussion.

As time goes on, the music grows louder and increasingly more ecstatic and cacophonous (which is not to be understood as a negative term), leading to what, following Lewis (quoted in Steinbeck 2008, 415) is often called an 'intensity structure'. This development is coupled with the increasing dominance of percussion: while the music is pitch-dominated at first, dense drumming patterns provide much of the connective tissue throughout the 24-minute track; at around 14 minutes, cymbals cover much of the texture, before melodic solos (notably an extended blues-drenched growl by Lester Bowie) provide the denouement. This track is not necessarily representative of the album as a whole; for instance, part two of 'Oh Strange' starts with a dreamy, dense polyphony, characterised not least by Malachi Favors's bowed bass (which remained seemingly unused in part one, during which Favors must have played percussion) and a much gentler flow, due to the absence (initially) and low prominence (later on) of un-pitched percussion. Later the music morphs into a sound field of sustained pitches, punctuated with rippling solo gestures.[18]

What interests me here is, once again, instrumental timbre, its expressive function and any metaphorical meaning we may ascribe to it. Among the most characteristic instrumental sonorities are what Archie Shepp (quoted in

68   Björn Heile

Steinbeck 2008, 415) has called 'energy-sounds', typically squeals and honks, particularly from the saxophones (Roscoe Mitchell and/or Joseph Jarman – both play soprano as well as alto sax and their sound and playing became quite similar over the years, which makes them hard to distinguish on an audio recording: cf. Jost 1994, 176). This has become a bit of a free jazz cliché, and it is worth stressing that the musicians employ a diverse and subtle mixture of timbres and textures, rather than the undifferentiated sonic barrage some may associate with the idiom. Indeed, some of the playing features a 'beautiful tone' as traditionally conceived, but this is only one option among many, and the performers are willing to explore harsher and more extreme sonorities.

It is in this area that the most direct parallels with Kagel and Hendrix can be found. All are investigating the outer ranges of instrumental possibilities where pitch blends into noise and traditionally sanctioned, pure sound into squeals, scratches and rasps. To be sure, the results of these explorations are as different as the instrumental means on which they are executed: the effects produced by *col legno sul ponticello* string playing, piano preparation, an overdriven guitar with wah-wah pedal, an overblown saxophone or a trumpet growl are not at all alike, but the rationale and spirit behind these expressive means may not be that dissimilar. In the case of Kagel and Hendrix, the use of technology to defamiliarise sound is also noteworthy: although the electric guitar had by that time become a conventional composite sonority, Hendrix's subtle use of the specific qualities of the Leslie speaker, as revealed by Clarke (2005, 49), goes beyond accepted models.

At the risk of banality or of overstretching what are essentially metaphors or homologies, this transgression beyond the traditionally approved ways of playing musical instruments, the liberation from sanctioned ideas of beauty and musical expressivity and the search for new forms of musical collaboration and creativity should be seen in conjunction with the challenge to tradition, authority and convention issued by the generation of 1968 and its experimentation with alternative social models and lifestyles. Of particular importance here is the expressive gesture of the (instrumental) scream that can be heard in Hendrix's overdriven guitar just as much as in Mitchell and Jarman's overblown saxes (less so in the Kagel, admittedly, although it occurs in other of his pieces). As an iconic (in a Peirceian sense) expressive gesture, it is immediately and viscerally experienced, without any need to 'understand its meaning'. Indeed, it is beyond meaning as denotation: we scream for joy, out of rage or protest, in terror, out of grief or in sexual ecstasy, or indeed out of a combination or mixture of those. Particularly in its musical variant, it is perhaps the sheer intensity that matters, more than the specific emotion that we may ascribe to it. Seen in this way, Murray's interpretation of Hendrix's performance may be spot on after all, even if any assumption of intentionality on Hendrix's part is problematic. This too is symptomatic of 1968: many of the new social movements cultivated the scream (Kutschke 2009) and there was a lot of the kind of passion that may give rise to it: anger and protest, but also joy and eroticism.

To sum up, then, their responses to and involvement with the events of 1968 provide a ground for comparison between Kagel's *Ludwig van*, Hendrix's Woodstock performance of the 'Star-Spangled Banner' and the Art Ensemble of Chicago's *Live in Paris* album. All artists were largely sympathetic to the new social movements or were at least regarded in this way. The most immediate expression of this affiliation, across the very different styles and technical means employed, can be found in their exploration of unconventional playing techniques and often extreme timbres. Also noteworthy is the very deliberate engagement with a model that is revered not only for its musical qualities but for the wider associations it evokes. This is quite obvious in the case of Hendrix's use of the US national anthem and Kagel's play with Beethovenian fragments. Similar points can be made about the Art Ensemble of Chicago: in their music too, there is a disparity between recognisable traditional idioms (although not identifiable pieces as such) and a more experimental sonic environment. Lewis (1998, 77) has commented on the collage-like aspect of some of their performances and their use of parody and irony. In all cases, the boundary between homage and critique, pastiche and parody is permeable, and the music is suffused with ambiguity. Finally, in the case of the Art Ensemble of Chicago, the search for new musical means of expression was connected and congruent with the experimentation with collective and communitarian social organisations. The same ideas are in evidence in Kagel as well, although he did not put them in practice with any consistency. Whether a similar argument can be made about Hendrix is almost a moot point. By the time of the Woodstock Festival, he had dissolved The Jimi Hendrix Experience due to conflicts, and he did not (yet) gel well with his new collaborators. He was obviously the bandleader and his name overshadowed all of his co-musicians, but that doesn't necessarily mean that he called all the shots. The irony is that it was Hendrix who, among the musicians considered here, comes closest to having provided the 'soundtrack to 1968', but who, in some respects, like his support for the Vietnam war and a traditional, leadership-oriented social organisation, was furthest from its ideals.

None of this is to minimise the differences in tradition, genre and technique between the artists. There is little suggestion here of mutual influence or the crossing, not to mention, breaking of boundaries. As regards the latter, the Art Ensemble of Chicago were very critical of what they regarded as confining categories, such as 'jazz', but, although neither artist can be associated with blinkered traditionalism, neither Hendrix nor Kagel seem to have been overly concerned about being largely identified as a blues-rock guitarist or classical composer (whether modernist, experimental or avant-gardist) respectively. Nor do I want to overstate the commonality or parallels between the artistic and political intentions between the artists: there are clear differences between the concerns of an African-American jazz collective, a rock superstar and a white avant-garde composer. The point is, rather, that an informed comparison can be undertaken and that

70   *Björn Heile*

this comparison can tell us more about the larger culture and society in which they all lived and to which they all contributed as well as illuminate what is specific to each of them.

Conclusion

The two case studies in this chapter are just that: they do not claim to present a comprehensive overview of twentieth-century music history, and if they are representative of anything, it is my own interests, concerns and priorities. A number of other topics and areas which allow for or require the comparative study of different traditions could be considered. One issue which suggests a partial convergence or potential mutual influence between popular, jazz and classical contemporary music is the prominent use of quotation and collage techniques during the period discussed here (cf. Metzer 2003; Gloag 2012). The term 'postmodernism' may denominate this phenomenon but fails to explain it.

The wide area of music politics likewise demands a holistic approach. For instance, the music policies of totalitarian regimes typically concern very different genres and traditions, composition, performance and consumption in equal measure. Although the effects tend to be less drastic, much the same holds true for any other system of government. While governments may prefer one type of music over another and subject them to different controls, rules and regulations, the reasons behind such judgments and the nature of the distinctions undertaken need to be properly understood. For example, the Nazis' conflicted and contradictory attitude to dodecaphony can be better understood through their similar response to jazz (and vice versa), since only that wider perspective allows uncovering the *criteria* by which music was regarded as desirable or undesirable, useful or harmful (that these criteria were by no means consistent or consistently applied does not affect the force of the argument). Again, the general point holds also for democratic governments: through subsidies, inclusion in or exclusion from teaching programmes and other rules and regulations, all governments have a direct and significant impact on musical culture and they all implicitly or explicitly discriminate between different types of music and music-making. A similar argument can be made about major institutions, such as, in the UK context, the BBC or the Musicians' Union. Both were and are in principle open to all types of music, but in practice this often led to conflicts as well as constant negotiation over priorities and scarce resources.

None of this, however, means that separate study of distinct musical styles and traditions or specific phenomena should be consigned to the past. Questions of style and compositional technique haven't lost their relevance, even though the significance we attach to these issues may change. Undoubtedly, the broader perspective I am advocating here can come at the expense of depth. Studying several musical genres and traditions together means that less time can be devoted to each of them. Likewise, any attention paid to

Integrative music history   71

what used to be considered 'contextual issues' impinges on the time spent on the analysis of compositional technique which used to be the focus of traditional music history understood as compositional innovation. Yet, we cannot escape the complexity of our past and present by reducing it to theoretical models that have no real validity.

A further consequence of an integrative history is that comprehensive, narrative histories are probably no longer possible. It is difficult to imagine a work like Taruskin's *Oxford History* incorporating the musical traditions that he has excluded (whether consistently or not) or indeed providing an account of the interaction between western and non-western music. The *Cambridge History's* attempt at inclusiveness seems to more often than not have alerted readers to what was excluded after all.

In this respect, the form of case studies I have employed here is of larger significance. Although both encapsulate a pre- and a post-history, they are largely synchronic rather than diachronic. This approach is substantially influenced by Hans Ulrich Gumbrecht's *In 1926: Living at the Edge of Time* (2009); comparable examples from music history would be Benjamin Piekut's *Experimentalism Otherwise* (2011)[19] or Hugh MacDonald's *Music in 1853* (2012), although the latter is quite narrowly conceived in terms of repertoire. But the comparison I have in mind is to photography: my case studies are a bit like snapshots capturing a 'decisive moment' which, in Henri Cartier-Bresson's (Cartier-Bresson and Sand 1999, 42) words, '[highlight] the significance of an event as well as of a precise organization of forms which give that event its proper expression'. They are fragmentary: they cannot tell 'the whole story', but ideally they, again in the words of Cartier-Bresson and Sand (1999, 24), 'depict the content of some event which is in the process of unfolding' exceptionally well. More than anything else, however, they are at best attuned to the complex social reality and the diversity of the musical culture we find ourselves in, engage with and contribute to.

Notes

1 I wish to thank John Butt, Nicholas Cook, David McGuinness, Eva Moreda Rodríguez and Ian Pace for advice, suggestions, ideas and materials received while researching and writing this text.

2 Although Clarke's article was only published in 2007, it is based on a talk given at the Royal Musical Association conference on Music Historiography in 2003 and in guest lectures at several UK universities.

3 I prefer the term 'classical' over 'art' music. Although its etymology and precise meaning are not without problems, the concept is readily understood and not quite as value-laden as 'art'.

4 It is worth interrogating the values underlying Huyssen's, Born's and van der Merwe's work. In all cases, it is suggested that it is somehow morally wrong for modernist music to part company with the popular (although not for popular music to reject its classical sibling). Although this inversion of traditional aesthetics, whereby popular culture is denigrated for its insufficient adherence to the standards of high art, is refreshing, it is only a limited advance.

72 *Björn Heile*

5 Clarke (2007, 11) quotes from the same passage.

6 It is worth mentioning here that the omnivorousness theory has been contested. It is neither possible nor necessary to outline that debate in every detail here, although an awareness of the complexity involved in making judgments about musical taste is relevant. Issues discussed include, for instance, to what extent the phenomenon could be specific to the USA, whether it really affects exclusively or predominantly 'high-brows', what changes can be observed over time, and whether high-brows have become genuinely more liberal and open-minded, or whether they simply demonstrate their distinction vis-à-vis 'univores' in different ways. Among the most virulent opponents of the theory is Atkinson (2011), according to whom it is based on simplistic questionnaires which don't provide genuine insight into the way people consume music and how they value it and often use unsuitably broad categories (e.g. 'Rock/Pop') which do not reflect the fine distinctions that many listeners undertake (see also Rimmer 2012). But these are relatively rare voices and the broad outlines of the theory are widely accepted (see also Chan and Goldthorpe 2007). While the phenomenon may be more marked and may have arisen earlier in North America, not least since status is typically more directly related to income, rather than education in that region, and although there are very significant national and regional differences, omnivorousness can be observed in a great variety of settings (Coulangeon and Roharik 2005). Furthermore, it appears to be on the increase, with increasing proportions of subjects reporting omnivorous tastes (Peterson and Kern 1996). It is not confined to 'high-brows' (Warde, Wright, and Gayo-Cal 2007), but the incidence of the phenomenon remains highest in that group.

7 Katz (2010, 39–40) lists a number of works which have been specifically composed for records. As will be seen later, Mauricio Kagel's *Ludwig van* can be seen as a related case. Nevertheless, the practice remained exceptional and relatively inconsequential for the wider culture of classical music.

8 Indeed, I contributed to one of a series of conferences organised by one of the editors which presumably played a role in the gestation of that volume – as well as leading directly to two others: (Jacobshagen, Leniger, and Henn 2007; Kutschke 2009), and this experience affected my thinking on the matter. The examples I want to focus on have not been discussed in detail in these publications, however.

9 Whether Kagel's title is indebted to Anthony Burgess's creation Alex from his 1962 novel *A Clockwork Orange* (2012) as popularised in Stanley Kubrick's (2001) film is uncertain. Even though the parallel is revealing: all three artists shared a sensitivity, if not necessarily approval, for (possible) counter-cultural appropriations of the Beethovenian legacy.

10 There is also a performance on CD by Alexandre Tharaud (2003), which seems to respond more directly to the score than Kagel himself did in his recording.

11 The performers on the recording are Carlos Feller (bass), William Pearson (baritone), Bruno Canino and Frederic Rzewski (piano), Saschko Gawriloff and Egbert Ojstersek (violin), Gérard Ruymen (viola) and Siegfried Palm (cello); the premiere of the 'live version' was performed by the Kölner Ensemble für Neue Musik: Gerhard Braun, Wilhelm Bruck, Chistoph Caskel, Vinko Globokar, Edward H. Tarr and Heinz-Georg Thor, under the composer's direction. The latter version would have been further removed from Beethoven's sound world on account of the instruments used alone: although the musicians from the KENM did not always perform on their primary instruments, Caskel is a percussionist, Globokar a trombonist and Bruck a guitarist. Only Braun, a flautist, Thor, a double bass player and Tarr, a trumpeter, would have had significant amounts of original music to play.

12 For *Ludwig van* see Kutschke (2010) and Heile (2006).

13 However one interprets it, there is no doubt that the film is controversial, portraying the *Führer* (guide) of the fictional Beethoven-Haus as Adolf Hitler and combining the strains of the choral finale of the Ninth Symphony with images of defecating elephants, among many other things.

14 See Clarke (2005) for a transcription and more detailed discussion of the performance.

15 This current description is clearly based on the original charter and an 'Informal Memorandum of Requirements and Expectations' (Lewis 2009, 116–17).

16 The homogenising forces of consumer capitalism are not so easily defeated however: the case of the Charly reissue displays the unequivocal demand: 'file under jazz'.

17 There are only two pieces on the double-CD: 'Oh strange' and 'Bon voyage', each divided into two parts of between around 22 and 25 minutes duration. It is to be assumed that these divisions were necessitated by the playing time available on the original LP sides. There is a curious, perhaps superficial parallel with the Kagel here which likewise uses the technical limitation of LP records to demarcate the piece: both sides of the record are about 25 min long.

18 I treat the music as essentially improvised here, which is the way it is often viewed. Steinbeck (2008) provides a more detailed analysis of another AEC performance from an insider's perspective, including a discussion of the relation between composition and performance. Jost (1994, 163–79) concurs that there are composed elements. On the CD cover, 'Oh, strange' is credited to Jarman and Bowie and 'Bon voyage' to Bowie. Without inside knowledge, it is impossible to know for certain which aspects of the music were pre-composed (the opening tune on 'Oh, strange'?) and this is arguably relatively unimportant for the argument pursued here.

19 Unfortunately, I only read Piekut's book after this chapter had been finished in draft form. There are obvious commonalities between his approach and mine.

Bibliography

AACM. 2013. 'About Us'. Accessed June 7. http://aacmchicago.org/about-us.

Adorno, Theodor W. 2002. 'On the Fetish-Character in Music and the Regression of Listening'. In *Adorno: Essays on Music*, edited by Richard Leppert, translated by Susan Gillespie, 288–317. Berkeley, CA and London: University of California Press.

Atkinson, Will. 2011. 'The Context and Genesis of Musical Tastes: Omnivorousness Debunked, Bourdieu Buttressed'. *Poetics* 39 (3) (1 June): 169–86. doi:10.1016/j.poetic.2011.03.002.Benjamin, Walter. 1999. 'The Work of Art in the Age of Mechanical Reproduction'. In *Illuminations*, edited by Hannah Arendt, 217–52. London: Pimlico.

Berliner, Paul F. 1994. *Thinking in Jazz : The Infinite Art of Improvisation (Chicago Studies in Ethnomusicology Series)*. 1st ed. University Of Chicago Press.

Berry, Jason. 1997. 'Declamations on Great Black Music'. *Lenox Avenue: A Journal of Interarts Inquiry* 3 (January): 42–54. doi:10.2307/4177061.

Born, Georgina. 1995. *Rationalizing Culture: Ircam, Boulez, and the Institutionalization of the Musical Avant-Garde*. Berkeley: University of California Press.

———. 2010. 'For a Relational Musicology: Music and Interdisciplinarity, Beyond the Practice Turn'. *Journal of the Royal Musical Association* 135 (2): 205–43. doi:10.1080/02690403.2010.506265.

74   *Björn Heile*

Bourdieu, Pierre. 2013. *Distinction: A Social Critique of the Judgement of Taste*. London: Routledge.

Burgess, Anthony. 2012. *A Clockwork Orange: The Restored Edition*. New York and London: W.W. Norton & Co.

Cartier-Bresson, Henri, and Michael L. Sand. 1999. *The Mind's Eye: Writings on Photography and Photographers*. New York: Aperture.

Chan, Tak Wing, and John H. Goldthorpe. 2007. 'Class and Status: The Conceptual Distinction and Its Empirical Relevance'. *American Sociological Review* 72 (4) (1 August): 512–32. doi:10.1177/000312240707200402.

Chanan, Michael. 1995. *Repeated Takes: A Short History of Recording and Its Effects on Music*. London and New York: Verso.

Clarke, David. 2007. 'Elvis and Darmstadt, or: Twentieth-Century Music and the Politics of Cultural Pluralism'. *Twentieth-Century Music* 4 (01): 3–45. doi:10.1017/S1478572207000515.

Clarke, Eric F. 2005. 'Jimi Hendrix's "Star Spangled Banner"'. In *Ways of Listening: An Ecological Approach to the Perception of Musical Meaning*, 48–61. New York: Oxford University Press.

Cook, Nicholas, and Anthony Pople. 2004. *The Cambridge History of Twentieth-Century Music*. Cambridge: Cambridge University Press.

Cottrell, Stephen. 2012. 'Musical Performance in the Twentieth Century'. In *The Cambridge History of Musical Performance*, 725–51. Cambridge: Cambridge University Press.

Coulangeon, Philippe, and Ionela Roharik. 2005. 'Testing the "Omnivore/Univore" Hypothesis in a Cross-National Perspective. On the Social Meaning of Ecletism in Musical Tastes'. https://hal-sciencespo.archives-ouvertes.fr/hal-01053502/document.

Daley, Mike. 2006. 'Land of the Free - Jimi Hendrix: Woodstock Festival, August 18, 1969'. In *Performance and Popular Music: History, Place and Time*, edited by Ian Inglis, 52–57. Aldershot, Hants, UK and Burlington, VT: Ashgate.

Day, Timothy. 2000. *A Century of Recorded Music: Listening to Musical History*. New Haven and London: Yale University Press.

DeVeaux, Scott. 1988. 'Bebop and the Recording Industry: The 1942 AFM Recording Ban Reconsidered'. *Journal of the American Musicological Society* 41 (1): 126–65. doi:10.2307/831753.

Garber, Frederick. 1995. 'Fabulating Jazz'. In *Representing Jazz*, edited by Krin Gabbard, 70–103. Durham, NC: Duke University Press Books.

Gloag, Kenneth. 2012. *Postmodernism in Music*. Cambridge: Cambridge University Press.

Gumbrecht, Hans Ulrich. 2009. *In 1926: Living on the Edge of Time*. Cambridge, MA: Harvard University Press.

Heile, Björn. 2006. *The Music of Mauricio Kagel*. Aldershot, UK: Ashgate Pub Co.

———. 2016. 'Play It Again, Duke: Jazz Performance, Improvisation, and the Construction of Spontaneity'. In *Watching Jazz: Encounters with Jazz Performance on Screen*, 238–266. New York: Oxford University Press.

———. 2007. 'Avantgarde, Engagement Und Autonomie: Mauricio Kagel in Den Sechziger Jahren'. In *Rebellische Musik: Gesellschaftlicher Protest Und Kultureller Wandel um 1968*, edited by A. Jakobshagen, M. Leiniger, and B. Henn, 1: 81–91. Cologne: Dohr.

Horn, David. 2003. 'The Identity of Jazz'. In *The Cambridge Companion to Jazz*, edited by Mervyn Cooke and David Horn, 9–32. Cambridge: Cambridge University Press.

Huyssen, Andreas. 1986. *After the Great Divide: Modernism, Mass Culture, Post-modernism*. Bloomington: Indiana University Press.

Jacobshagen, Arnold, Markus Leniger, and Benedikt Henn. 2007. *Rebellische Musik: gesellschaftlicher Protest und kultureller Wandel um 1968*. Cologne: Dohr.

Jost, Ekkehard. 1994. *Free Jazz*. 1st Da Capo Press pbk. ed. New York: Da Capo Press.

Kagel, Mauricio. 1970a. *Ludwig van [Record]*. Deutsche Grammophon Gesellschaft 298687.

———. 1970b. *Ludwig van [Score]*. London: Universal Edition.

———. 1975. *Tamtam: Monologe und Dialoge zur Musik*. München: R. Piper.

———. 2008. *Ludwig Van [DVD] [2005]*. Winter and Winter.

Kagel, Mauricio, and Felix Schmidt. 1970. 'Beethovens Erbe Ist Die Moralische Aufrüstung'. *Der Spiegel*.

Katz, Mark. 2010. *Capturing Sound: How Technology Has Changed Music*. Rev. ed. Berkeley, CA and London: University of California Press.

Kelley, Robin D. G. 1997. 'Dig They Freedom: Meditations on History and the Black Avant-Garde'. *Lenox Avenue: A Journal of Interarts Inquiry* 3 (January): 13–27. doi:10.2307/4177059.

Kubrick, Stanley. 2001. *A Clockwork Orange [DVD] [1971]*. Warner Home Video.

Kunkel, Michael. 2011. 'À La Recherche Des Joueurs Perdus: Wo Sind Die Spieler in Kagels Zwei-Mann-Orchester'. In *Mauricio Kagel - Zwei-Mann-Orchester: Essays und Dokumente*, edited by Matthias Kassel, 31–40. Basel: Schwabe.

Kutschke, Beate. 2009. 'The Scream in Avant-Garde Music: The New Left and the Rediscovery of the Body'. *The Modernist Legacy: Essays on New Music*, edited by Björn Heile, 61–80. Farnham: Ashgate.

———. 2010. 'The Celebration of Beethoven's Bicentennial in 1970: The Antiauthoritarian Movement and Its Impact on Radical Avant-Garde and Postmodern Music in West Germany'. *The Musical Quarterly* 93 (3–4): 560–615. doi:10.1093/musqtl/gdq021.

Kutschke, Beate, and Barley Norton. 2013. *Music and Protest in 1968*. Cambridge: Cambridge University Press.

Lewis, George E. 1998. 'Singing Omar's Song: A (Re)construction of Great Black Music'. *Lenox Avenue: A Journal of Interarts Inquiry* 4 (January): 69–92. doi:10.2307/4177069.

———. 2009. *A Power Stronger Than Itself: The AACM and American Experimental Music*. Reprint. Chicago: University of Chicago Press.

Macdonald, Hugh. 2012. *Music in 1853: The Biography of a Year*. Woodbridge, UK: Boydell Press.

Metzer, David. 2003. *Quotation and Cultural Meaning in Twentieth-Century Music*. Cambridge: Cambridge University Press.

Moore, Robin. 1992. 'The Decline of Improvisation in Western Art Music: An Interpretation of Change'. *International Review of the Aesthetics and Sociology of Music* 23 (1): 61–84. doi:10.2307/836956.

Peterson, Richard A., and Roger M. Kern. 1996. 'Changing Highbrow Taste: From Snob to Omnivore'. *American Sociological Review* 61 (5): 900–907. doi:10.2307/2096460.

Peterson, Richard A. and Albert Simkus. 1992. 'How Musical Tastes Mark Occupational Status Groups'. In *Cultivating Differences: Symbolic Boundaries and the Making of Inequality*, 152–86. Chicago: University of Chicago Press.

Philip, Robert. 2004. *Performing Music in the Age of Recording*. New Haven and London: Yale University Press.

76 *Björn Heile*

Piekut, Benjamin. 2011. *Experimentalism Otherwise: The New York Avant-Garde and Its Limits*. Berkeley and Los Angeles and London: University of California Press.

Rasula, Jed. 1995. 'The Media of Memory: The Seductive Menace of Records in Jazz History'. In *Jazz among the Discourses*, edited by Krin Gabbard, 134–62. Durham, NC: Duke University Press.

Rimmer, Mark. 2010. 'Beyond Omnivores and Univores: The Promise of a Concept of Musical Habitus'. *Cultural Sociology* 6 (3) (1 September): 299–318. doi:10.1177/1749975511401278.

Scott, Derek B. 2008. *Sounds of the Metropolis : The 19th Century Popular Music Revolution in London, New York, Paris and Vienna: The 19th Century Popular Music Revolution in London, New York, Paris and Vienna*. New York: Oxford University Press.

Souchon, Edmund. 1957. 'Jazz in New Orleans'. *Music Educators Journal* 43 (6): 42–45. doi:10.2307/3388229.

Steinbeck, Paul. 2008. '"Area by Area the Machine Unfolds": The Improvisational Performance Practice of the Art Ensemble of Chicago'. *Journal of the Society for American Music* 2 (03): 397–427. doi:10.1017/S1752196308080127.

———. 2013. 'The Art Ensemble of Chicago's "Get in Line": Politics, Theatre, and Play'. *Twentieth-Century Music* 10 (01): 3–23. doi:10.1017/S1478572212000394.

Stephan, Rudolf. 1994. 'Zum Thema Historische Aufführungspraxis'. *Jahrbuch Des Staatlichen Instituts Für Musikforschung Preußischer Kulturbesitz*, 9–19.

Taruskin, Richard. 2010. *The Oxford History of Western Music*. Oxford: Oxford University Press. www.oxfordwesternmusic.com.

Tharaud, Alexandre. 2003. *Kagel: Ludwig van*. Aeon.

The Art Ensemble of Chicago. 2008. *Live In Paris*. Charly.

The Dick Cavett Show, Sept. 9, 1969- Jimi Hendrix. 2013. Accessed June 6. http://blip.tv/ipodlife/the-dick-cavett-show-sept-9-1969-jimi-hendrix-4594128.

Tucker, Bruce. 1997. 'Narrative, Extramusical Form, and the Metamodernism of the Art Ensemble of Chicago'. *Lenox Avenue: A Journal of Interarts Inquiry* 3 (January): 29–41. doi:10.2307/4177060.

Van der Merwe, Peter. 2004. *Roots of the Classical: The Popular Origins of Western Music*. Oxford: Oxford University Press.

Wadleigh, Michael. 1970. *Woodstock*. Documentary, History, Music.

Warde, Alan, Mark Tomlinson, and Andrew McKeekin. 2000. 'Expanding Tastes?: Cultural Omnivorousness & Social Change in the UK'. www.cric.ac.uk/usercgi/cric/cricpaperdl.asp?paper=dp39.

Warde, A., D. Wright, and M. Gayo-Cal. 2007. 'Understanding Cultural Omnivorousness: Or the Myth of the Cultural Omnivore'. *Cultural Sociology* 1 (2): 143–64.

4   The many voices of 'art song'

David J. Code

Why, after a century whose lyrical legacy extends (for a wildly random sample) from Cole Porter and Duke Ellington through Elvis Presley and Stevie Wonder, and from the Lennon and McCartney partnership through the individual *oeuvres* of Björk and Joni Mitchell and Amy Winehouse, would anyone choose to base a song course, yet again, on the arch-canonical repertoire of the early German Romantics? Even if we put aside all questions of origin – that is, about what exactly grants such precocious creations as 'Gretchen am Spinnrade' their genre-defining status within the immemorial history of words sung to music – a larger question remains. Why would anyone still want to re-inscribe, as mythic well-spring of 'art song', the work of Franz Schubert and Robert Schumann, who bring with them not only a language now much less central to music scholarship than it once was, but also a conception of musical art rooted in Goethean organicism (and Germanic Idealism) that has come under repeated critique within recent reflections on the scope and values of a University music curriculum?

I do not intend this opening note of post-canonical self-consciousness as a mere hand-wave in the direction of 'musicological correctness'. My choice of the subject and content of the course I have long taught at the University of Glasgow under the heading 'Romantic Song' undoubtedly rested, initially, on good old-fashioned reverence for the 'greatness' of the musical and literary materials in question, buttressed by a keen interest in the cross-disciplinary complications their interplay brings in tow. But as the course has evolved over several years, I have also found these same materials ever richer as nodes for critical exploration of the very questions I have raised above – about canonicity and tradition; and about the modes of cultural transmission, understanding and evaluation. Which is to say, ultimately, about the aims and ideals of music education itself.

For a start, however, the chimerical creature 'art song' calls for explanation. Here, we should note that most students in this course will have taken our introductory 'Listening and Repertory' course, under whose inclusive remit they will have had ample opportunity to consider the specious nature of all attempts to elevate any kind of musical art over any other. But they will also have had the chance to weigh the categorical value that may still

78   David J. Code

remain in 'art song' as the label for a relatively distinct subset of all songs, in which a composer appropriates a pre-existing piece of literary art, hitherto complete unto itself, and by drawing it into the realm of music inevitably 'makes it their own' to some significant extent. The inexhaustible richness that arises from this collision of voices – crudely: a poetic one and a musical one, though neither proves easy to pin to a single speaker – renders this genre a rich field for reflection on the very idea of 'art', as it informs (if it does) countless individual experiences of contemporary musical culture.

Still, even if we accept this provisional generic boundary a more basic question soon follows. Surely the challenge to confront critically both musical artistry and the myriad verbal arts that gather under the rubric of 'poetry' would be far easier if we were to start, at least, with a familiar language? It could well make pedagogical sense, these days, to focus first on the art songs of (say) Benjamin Britten or Aaron Copland, and thus the poetic craft of John Donne or Emily Dickinson, in order to bring unfamiliar literary principles into view unimpeded by a foreign tongue. But I find that the task of translation itself carries crucial lessons about the close, recursive engagement needed to draw any (native or foreign) poetry into feeling and understanding. Musty whiffs of Teutonic exceptionalism aside, the language of Goethe et al. now offers most of our students the invaluably unsettling effect of any encounter with a linguistic 'Other' – much like those that likely gave many scholars their first clear sense of verb tense, sentence structure and linguistic personhood in their own over-familiar mother tongue.

This interdisciplinary exploration thus begins, as it must, by confronting the polysemous voices intrinsic to language even before it is shaped into poetic utterance. The degree to which any such artful writing remains at basis untranslatable can begin to come vividly into focus even through a first, close pursuit of the shades of meaning that escape any attempt to bring Goethe or Heine into English. At the next level of inquiry, the attempt to trace the ways in which poetic craft compounds the implications of some unique structure of words may, paradoxically, only heighten a sense of foreignness even as it gives a distorted glimpse of the humane messages or (more likely) questions it carries. But the attempt can also begin establishing a personal relationship to the literary work – and thus a standpoint from which to assess the inevitably rather different relationship that will appear in someone else's musical setting.

Turning finally to song, we reach the most treacherous stage of exploration. It can be all too easy to see the (great) composer's 'reading' as not only successful (as if by definition) but entirely natural, and thus to overlook those creative decisions that escape explanation in mimetic or affective (or even literary) terms – let alone those at odds with the expectations fostered by our own poetic analysis. The hope is that even a faint sense of *surprise* at someone else's reading might inspire further thought about creative 'Otherness' and open paths of explication that will likely bend, soon enough, towards the thorniest domains of criticism.[1] But we cannot cut off the chain of voices even here, for we cannot really *hear* a compositional reading without some (private or public) performance – and thus some further mediation by unruly minds and bodies (if only our own). Once, it may have been easy to dismiss this last layer of reading as extrinsic to 'the music' in question. But nowadays we are more solicitous about the role of performance in musical experience. And it proves fascinating, later on, to turn to actual recorded voices – and to radical re-voicings by composers and arrangers – to hear just how much latitude they claim in their service, respectful or otherwise, to the living tradition of art song.

Some generalities

Before embarking upon close critical study, I generally try and elicit a few shared notions about Romanticism, and briefly consider the historiographical question about why the *Lied* attained a new status, after 1810, as a central genre (Dahlhaus 1989; Rosen 1995; Rushton 2002; Taruskin 2005). If any number of familiar ideas might emerge from the first venture, for the second it seems particularly crucial to emphasize the new interest in a *Volkston* or *Volkstümlichkeit* that was to prove so influential across all of nineteenth-century music history. To give some emphasis, as well, to the development of the fortepiano can usefully add one technological concern that utterly eludes explanation in terms of 'great artists' alone.

Zeroing in on aesthetic challenges, I present from the start a provisional list of all the discrete points of analytical purchase that might serve to illuminate both poetic craft (e.g. prosody, grammar, voice and point of view, allegorical implication) and musical setting (e.g. rhythm, melody, texture and register, affect). I imagine such a list may seem artificial in isolation from critical practice. But I particularly want to have the following question in view from the start:

> QUESTION: is such compositional 'reading' often, or always, a kind of *mis*reading? (Goethe actually preferred the bland accompaniments by Zelter to the imaginative, psychologically rich settings by Schubert!)

And in a broader view, this vision of an orderly analytical discipline (idealistic as it may prove) can offer a useful *point de repère* for the attempt to let careful encounters with poetry forestall all illusions of 'natural' song setting.

In outline, finally, the 'Romantic Song' course proceeds from a single Schubert *Lied*, to one of his song cycles, to several selections from Robert and Clara Schumann, before returning to the Schubert discography for thoughts on performance and arrangement. Here I will trace a more streamlined trajectory focusing on Schubert alone. Methodologically speaking, finally, while drawing selectively on relevant professional literature, I also use the dialogic context of the course to illustrate how critical insights might also emerge from a relatively *ad hoc* approach to poetry and music – which can help to encourage a lasting metacritical perspective on more 'disciplined' approaches encountered later on.

80 *David J. Code*

Part 1: Schubert and Goethe, from lyric to ballad

Saving such much-discussed instances as 'Der Erlkönig' and 'Gretchen am Spinnrade' for independent student inquiry, I start with a later, more succinct example from Schubert's Goethe songs. The tiny 'Wandrers Nachtlied' D. 768 brings a text that finely encapsulates many central concerns of the perennially problematic idea of 'lyric poetry'.[2] By all accounts Goethe's single most famous poem, this little shred of artful utterance inspired the song published in 1824 as op. 96, no. 3 – which richly exemplifies, in turn, Schubert's skills as a musical reader and the transformation such reading implies.

This song also boasts a thorough analysis by Thrasybulos Georgiades, which can show how an eminent specialist negotiates our critical challenges (Georgiades 1986). But in keeping with the notional discipline, I like to start by considering the puzzles even this tiny poem poses to a translator. Here is the text from the *Sämtliche Werke* (Goethe 1988, 65) along with a prose translation and a few of many attempts, over the years, at a poetic English equivalent:

Wandrers Nachtlied
Über allen Gipfeln
Ist Ruh',
In allen Wipfeln
Spürest du
Kaum einen Hauch;
Die Vögelein schweigen im Walde.
Warte nur! Balde
Ruhest du auch.[3]

Over all the hills is peace, in all the tree-tops you feel hardly a breath; the little birds are silent in the forest. Only wait, soon you [will] rest too.

(1) Over all the hilltops
Is rest,
In all the treetops
Thou feelest
Scarce a breeze;
The birds are stilled in the forest.
Only wait, soon like these
Thou too shalt rest.

(2) Over every hill
Is repose.
In the trees, you feel,
Scarcely goes
The stir of a breeze.
Hushed birds in the forest are nesting.
Wait, you'll be resting
Soon too like these.

(3) O'er all the hill–tops
Is quiet now,
In all the tree–tops
Hearest thou
Hardly a breath;
The birds are asleep in the trees:
Wait, soon like these
Thou, too, shalt rest.

(4) Over mountains yonder,
A stillness;
Scarce any breath, you wonder,
Touches
The tops of all the trees.
No forest birds now sing;
A moment, waiting–
Then take, you too, your ease

The many voices of 'art song' 81

No doubt – as a colleague once exclaimed at the photocopier – each verse translation is, in its own way, atrocious.[4] But that is precisely the point. And if it is hard to choose a 'least worst' in overall quality, they can all serve together to highlight those ideas that prove most elusive to foreign readers.

An initial invitation to students to note any striking discrepancies might elicit a few comparatively straightforward observations that are nonetheless open to 'poetic' elaboration (e.g. the setting, in 'hills' or 'mountains'; the various shades of anthropomorphic inflection given for 'Ruhe'). More telling points of interest start to emerge, I find, with the questions raised by the first verb (line 4). Almost every translator reads 'spüren' as 'to feel'. But a telling instability – one 'to hear'; one shift of agency so that the object, 'Hauch', does the 'touching' – might serve to suggest a question about what exactly the verb's subject ('du') is 'scarcely' experiencing. A 'feeling' of something implies an intimate *feeling into* nature (the branches) rather than a simple 'hearing'. And the slight hesitation on this point across the translations can bring focus to the sensory trajectory through these lines – that is, the incremental drawing in of focus and access, from a first embracing gaze 'over' summits, *down into* treetops (close enough to 'feel'), and then, in the next line, even closer, to the living creatures, the 'Vögelein' within, who somehow reach our awareness. With this diminutive of endearment – think of all the 'Bächleins' and 'Rösleins' in Goethe and Schubert – the questions about sense perception become most acute.

The action of these 'little birds' proves hardest of all to translate. As with 'Ruh'', previously, we find both human and non-human shadings ('asleep' or 'hushed'; 'silent' or 'stilled'). But perhaps the two oddest contortions – a new verb, 'nesting'; a resort to what the birds do *not* do ('sing') – bring us closer to the problem. For these creatures are actively *doing* something that escapes simple translation: they are 'holding still', or 'being silent'. (Might we say they are '*being*, silently'?) And a question immediately arises: how do we know? Given the nocturnal setting, it seems odd to suppose that the birds – in their non-action, up in the trees – are *visible*. We can imagine seeing high, dark vistas and hearing/feeling a faint 'breath' or 'breeze' in (with) the trees. But our sense of the 'little birds' implies something more mysterious – an attunement to shared liveness, let us say, which transcends sense perception.

The pivotal mystery sets up a striking change in tone. The imperative 'Warte nur!' ('Only wait!') startles for its directness, and then for its recasting of the noun 'Ruh'' as a decisively humanised verb, 'Ruhest du'. This second 'du' revisits a previously overlooked problem. These days, to ask why two readers opt for 'thou' instead of 'you' might elicit student answers that circle, ironically, around the old-fashioned formal effect of the former. The truth, of course, is that this is how English speakers try to capture the *informal* second person so crucial to this poetic intimacy. And neither translation ('thou' or 'you') really catches the transformation from a somewhat impersonal 'spürest du' to the most iconic lyric gesture of all: the direct 'I- You' address from poetic persona to reader.

82   *David J. Code*

I have found it helpful, in furthering class discussion at this point, to refer to a fine essay by one-time US poet laureate Robert Hass, in which he suggests that '*the form* of any given poem [as distinct from its generic 'form', i.e. sonnet or sestina] consists in the relation between its music and its seeing' (Hass 1984, 65). Taking the 'seeing' of Goethe's little poem to mean *all* the finely calibrated senses that we have found to give access to its world, we might add a few helpful hints towards thought about what its prosodic 'music' adds to the formed experience:

1	Über allen Gipfeln	a	6
2	Ist Ruh',	b	2
3	In allem Wipfeln	a	5
4	Spürest du	b	3
5	Kaum einen Hauch;	c	4
6	Die Vögelein schweigen im Walde.	d	9
7	Warte nur! Balde	d	5
8	Ruhest du auch.	c	4

Numbering lines, indicating rhymes, counting syllables – even these simple exercises, I suggest, can unearth a few points of interest. For one, we see that the seemingly improvisatory utterance is actually projected through a delicate matrix of order: a rhyme scheme built from the two most common poetic quatrains. Closer scrutiny, furthermore, finds a hidden pattern of 8-syllable pairings (6+2, 5+3 – here it can be useful to demonstrate a little exercise in 'counting fingers') that gains its strongest presentation in the framing four-syllable lines – 'Kaum einen Hauch'/ 'Ruhest du auch' – of the second rhyming quatrain. But if this prosodic embrace of the line with the birds (and its companion) seems a fine marriage of form and feeling, it can only be exposed by reading across a different, equally strong formal pattern: the steady, irregularly paced deepening of grammatical 'breaths', from comma, to semi-colon, to full stop.

Turning to Georgiades now, we find that he, too, notes many of these intricacies on the way to suggesting that the 'sixth line functions – from whichever angle we choose to look at it – as an island within the poem' (Georgiades 1986, 86). But there is more mileage to derive from one last level of craft he brings into view. Parsing the poem's metre and accents, he gives this stress pattern for line six:

˘ / ˘ ˘   / ˘ ˘   / ˘

Die Vögelein schweigen im Walde.

As he notes, the hint of 'triple rhythm' and 'feel of a regularly built song-like form' are highly appropriate to the 'naïve, folklike' images ('Vögelein'; 'Walde'). As an example of the fine qualification we might bring to even such refined criticism as this, I add, more esoterically, that the nine-syllable fragment is structured symmetrically around the pivotal sound '*scwhei-*': a

The many voices of 'art song' 83

'weak-strong-weak-weak' rhythm on either finds support in faint sonorous echoes ('D_V' becomes the softer 'w_D'; 'l' and 'n' sounds are scattered, more haphazardly, to either side). Even while audibly evoking song-like *Volkstümlichkeit*, the form also articulates a more secretive, inaudible focus on the sensual and spiritual mysteries encapsulated in that pivotal verb.

Perhaps this level of scrutiny exceeds what we might expect in a course – or chapter – of this nature. But such a suspicion can be turned towards basic questions about the degree to which poetry, in its simultaneous shaping of sounds and accreted meanings, always delivers a rich admixture of chance and intention. The turn to Schubert's song brings yet more complexity to this blend.

To prepare this new level of analytical scrutiny we can also turn to an article by Kofi Agawu that directly challenges the procedure outlined so far. As he puts it, the common presumption that we should start an analysis of song by 'doing as the composer did' – i.e. reading the poem – risks importing literary assumptions into a genre better approached with sensitivity to the distinct concerns of 'text-setting' and 'composition' broadly construed (Agawu 1992, e.g. 10). While his absolute-musical conception of the latter might be somewhat overstated, Agawu's intervention can support useful warnings to students against the perennial temptation to discern hilltops in harmonies or tree branches in tunes, while reminding us all of the eternally open implications of any poetic-musical interaction.

The first bars of Schubert's 'Wandrers Nachtlied' nicely illustrate the point (see Example 4.1). While it would be absurd to discern anything as precise as a 'hilltop' in the first, processional chords, it still seems crucial to highlight, for ears accustomed to modern amplification, how effectively that low-register, octave-doubled, *pianissimo* scoring responds to Goethe's invocation of wide, dim spaces. But the slinky, chromatic inner voice in bar 2 – the most distinctive feature of the opening – is harder to tie back to poetic precedent, unless we want to riff extravagantly on the wayward Romantic interiority that both co-exists with and resists the 'symbolic order' of cadential syntax. With Georgiades, finally, we might note how the intro sets the stage for the voice, through an anticipatory approximation of both the rhythm (slightly plainer) and the melody (similar, but on the mediant) of the first line of song.

To scan through the initial vocal phrases is to find, first, a melody whose articulation according to grammatical breaths largely subsumes most intricacies of rhythm and rhyme; and then, a finely calibrated emergence of expressive lyricism. At first, a near-monotone syllabic declamation, inflected by the barest stepwise turn, marks a 'zero degree' of melodic expression. The breath after 'Ruh'' brings a first melodic reach, to a warmly harmonized subdominant (also anticipated back in bar 1), and then a gradual accumulation of archetypical lyrical devices. A first appoggiatura (the octave-doubled D) and a first touch of melisma both come with 'Wipfeln', even as a first shadow of Schubert's characteristic modal mixture (in an inner voice) expressively

Example 4.1 Schubert, 'Wandrers Nachtlied', op. 96 no. 3, D 768.

The many voices of 'art song' 85

softens the move in to a closer sense of branches. As the accompaniment gains a syncopated throbbing, the minor-mode shading carries forward to darken 'spürest' – crucial verb – before imparting a pang to the voice as well for 'kaum'.

In a broader view, we see that Goethe's incremental *drawing in* finds a textural equivalent, starting with the release of the bass from doubling octaves (under 'allen') and continuing, after the rising chromatic bass – expanded inversion of the slinky inner voice – to a more radical registral shift, up another octave, for the 'Vögelein'. Here, the closest accompanimental texture gains further intimacy through a recasting of the rocking quavers, which lifts the chord root to the offbeat to hint briefly at weightlessly idyllic lullaby. The pivotal line also brings a surprise. Schubert now repeats the crucial verb 'schweigen' across two bars multiply marked as an island of archetypical song: a near-exact melodic repetition bar by bar; a climactic proliferation of melismas and appoggiaturas.

The moment nicely encapsulates those questions about musical 'reading'. Maybe the lyrical flowering seems a perfect realization of the expectations fostered by that 'island' of a line. But in truth, musical song only emerges, here, through an effacement – by the contraction ('Vög'lein') and the word repetition – of the metrical 'song' Georgiades heard in the text. Yet more radical transformation follows. The imperative 'Warte nur', declaimed sequentially, brings an abrupt change of texture to prepare the rise to the vocal high point, and an enactment of 'waiting' with a pause on the weak second syllable of 'balde'. And after the slinky chord-voicing returns for the newly personal 'du' the whole, newly repetitive address receives another full repetition before one 'extra' bar echoes the piano cadence once more to bring the reading to a close.

In sum, while it is surely excessive to invoke 'misreading' in this case, if we grant to Goethe's poem an expressive plainness and simplicity the equal of any haiku or Zen koan (we know he was fascinated by the East), we might find excellent cause here to open a broad, evaluative or diagnostic question about whether or not Schubert's emphatically repetitive personalization of those closing phrases actually comes at some loss. Generally finding student response to this question intriguingly mixed, I also suggest that a bit more formal inquiry invites a last critical turn. That seemingly exact repetition of the closing phrase (from 'warte nur') actually features a telling variation: a metrical shift within the 4/4 bar. Locally, the effect of the expansion is to allow the pair of two-and-a-half bar phrases to settle, finally, onto two metrically correct statements of the slinky cadence. But in a longer view, the time it takes to 'correct' this metrical focus results in a total number of bars (fourteen) that places the first textual alteration – the repeated 'schweigen' – precisely across the midpoint of the work. This deft structural calculation brings to mind the interplay in Goethe between seeming improvisation and secret formal control – and thus offers a preliminary grasp of this song's encapsulation of some central aesthetic dialectics (i.e. the interplay of formalist and expressive priorities) of its historical moment.

In presenting such detailed scrutiny of this little song as a compact model for the kinds of close attention students might summon more selectively for

86   *David J. Code*

any other, I also use it as a springboard for two kinds of theoretical reflection. The first concerns ultimate goals. For even after all this parsing of rhythms and proportions, we have only *prepared the ground* for an interpretation of what the poem and song might conceivably 'mean'. Invited to this broader view, students generally have no trouble discerning the metaphorical resonances in that final promise of rest. But if the intimation of death – the end of all our wanderings – is plain enough, that is only one aspect of the possible allegorical implications of the poem and song as crafted wholes. Full appreciation of these hinges, again, on a recognition of the mysterious sense of shared liveness in the 'island' of silent birds, and a question about what it might offer all of us in our nocturnal awareness of mortality.

An acceptance that the discussion must remain open at this point can lead into a second theoretical realm. As an attempt to give context both for the crucial role of lyric address and the open nature of lyric form, the table below sketches a serviceable summary of a much-contested domain (Figure 4.1).

Suggesting a generic context for the open-ended reading just accepted for one little lyric, this scheme also offers a means to begin introducing other kinds of poetic language, notably including the ballad form that proved a key forum for composers to extend their literary-musical explorations over broader spans.[5]

It is in light of this scheme that I now briefly introduce one of the most celebrated ballads, Goethe's 'Der Erlkönig', as a vivid instance of the possibility for literary art to bring *all three* categories into intricate interplay. Here is the text and translation, lightly annotated as a goad to more detailed inquiry (Figure 4.2).

Literary type:	LYRIC	EPIC (narrative)	DRAMA
VOICE	– the poem is a direct expression in the first person – the lyric 'I' (the authorial voice) can be implicit or explicit – diret address, either to the reader or someont else: the lyric 'I-You'	– the poem is a story told in the third person about other individuals and their experiences – 'he/she'	– the aouthor gives named characters direct expression os their own experience – 'I' is spoken from other fictional perspectives
TIME (verb tense)	– tends to be an expression/ observation about the present	– tends to be in the past tecse: 'once upon a time'	– present situations, enacted
FORMAL PROCESS	– a 'frozen moment' in time; no clear plot or progression of events – new insight emerges throgh circulation of imagery, juxtaposition, combination, reflection, etcetera	– both tend to be 'plot-driven', i.e. telling (or enacting) a series of events across a directed, seuential development – the ending presents a markedly different situation from the beginning	

Figure 4.1 The basic types of poetic discourse (as adapted by Renaissance and Romantic theorists from the Greeks).

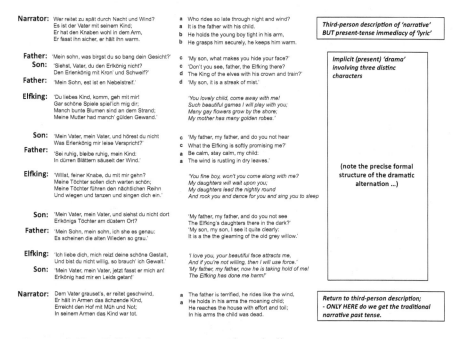

Figure 4.2 'Der Erlkönig' as a structure of poetic discourse.

I tend to withhold further comment of my own at this point, suggesting only that students might approach Schubert's setting (and the many commentaries it has spawned) with eyes and ears attuned to textual – i.e. vocal – hybridity and its possible effects on compositional choice.

Part 2: Schubert and the song cycle

Beyond the poetic or vocal 'types', my glance at 'Der Erlkönig' also notes only the recurring end-rhymes that impart long-range formal coherence to a highly varied strophic scheme. This small point adumbrates a new central concern as we turn to the 'song cycle' – an even more significant forum than the ballad for the extension of lyrical expression across truly epic scale. The turn to *Die Winterreise*, as my Schubert example, offers an occasion to address, as well, some new and distinct questions for the setting of strophic poems, as compared to one-stanza lyrics (Tunbridge 2010; Youens 1991).

To prepare our first look into this new genre, it can help to present a summary overview of the more straightforwardly 'narrative' progression of Schubert's earlier Müller cycle, *Die schöne Müllerin*, as a foil to the more elusive, meta-lyrical outline of *Die Winterreise*. While it is impractical to sample extensively from either set, students can be invited to *place* any song they choose for analysis, provisionally, within the distinct progression of its source cycle. Here, I will concentrate only on the first and last songs of *Die Winterreise*, a pairing that (however distant) can also serve to give a brief glimpse of the thorny problem of 'cyclicity' itself.

A familiar scheme of options for the setting of a strophic poem might help orient the discussion (Figure 4.3).

The first song, 'Gute Nacht', nicely illustrates the creative challenges lying behind the 'modified strophic' approach Schubert chose for so many of his finest settings.

Presenting the poem for discussion in these terms (see below), we readily note the *Volkstümlich* simplicity of metre and rhyme, but also quite easily recognise, through discussion, two pressing questions for anyone considering a strophic setting. First, it is hard to see how the internal structure of all four strophes can fit comfortably with a recurring musical underlay. Second, some of the strophes seem distinctive enough in tone to require more substantial departure from strophic recurrence (Figure 4.4).

My brackets alongside the first two strophes indicate one challenge of the first kind. In the first strophe, the abrupt shift to a remembered 'May', with 'flowers', after two lines (and before a two-line return to snowy 'Now'), clearly frames the (four-line) past within a darker present. But the second strophe, temporally a more continuous 'eight line' structure, falls grammatically into a simpler 'four plus four' pattern. It is hard to imagine how the same music could serve both without compromise.

The second question, about distinctive strophes, admits of a range of possible responses. Some students sense a marked shift in tone with the question that launches the third strophe (whose howling dogs also stand out); others note the possible further anomaly when the speaker's – perhaps unconvincing – reach for proverbial compensation ('Love loves to wander …') unfolds through three lines before breaking off for a single line of direct address. The scheme of literary types again proves relevant here, if we note how this sudden address to the 'Liebchen' sets up a strikingly personal last stanza, rife with second-person forms.

Suggesting that all such detail suffices to guide an assessment of the setting, I also preface analysis with two new musical considerations – both extrapolations from the idea of 'mode'. The first derives from a simple question: What makes for a good melody? Impossible to answer in universal terms, the query can nonetheless inspire thought about what makes any given melody an

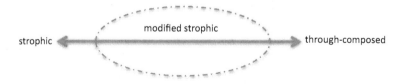

Figure 4.3 Options for strophic setting.

The many voices of 'art song' 89

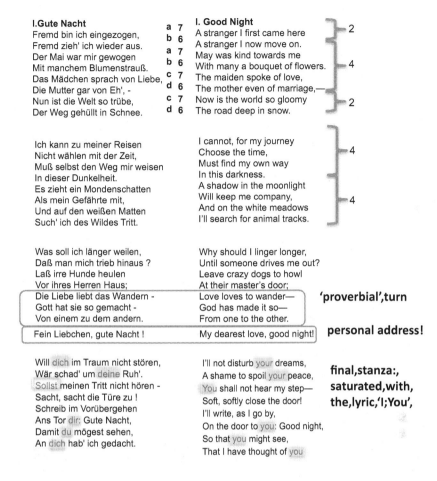

Figure 4.4 Strophic intricies in Müller, 'Gute Nacht'.

admirable exemplar of lyrical possibility within its own musical style. I find that the pursuit of this question for *Die Winterreise* profits from the attempt to recover the deeper, historical meaning of 'mode' – that is, a *way* or *kind* or *fashion* of melodic behaviour (like a *raga* or *maqam*), rather than an abstract 'set' of available pitches.[6] To this end, we might usefully review the deepest bedrock of tonal rudiments: the distinct series of tones and semitones that define the major and minor scales as two interdependent realms of expressive implication. If we can thus approach the melody of 'Gute Nacht' with an ear for its crafted navigation of a 'd minor' modal environment, another slab of rudimentary bedrock – the expressive 'palette' of triads built on the major and minor scale degrees – can also prove illuminating of some larger formal choices. Indeed, I find that 'Gute Nacht' proves a suggestive instance for the case that this theoretical 'ABC' is a resource Schubert worked just as deftly as he did the more elaborate riches of his early Romantic harmonic syntax.

Example 4.2 Schubert, 'Gute Nacht', song 1 from *Die Winterreise*, D 911.

Example 4.2 (Continued).

Example 4.2 (Continued).

Example 4.2 (Continued).

Turning now to the song (see Example 4.2), we find another delicately approximate piano prefiguration of the voice, which in this case could not better exemplify modal thinking. After tersely establishing the song's plodding quavers, the solo piano phrase unfurls a melodic line that emphatically marks – or claims – the defining turns and spans of its modal environment. Beginning with a pick-up move through the ^3-^2 semitone, the line droops down through the octave to an accented, re-rhythmicized statement of the same semitone, newly supported by the other characteristic 'minor' move (^6-^5, B♭-A) in an inner voice. Then, a brief repetitive play with the falling tonic-dominant fourth leads to a last little descent that decoratively highlights the F-E move once more (over B♭-A in the bass) before the cadence ushers us in the first vocal strophe – and a highly inventive response to the puzzles in Müller's strophic structure.

Echoing and varying that drooping line for the first line of text, the singer's antecedent phrase further emphasises the F-E move by reiterating it down the octave, as pick-up to yet another turn on the same modal node. The new consequent phrase, more simply triadic at first, then gives yet another little F-E turn before coming to rest on the tonic. When we now find the third and fourth lines of the poem – in both stanzas – set to exactly the same antecedent-consequent melodic pair, it appears that Schubert solves the first strophic puzzle by simply ignoring the structure of the first stanza and letting the setting be guided by the second. (Note how the compromise tramples over the imagery of 'May' and 'flowers'.) But to listen on is to find that the response to competing strophic options is more complicated than it first seems.

Again, Schubert significantly alters this poem by repetition. The resulting new structure deserves schematic representation (Figure 4.5).

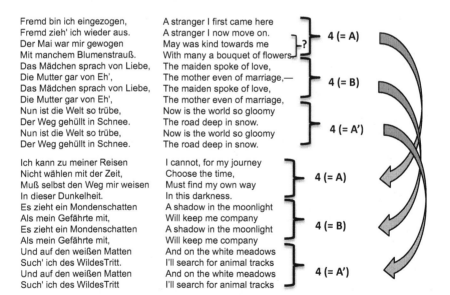

Figure 4.5 'Gute Nacht', Schubert's formal alteration to strophes 1 and 2.

The many voices of 'art song' 95

As shown, the extensive repetition, two lines by two lines, of all but the first four lines of each strophe, results in a new, 12-line version (4+4+4) of the framing dynamic initially carried by that 2+4+2 structure. The small initial compromise (for 'May') thus facilitates a refashioning of Müller's initial two formal alternatives into two more fully realised 'ternary' structures. In both cases, a middle section now names a companion (a maiden, a shadow) for the speaker, and a last section returns him to wintry solitude (the 'road deep in snow', the 'white meadow'). The re-sculpted textual form thus gives new weight to a question – lightly prefigured in Müller – about lost or illusory alternatives to alienated loneliness.

The new ternary conception thoroughly informs the musical setting (see Example 4.2). An *almost* regular series of eight-bar phrases, constructed out of repeated four-bar pairs on either side of a four-plus-four-bar sequence, sets the three new sections. The newly expansive central glimpses of companionship receive expressive support both from a warm harmonic move and a change in predominant melodic character, from downward droop to upward stride. The two close 'modulations' through F and B♭ major are better recognised as lightly tonicised ventures through the two major colours (III and VI) available in the home modal palette. The one anomaly in the phrase structure – the accented gesture inserted twice after this excursion (bars 24-25) – seems like a pointed, admonitory reminder of the true modal semitones. The interjection ushers in (and carries on into) a final section whose emphatic reiteration of the 6^-5^ (B♭-A) semitone (downbeats of bars 26-27) for the return to repetitive melodic droop modally underlines the return, in both strophes, to wintry solitude.

As expected, the third strophe – expanded in its turn – inspires initial departures from musical repetition. The drooping antecedent phrase, almost intact, gains a newly energetic, upward tail; the consequent phrase, setting the bitter question '... daß man mich trieb' hinaus?', voices a searching rise rather than a dying fall. When a closer return to precedent for the middle section now brings back the major melodic-harmonic excursion for the unctuous proverbial turn, it is hard not to hear a whiff of irony tainting the previous idyllic sweetness. The address to the 'Liebchen' draws a less marked musical response, but the strophe does end with two further alterations to the vocal cadences: the first, a ^2-^7-^1 turn that strengthens the titular 'good night'; the second, a last high reminder of the F-E semitone with which the voice had begun.

Slight as it might seem, this second alteration proves telling preparation for the most substantive departure from strophic repetition, when the change to D major for the most personal final strophe (slipped in almost casually by the piano) comes keenly into relief with the high vocal F♯-E. Schubert suffuses the new environment with further touches of modal warmth: a new E dominant seventh shading (bars 73 and 77) that seems as much a local 'Lydian' coloration as a true 'V^7 of V'; a melodic variant that adds the new major sixth degree B♮ (further brightened by an inner-voice E♯) as pick-up to bars 74 and 78.[7] But it is in the last middle section that the craftiness

96 David J. Code

of the song's modal-harmonic conception emerges most clearly, through a deft musical alteration best understood in light of a further change to the strophic form (Figure 4.6).

The third strophe conforms to the precedent of two-by-two-line repetition. But in the fourth, a repetition of all four lines, as a complete section, creates a new textual 'bar' form (ABB) in place of the previous ABA structures.

Looking to the setting of the final stanza, we find a hybrid of ABA and ABB forms. Broadly speaking, the first B section revisits the prior contrast in melodic character – but with a slight change to harmonic precedent. To pass through the mediant and submediant (as before) would be to reverse the contrast in expressive hue (i.e. III and VI in minor would become iii and vi in major). But the new textual structure has shed the expressive contrast between sections. Tweaking his setting (doubly) to place these central melodic phrases on IV and I instead, Schubert discovers a more affectively uniform variant within which he can highlight, once more, the major E-F♯ whole step (against chiming high dominant pedal) on the most intimate words 'so that you might see'. The accented interjections, again breaking the phrasal regularity, now serve to affirm the whole steps (one, again, over Lydian warmth) rather than to insist on minor semitones. The final vocal phrases, modally translating both cadential variants from the previous strophe, prepare a last, close juxtaposition of major and minor ^3-^2 moves before the piano plods to a close through an extended final droop.

A glance back over text and music sees how multiply Schubert's 'Gute Nacht' transcends any notion of 'natural' song setting. His response to

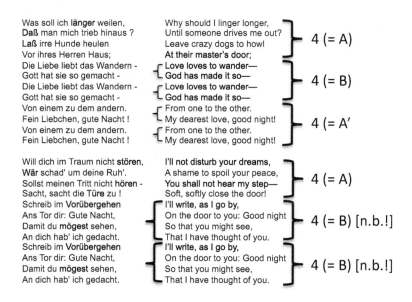

Figure 4.6 'Gute Nacht', Schubert's alteration to the final strophe.

Müller's strophic form overlooks some local details ('Mai', 'Liebchen') in order that larger motivations – a new ternary formal understanding; a long-range play with modal shadings – can gain clearer focus. By contrast, a brief glance at 'Der Leiermann' brings into view a different kind of artistry altogether, whose exemplary power is harder to pin down to detail. In stark contrast to the formal subtleties just discussed, 'Der Leiermann' offers a new critical challenge: to encompass an art of extreme impoverishment, which accomplishes a great deal by doing very little.

The text of 'Der Leiermann' (see below) offers a limit case, in the cycle, of stripped down prosody. Its lines are the shortest in the set; its pervasive weak rhymes ('e', 'er', 'en' etc.) compose numbness into poetic music itself. The overall structure – four strophes of description, one of address – also seems simple enough, though one recurring rhyme and one close textual variant ('sein [...] Teller', 'immer Leer' / 'sein Leier', 'nimmer still'), together suggest a 2 + 2 + 1 strophic parsing (Figure 4.7).

Within a setting that takes two poetic lines as the basis for each vocal phrase, Schubert strengthens these formal hints through new repetitions only of the final lines in each strophic pair. This one poetic intensification aside, he multiply infuses the song with his own version of frozen numbness.

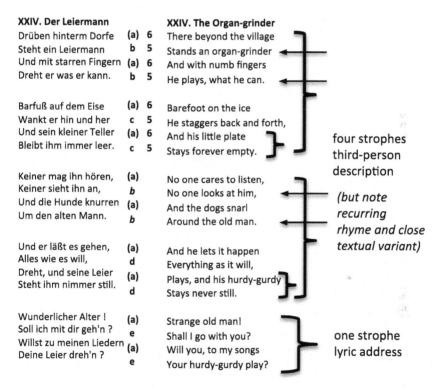

Figure 4.7 'Der Leiermann', with implications for strophic setting.

Example 4.3 Schubert, 'Der Leiermann', song 24 from *Die Winterreise*.

Example 4.3 (Continued).

Example 4.3 (Continued).

Most obvious is the unrelenting harmonic poverty (see Example 4.3). Set entirely over a hollow A-E pedal, the melody lurches, without respite, between implicitly 'tonic' and 'dominant' arrivals. A similar sense of entrapment multiply informs the temporal conception. A blankly declamatory quaver rhythm is enlivened only fleetingly by dotted figures; almost every vocal phrase is contained – constrained – within a two-bar frame. The rigorously exact repetition of each two-strophe section takes on, in this case, an aesthetic force in keeping with the pervasive sense of impotent circularity. Only in the final, personal strophe does a vestige of human warmth emerge. With the direct address to the 'wonderful old man', the phrase spills, for the first time, beyond the second bar; the beseeching final question then claims the more flexible dotted rhythm for a pair of extravagant octave leaps and a last arrival that also carries across the bar line. As if in response, the piano – hitherto coiling and hiccupping in *pianissimo* handle-cranks – finds one exceptional burst of *forte* before wheezing down to a final cadence.

As noted in my summary comparison of the two Müller cycles, the ending of this meta-lyrical series is disconcertingly inconclusive – and the lessons we might take from its last, pathetic human encounter have been posited in various ways. I will take those last questioning vocal gestures way to open, instead, a slightly different domain of inquiry, concerning the degrees of musical unity we might appropriately seek in this 'cycle'.

The disparate sequence of keys, textures and vocal characters across the twenty-four songs strongly cautions against assuming any meaningful relationship between the 'a minor' on which 'Der Leiermann' ends and the 'd minor' with which 'Gute Nacht' began. But without wishing to come down too strongly on either side of a debate about tonal unity, I would suggest that the question might again benefit from the adoption of a *modal* sensitivity. The cycle ends, vocally, on the same mode-defining semitone – the high F-E, now as ^6-^5 rather than ^3-^2 – that once launched 'Gute Nacht'. Absolute pitch aside, such a modal inflection – in such a vocal tessitura – will retain its audible expressive and coloristic identity across any transposition. Perhaps it is with an ear to unity (or 'connection' or 'recall') in this looser sense, rather than in any more rigorous sense of tonal structure, that we can discern the more delicate cyclic implications across this whole diverse set.[8]

Part 3: Singing, playing and adapting Schubert

If 'Der Leiermann' might best serve to illustrate both the power of starkly limited musical means and the expressive force of a studied phrasal discipline, one further concern glimpsed in passing above can adumbrate the turn to a last layer of encounter with 'art song'. The piano's late *forte* outburst, I suggested, sounds like a quasi-dramatic reaction to the singer's query. To hear it this way is to open questions about incipient dramatic interplay that can usefully inform critical hearing of performance and arrangement.

At this point in the course, having introduced various (*ad hoc*) tools for poetic and musical analysis, I find it best to acknowledge (in all awareness of the burgeoning recent interest in performance criticism) that these last critical challenges remain even harder to encompass within a precise methodological discipline.[9] But I also suggest that there may still be some value, for thoughtful rehearing of this particular genre, in the provocations offered long ago by Edward T. Cone in his 1974 book *The Composer's Voice*. When introducing Cone's idiosyncratic attempt to delineate the notional 'personas' audible in song, I emphasize that its value does not lie in any clear 'success' at systematic description, but rather in the interrogative approach most clearly evidenced by the fact that we encounter, at various points, three quite different schemas for song's internal relationships:

Proposition One:

Accompaniment : Vocal persona :: Narrator : Poetic character
[i.e. 'The accompaniment is related the vocal persona as the Narrator is related to the poetic character'.]

Proposition Two [two alternatives]:

a   Accompaniment : Vocal Persona :: Unconscious : Conscious aspects of character
b   Vocal identity : Verbal identity :: Unconscious : Conscious aspects of character[10]

102 *David J. Code*

There is no need to choose between these various options in order to weigh the critical utility of a passing comment like this one, on the very songs here under discussion:

> Even when the accompaniment produces appropriate sounds, it is rarely to be considered as directly heard by the vocal persona. The protagonist of 'Der Leiermann' hears a hurdy-gurdy, but not what the singer and audience hear: a pianist playing a stylized version of what a hurdy-gurdy might sound like.
>
> (30)

Cone goes on to characterize this particular 'split' more precisely:

> The accompaniment suggests both the impingement of the outer world on the individual represented by the vocal persona, and their subconscious reaction. In 'Erlkönig' and 'Der Leiermann' we hear, not the actual sounds of hooves and hurdy-gurdy, but a transformation of those sounds – their resonance in the subconscious of the protagonist as interpreted by the consciousness of the instrumental persona. Even when the accompaniment appears to be dealing with external circumstances, it is usually revealing their effect on the protagonist.
>
> (35–36)

Both the simple emphasis on stylization and the more complex sense of a refracted or transformed musical mimesis potentially offer fresh aural purchase on what might all too easily pass as a straightforward case of musical imitation.

Before proceeding, I like to add – as one further complication – Carolyn Abbate's well-known challenge: 'To Cone's monologic and controlling "composer's voice", I prefer an aural vision of music animated by multiple, decentred voices localized in several invisible bodies' (Abbate 1991, 13). With these twin provocations in mind, we now turn an interrogative ear on a few of the countless available recordings. I will here trace just one of the possible paths along which such a discussion – pursued openly, and thus unpredictably, in the classroom – might proceed. Focusing largely on 'Der Leiermann', I will consider just a handful of recordings, starting with three of a relatively conventional nature (Matthias Goerne and Alfred Brendel in 2004; Mark Padmore and Paul Lewis in 2009; Christine Schäfer and Eric Schneider in 2006) and proceeding to two more unconventional versions (Hans Zender's 1993 'composed interpretation' of *Die Winterreise*, as recorded in 1999; the composite cycle *Im wunderschönen Monat Mai: Lieder nach Robert Schumann und Franz Schubert* written by Reinbert de Leeuw in 2007 for Barbara Sukowa). The exploration will occasionally bring me into dialogue with Cone, but it might best be read as a preliminary sketch of an answer to the questions about history, canonicity and tradition with which I began.

The many voices of 'art song'   103

Predictably, of all these versions the one from the live 2004 Wigmore Hall performance of *Die Winterreise* by Goerne (a student of Dietrich Fischer-Dieskau and Elisabeth Schwartzkopf) and Brendel (whose pianistic – and Schubertian – pedigree needs no elaboration) presents the most traditional interpretation. At first, this 'Leiermann' wholly meets the expectations fostered by their conjoined eminence. A transcription by ear of the reverentially text-faithful piano introduction could recover Schubert's notation to an astonishing precision, down to the slurs, accents and rests. But Brendel's reverent 'realisation' becomes considerably complicated by the entry of Goerne with an indulgently 'lyrical' approach – taking as much time as possible within this rhythmic environment, giving almost every quaver and semiquaver its warm vocal bloom. The sense of a conflation of quite different temporal conceptions occasionally becomes marked: the singer, for example, stretches the return of the A-E leaps for the third phrase (second time) with an expansive *bel canto* rubato, explicable (in the absence of clear textual cause) only by a generic urge for expressive variety. And at the end, Goerne gives the question 'will ich mit dir gehn?' such local deliberation that any larger point about its escape from two-bar strictures – already forestalled by the way he lets each phrase ending taper resonantly into the next bar – feels somewhat defused.

It would not be accurate to describe these two temporal 'personae' as wholly at odds: Brendel, too, occasionally finds his own version of lyrical expressive flexibility. But even so – thinking back to Cone – there is something about the primacy of the 'vocal' here that, while it may not precisely override the 'verbal' (Goerne's diction is meticulous), pushes larger-scale, formal and imaginative dimensions of Schubert's reading decisively into the background. This is no formally embodied experience of frozen alienation, but an insistent expression of how we should feel about it – and who should determine that feeling. The point becomes most vivid when in closing, after *portamenti* that render the octave leaps in a fully lyrical legato, Goerne's full- chested swell on the final, tied E effaces any strong sense of dramatic exchange beneath a last strong assertion of vocal priority.

To turn to the studio recording of 'Der Leiermann' by Padmore and Lewis (sung in B minor – the key of Schubert's first version) is to find starkly different conceptions of text-fidelity, of vocality and pianism, and ultimately of the song as a reading of Müller's poem. In a strikingly imaginative re-alisation of the initial notation, first of all, rather than treating the grace notes as the usual fast 'pick-ups' (i.e. E♯-F♯), Lewis strikes the three notes simultaneously, then slowly releases the bare fifth from a sour initial smear. He then carries this sound idea forward through the entire song, every time the bare fifth sounds alone in the bass (i.e. without added tenor). It is easy to imagine textual literalists crying foul. But if we take music notation as a suggestive rather than a prescriptive medium, the reading makes considerable sense as a response to a stylized mimesis. For if the written grace notes hint at a slightly mistuned rustic drone, the element of 'noise' would surely

104   *David J. Code*

carry through every time the drone is re-struck, rather than being restricted to two initial instances.

Bringing a reedier tenor timbre, recorded more distantly than Goerne's, Padmore's vocal rendition also melds text-fidelity with imaginative response. His occasional touches of rubato never perturb a stricter rhythmic discipline; his final crotchets taper quickly enough to project the regular phrasing. But he, too, reads the score flexibly – for example, by taking Schubert's few notated dotted rhythms as an invitation to add his own. We might hear these as an inflection of the vocal line in response to the insistent trochaic rhythms in the text. But they are also redolent of close attentiveness to the piano, whose sectional perorations in bars 27–28 and 49–50 come to feature one melodic bar explicitly foreshadowed (bar 26) and echoed (bar 48) through Padmore's re-dotting.

Whatever the cause, the markedly stronger impression, in this recording, of a unitary interpretation need not imply anything like the authorial unity of Cone's 'composer's voice'. The effect of closely collaborative reading arises as much from the interplay of distinctive departures from the score as from any 'realisation' of a fully notated *Lied*. Indeed, we might describe the result as something like a new embodiment, in its own varicoloured sounding medium, of the expressive deep freeze once suggested, much differently, in the media of poetic and compositional writing.

The recording by Schäfer and Schneider brings yet another performative recasting, which – while cannily displacing any sense of the accompaniment as narrator – further deepens the suspicion that faithful rendition and overt adaptation may differ only by degree. Schneider's introductory evocation falls somewhere between the other two: he strikes the D sharp together with the A but as clean pick-up to the E (and plays it only twice); a slight pedal blur through the melodic coils can also be heard as part of the stylized mimesis. But Schäfer's vocal entry brings something more radically new to the mix. Here it is not a case of a few extra dotted rhythms but of a fresh temporal feel throughout. Pushing far beyond Padmore in her flexible response to the written quavers, she imparts a playful, dance-like *Schwung* to many wider leaps, delivering a reading that is by far the most rhythmically vivid of the three.

If this seems a perverse response to the bleak text, that may be because it is misleading to describe it solely as a technical aspect of *rhythm* rather than as a broader effect of *characterization*. In a word: Schäfer *acts* her delivery of the text, with dancingly emphatic diction, as if in the garb and mask of a storyteller; we can almost see the wide eyes and witty gestures of a stage entertainer who knowingly indulges our shared taste for bleak gothic imagery. More precisely, the singer here vividly brings to mind her own recording of Schoenberg's *Pierrot lunaire* – that mongrel offspring of song cycle, melodrama, commedia dell'arte and Berlin cabaret.[11] And it is the tradition of Schoenberg's muse Albertine Zehme and the Parisian café-concert *diseuses* – virtuoso characterizers of language all – that vividly comes to mind as Schäfer opens a wholly new narrative space around music so ready prey to self-indulgent pathos in more earnestly 'Romantic' renditions.

Of course we can dismiss such modernisation as an inappropriate twenty-first-century response to nineteenth-century art. But even from these few instances it is possible to glean a deeper point: that the most ostensibly text-faithful rendition will inevitably also spring from performance traditions no less anachronistic than any post-*Pierrot* stylings. Goerne's approach would be more at home in an opera house (where he made his name singing Wagner, among other things) than a Biedermeier drawing room; the rich expressivity that drenches every note of his 'Leiermann' could be criticised (from a different angle) for turning an eerily idiosyncratic musical reading into one more straightforwardly lyrical outpouring. On the other hand, to hear the less text-faithful rendition of Padmore and Lewis as a deeper (because more *in*expressive) response to those spare musical means is not to make any stronger claim for its historical 'authenticity'. This version, too, brings own historically alien sonorous halo, redolent of the Oxbridge chapels in which Padmore first trained.

In contrast to the timeless, somewhat abstract personas Cone once invited us to hear, what emerges from this brief exploration is a sense of the thorough saturation of all real, embodied voices with traces of the spaces and histories that nourished their development. Putting aside any idea of fidelity to a fictive, unchanging original, then, we might best inquire: what does *this* unique accretion of audible spaces and contexts bring to a score's suggestive invitations, and how does *this* new voice re-frame – and navigate – the histories through which the song has passed? It is in the same terms, finally, that we can best proceed to consider those versions whose more extravagant transformations pose a much greater challenge to purist hearers.

Lest we doubt that such purism still persists, one of the performers just named conveniently offered clear proof even as this chapter was being written. Reviewing Ian Bostridge's recent book on *Die Winterreise* for *The New York Review of Books*, Brendel felt the need to assert: '*Winterreise* doesn't need updating, embellishing, transcribing, or paraphrasing' (Brendel 2015, 29).[12] Of course it doesn't. But Müller's (and Goethe's) poems didn't need to be set to music either, nor formally altered in the process. Pious reverence for un-embellished Schubert songs is at odds with the creative attitude to poetic texts that gave rise to the music in the first place. Brendel inevitably updates his *Winterreise* recordings to suit modern sound ideals; Zender's more extravagant paraphrase offers one more creative response to expressive invitations, one step further down the line from the initial compositional embellishment of Müller.[13]

As it happens, 'Gute Nacht' and 'Der Leiermann' feature Zender's most extensive additions to the Schubert model. His cycle begins with a lengthy new introduction based on the quaver plodding and modal inflections of the first song, whose unpredictably accented lurches and swells hint at unruly forces beneath. After settling onto a respectfully literal string transcription

106   *David J. Code*

of the original introduction to prepare the vocal entry, the setting continues with a largely restrained arrangement – voice part unaltered – through two strophes delicately differentiated by variations in scoring. But the second return of the original intro brings abrupt reminders of underlying turbulence – and in the third strophe, composed interpretation erupts fully into hearing.

The image of 'hounds' now seems to trigger irrepressible memories of modern music, for a sudden break in metrical decorum – like a filmic cut – inserts a violently scored *ff* repetition, set rhythmically off by one quaver, and sung 'mit Verstärkung' (with great force). Normality briefly resumes for the first proverbial consolation – but the taint of irony previously noted now triggers another violent response. Just before the first cadential 'gute Nacht', the music explodes again (as if against its own falsity), and with another lurch to *ff*, the singer snarls his address to the 'Liebchen' in a deranged *Sprechstimme*. More blatant than Schäfer's subtle echoes of the same *milieu*, this Schoenbergian reference does not stand so singularly, here, as an audible trace of intervening generic history. For after a quick shift back to 'song' for the last 'gute Nacht' we reach a delicate rescoring of the blithe slippage from minor to major – and then, in place of *one* transitional bar, fully *fifteen* bars of loosely canonical play on the new D major hues. Clearly no further Expressionist revenant, this new expansion instead brings to mind a slightly earlier phase of generic history, in the orchestral songs of Mahler – pre-eminent *fin-de-siècle* translator of Schubert's fading modal expressivity.

Some implications of these stylistic echoes might seem relatively obvious. By allowing latent aspects of the poetry to burst into consciousness, for example, the Expressionistic turns can be heard as blatant sonorous markers of the post-Freudian perspective from which we now regard early Romantic alienation. But perhaps the Mahler-esque expansion offers a more poignant opening to historiographical reflection. For if we consider how thickly the device of modal mixture was to be overlaid, later, by vari- and multi- and post-modal styles, then we might also acknowledge that it would become ever harder to recover its original, Schubertian expressive acuity – and thus understand why an attempt to do so may have found post-Mahlerian expansion a near necessity.

Zender's 'Der Leiermann', also much expanded, proves a somewhat more consistent adaptation. The vocal phrases remaining entirely unchanged, its main transformation seems – however fortuitously – a strikingly precise instantiation of the very 'split' Cone once imagined for this stylized instrumental mimesis. A brief new introduction delivers us to the grace-noted drone scored for folksy accordion. Then, the hurdy-gurdy tune appears, multiply refracted through a temporally and timbrally flexible canon, whose unpredictably layered exchange evokes, at once, both a rustically improvised musical 'reality' and its proliferating echoes within a resonant mental space. After a few instances of more blatant worldly mimesis (e.g. a violent *ff* variant following upon the howling dogs) and a dramatic exchange much intensified by a viscerally dissonant harmonic lurch, the cycle closes with a

The many voices of 'art song'   107

registrally extravagant postlude that adds post-Ligetian 'colour field' composition to the range of resources evoked.

Inspired as the multiply refracted hurdy-gurdy may be, it could be that the new, timbrally vivid psychological space here comes at the cost of a dismembered vocal-verbal continuity, and a relinquishing of those very hints of frozen temporal automatism – i.e. the two-bar units traded quasi-metronomically between the two personae – that ironically render the thinner and paler Padmore/ Lewis version *more* modern in overall effect. By comparison, the more consistent compositional – and performative – flexibility across *both* vocal and instrumental components of a last, even more radically iconoclastic instance, Reinbert de Leeuw's 2007 set of *Lieder nach Schubert and Schumann*, 'adapted and recomposed' for Barbara Sukowa (as per the liner note – which attributes the 'artistic concept' to both of them), arguably seems the more fully-realized instance of explicit reflection, through sounding means, on the questions raised about 'Romantic song' by an awareness of the genre's tangled subsequent histories.

The De Leeuw/ Sukowa cycle frames the nineteenth-century progenitors of the genre even more explicitly within a historical vista determined primarily by their most influential modernist descendant. In broad structure – twenty-one songs in three groups of seven – the composite form precisely follows *Pierrot lunaire*; the first section begins by recalling the famous seven-note motive from that work's first song, 'Mondestrunken'. Following from this nod to Schoenberg, we find eight songs by Schumann freely distributed amongst thirteen by Schubert (including five from *Die Winterreise* and five Goethe settings); snippets from other works by both composers slip in as interludes or added layers of accompaniment. An investigation of the logic of the sequence must await another time, but for now we might at least note a partial counterweight to Schubert's proportional pre-eminence in the formal shape of the whole, which begins and ends with the first and last songs of *Dichterliebe*.

The wildly variegated sonorous means featured across this cycle place it even further beyond methodologically disciplined critique than most other performances. Sukowa ranges vocally from near-straight declamation ('Heidenröslein', no. 19) through whispering, shouting and *Sprechstimme*, to lyrical singing and even caricatural cabaret croon ('Ständchen', no. 18). Within a single song, she might sing one line exactly as written only to switch, for the next, into whispered or heightened speech; haphazardly leaving out some words, she slips others in early, or late, or with the loosest relation to the accompaniment. Meanwhile, de Leeuw's expanded *Pierrot* ensemble also ranges, extravagantly, from chillingly sparse harp and pizzicato textures ('Ich hab' im Traum geweinet', no. 12) to frenzied supplement to vocalized sexual hysteria ('Gretchen am Spinnrade', no. 5), to *Erwartung*-level expressive intensification ('Der Doppelgänger', no. 14). But beyond all these sonorous transformations (which differ only in particulars from Zender's) there remains one singular aspect of this version that most deserves an attempt at critical appraisal.

108 *David J. Code*

De Leeuw and Zender approach the *temporal* identity of each song with a flexibility that renders their joint response to generic history distinct from all others discussed. Only rarely do they trace a formally complete rendition of what Schubert wrote. Instead, they continually drop or elide selected passages of text, or melody, or both. At times, the result can be heard as a wry play with canonical over-familiarity – as when they leave the last two words of 'Der Erlkönig' unsung, forcing knowing hearers to fill them in from memory. But at others, the seemingly haphazard omissions deliver what sound like partially eroded recollections – or imperfect recreations from incomplete sources. This sense of frayed or eroded musical objects is particularly clear in two early adaptations from *Die Winterreise*: 'Gute Nacht' (no. 2) and 'Im Dorfe' (no. 4). Following the precedent of these companions, 'Der Leiermann' also revisits this idea when it emerges as the first song of 'part III' (no. 15) – but brings new variants as well.

The dreamy instrumental intro to this third section darkens to sour dissonance before emitting two annunciatory signals of the song. The first, a spasm-like low string spiccato, *sur la touche*, will recur haphazardly like a stuttering new sonorous sign of inertia; the second is the familiar grace-note figure on piano. Over this composite background, an oboe takes up the coiling hurdy-gurdy tune – now fissured with gaps (we only get the last three notes of bar 3, and only the E chord, not the second hiccup, in bar 5, etcetera). Soon the vocal part too starts to erode: the third textual phrase is erased up to the (half-declaimed) words 'wankt er hin und her'; the fourth ('un sein kleiner Teller') has lost its second repetition. Yet more erasures pockmark the second large 'strophe': the third line ('und er lässt es gehen') only belatedly appears as a blurted declamation; both versions of the fourth ('dreht, und seine Leier...') drop away entirely. Much sooner than expected, we are hearing the last questions to the 'wonderful old man', delivered in an intimate whisper that has left all melodic lyricism behind.

Brendel is right: there was no need to treat the song this way. But a signal value of this version, as a pedagogical provocation to students whose relation to the conservatoire mind-set central to classical music education for decades has long been much enriched by approaches adapted from folk or jazz or pop, is the clarity with which it forces us to ask why anyone would *want* to – in other words, just what obligation we now bear to the canonical scores whose inviolable integrity has been so often assumed, in history surveys, theory texts and recital programmes alike. It can thus also conceivably goad us towards our own ideas about how best to incorporate into 'composed and performed interpretation' a vivid reflection of our own evolving perspectives on the moth-eaten bundle of ideas about 'art' we have inherited from the early Romantics. Perhaps we glimpse here one compelling reason for returning as teachers, again and again, to the canonical 'art songs' about which some musicians remain so preciously defensive. They may, when all is

The many voices of 'art song' 109

said and done, differ only in kind from other repertoires (e.g. jazz standards, pop songs), which boast their own vibrant histories of successive appropriations and 'cover versions'. But the hall of mirrors opened by these older songs extends back more deeply, into the very wellsprings of the traditions that, by some accounts, have made us – or continue to make us – 'modern'. They thus can help us affirm the powers of the final voice in a chain that winds all the way forward from eighteenth-century poetry, through nineteenth-century song, into twentieth- and twenty-first-century composed and performed interpretation: our own voice, *talking back*.

Notes

1 One of the more extreme formulations of this potential (or expectation) of 'surprise' can be found in Kramer 1984. In what follows, I will not cite the vast literature that could open at every point, but will note only directly relevant resources.
2 It can prove suggestive, in this context, simply to note that this tiny text has given rise to at least two full-length critical monographs: Seggebrecht (1978), and Fischer et al. (1999).
3 The poem, here printed right after a different 'Wandrers Nachtlied' ('Der du von dem Himmel bist …'), carries the title 'Ein Gleiches' (another one) (65).
4 They are taken from: (1) Viëtor (1949, 60) (trans. credited to Emery Neff); (2) Zeydel (1955, 78–79); (3) and (4) Goethe, ed. Middleton (1983, 59). (3) is credited to Longfellow, (4) to Middleton himself.
5 Amongst a vast literature on these basic categories, see e.g. Genette (1992), which touches on many key stages in the centuries of debate.
6 I know no of precedent for this modal-melodic approach in the specialist Schubert literature, which tends to exemplify the institutionalized music-theoretical emphasis on harmony and structural voice leading (see e.g. Damschroder 2010). However alien it may appear for Schubert, the focus on harmonic 'palette' and characteristic modal inflections proves useful preparation for the more elaborate, multi-modal explorations in the fin-de-siècle French *mélodie* repertoire, which I often present as a later unit on the same course.
7 Recall that Beethoven, just two years before, had included within his string quartet op. 132 (1825) a 'Heilige Dankgesang […] in der lydischen Tonart'.
8 I don't take this modal focus as a 'universal solvent' to the thorny question of cyclicity, but rather find it useful to broach the question, at least, as to whether there may be an interesting difference (in degree if not kind) between this sort of modal tendency in Schubert and a more thoroughly 'functional-harmonic' cyclic imagination in Schumann, e.g. in the much-debated case of *Dichterliebe*.
9 A useful instance of contemporary performance criticism, and a convenient orientation to the wider literature, is Cook (2014).
10 I have redacted these formulations from across the first two chapters of Cone (1974): the first two as stated on 12 and 16, the last drawn from a more diffuse discussion of the 'subconscious' on 34–37.
11 For the multiple traditions behind *Pierrot* see Dunsby (1992).
12 The review is of Bostridge (2015).
13 An obvious reference point here is the essays of Roland Barthes, notably 'The Death of the Author' and 'From Work to Text'. For both (and also 'The Grain of the Voice', which I find less applicable) see Barthes (1977).

110   *David J. Code*

Bibliography

Abbate, Carolyn. 1991. *Unsung Voices: Opera and Musical Narrative in the Nineteenth Century*. Princeton University Press.

Agawu, Kofi. 1992. 'Theory and Practice in the Analysis of the Nineteenth-Century "Lied"', *Music Analysis* 11, 1 (March 1992).

Barthes, Roland. 1977. *Image, Music, Text*, ed. and trans. Stephen Heath. The Noonday Press.

Bostridge, Ian. 2015. *Schubert's Winter Journey: Anatomy of an Obsession*. Faber & Faber.

Brendel, Aflred. 2015. 'Some Winter Wonders', *The New York Review of Books* LXII, 10: 28–29.

Cone, Edward T. 1974. *The Composer's Voice*. University of California Press.

Cook, Nicholas. 2014. *Beyond the Score: Music as Performance*. Oxford University Press.

Dahlhaus, Carl. 1989. *Nineteenth Century Music*, trans. J. B. Robinson. California University Press.

Damschroder, David. 2010. *Harmony in Schubert*. Cambridge University Press.

Dunsby, Jonathan. 1992. *Schoenberg: Pierrot Lunaire,* A Cambridge Music Handbook. Cambridge University Press.

Fischer, Volker, Soltek, Stefan, Bradburne, James M., Schulenburg, Stephan, and Leutner. Petra. 1999. *Über allen Gipfeln ... : Naturerfahrung zwischen Goethe und Gegenwart*, exhibition catalogue. Verlag Hermann Schmidt.

Genette, Gérard. 1992. *The Architext: An Introduction*, trans. Jane E Lewin. University of California Press.

Georgiades, Thrasybulos. 1986. 'Lyric as Musical Structure: Schubert's *Wandrers Nachtlied* ("Über allen Gipfeln", D. 768)', trans. Marie Louise Göllner, in *Schubert: Critical and Analytical Studies*, edited by Walter Frisch, 84–103. University of Nebraska Press.

Goethe, Johann Wolfgang von. 1983. *Selected Poems* (Goethe Edition vol. I), ed. by Christopher Middleton. Suhrkamp/Insel Publishers.

Goethe, Johann Wolfgang von. 1988. *Sämtliche Werke*, vol. 2 *Gedichte, 1800–1832*, edited by Karl Eibl. Deutsche Klassiker Verlag.

Hass, Robert. 1984. 'One Body: Some Notes on Form', in his *Twentieth Century Pleasures*, 56–71. The Ecco Press.

Kramer, Lawrence. 1984. *Music and Poetry: The Nineteenth Century and After*. The University of California Press.

Rosen, Charles. 1995. *The Romantic Generation*. Harvard University Press.

Rushton, Julian. 2002. 'Music and the Poetic' in *The Cambridge History of Nineteenth-Century Music*, edited by Jim Samon, 151–77. Cambridge University Press.

Seggebrecht, Wulf. 1978. *'Über allen Gipfeln ist ruh': Texte, Materialen, Kommentar*. Carl Hanser Verlag.

Taruskin, Richard. 2005. *Oxford History of Western* Music, vol. III *Music in the Nineteenth Century*. Oxford University Press.

Tunbridge, Laura. 2010. *The Song Cycle*, A Cambridge Introduction to Music. Cambridge University Press.

Viëtor, Karl. 1949. *Goethe the Poet*. Harvard University Press.

Youens, Susan. 1991. *Retracing a Winter's Journey: Schubert's Winterreise*. Cornell University Press.

Zeydel, Edwin H. 1955. *Goethe, The Lyrist*. The University of North Carolina Press.

Discography

Barbara Sukowa (soprano), Reinbert de Leeuw (composer and conductor) and the Schönberg Ensemble, *Im wunderschönen Monat Mai: Lieder nach Robert Schumann und Franz Schubert*, Winter & Winter 910 132-2 (2007)

Hans Zender, *Schubert's 'Winterreise': Eine komponierte Interpretation*, Christoph Prégardien (tenor), Sylvain Cambreling (conductor), Klangforum Wien, Kairos 0012002KAI (1999).

Schubert: Winterreise Live from Albert Hall, Mathias Goerne (baritone) and Alfred Brendel (piano), Decca 467 092-2 (2004).

Schubert: Winterreise, Mark Padmore (tenor) and Paul Lewis (piano), Harmonia Mundi HMU 907484 (2009).

Schubert: Winterreise, D911, Christine Schäfer (soprano) and Eric Schneider (piano), Onyx Classics ONYX4010 (2006).

5 The music industries
Theory, practice and vocations – a polemical intervention

Martin Cloonan and John Williamson

... with thousands and thousands of young people still journeying to New York and Hollywood for music careers which simply do not exist.... too many young people are being prepared for a social and professional future that is but a misty, impossible dream.

(Cahn 1948)

Introduction

The (almost) seventy-year-old quote above is striking for its contemporary relevance. The impossible dreams remain and thousands of young people still seek careers in music. So, *plus ça change*. However, one thing which *has* changed is the relationship between higher education and the music industries. If in 1948 the perceived route to a career in music was via towns such as New York (and its UK equivalent, London), then today in the UK it is often via universities and their Music Departments. In addition, whereas in 1948 UK higher education was the domain of the elites and music part of a limited provision (see John Butt's contribution in this volume), today the system annually produces thousands of students who wish to work in music and its allied professions. Such a scenario raises hard questions for both educators and students alike which this chapter seeks to address.

We think that Music students in higher education need to be asked some very important questions such as: What are you doing here? Why are you studying music? What do you want to do with that study? What benefit do you think you will gain via the *academic* study of music? Do you want to be educated (as in asked to explore a range of ideas and possibilities) or trained (as in shown how to do something, or how to do it better)? Are you happy to learn more about the music itself and how to play it (better) or do you think that such study needs to be located in the material conditions under which it takes place? What do you expect to be taught? How do you think that your degree content will affect your career prospects? Put bluntly: Do you expect higher education to prepare you for working in the music industries without the degrees themselves containing at least one compulsory course on those industries? While our focus here is on undergraduate degrees, our arguments have implications for all those seeking to use a higher education programme to progress a career in music.

As will be apparent, our answer to the last question is implicit in the way it was posed and we will explain our views as the chapter progresses. Here we build on our joint and individual endeavours over a number of years. This includes our recent work in theorizing the music industries (plural, rather than singular – Williamson and Cloonan 2007, 2012), our experience in teaching Popular Music Studies (PMS) in UK higher education for over twenty-five years and our individual work within the music industries.[1] We write from within the broad field of PMS (Cloonan 2005) which we see as still being differentiated from a mainstream teaching of music in higher education which remains dominated by the western classical music canon. We also locate ourselves within the broadly leftist tradition with which PMS has been associated (Griffiths 1999). We see our arguments here as applicable to all seeking to work in and around music, from what might be characterized as the 'music profession' centred on the western tradition and modern 'art music', through those working in the 'popular' musical forms – pop, rock, hip hop etc. – to those seeking to work in the business of music and in music education. We regard all such people as working within the music industries[2] and, as such, believe that in order to empower themselves they should seek to understand the nature of those industries.

Readers will have already noticed that we intend to be polemical. We want to raise the fundamental question: What are Music degrees *for*? We do not ask this in abstraction but in a context where higher education has become increasingly marketized (the introduction, in 2012, of annual fees of £9,000 per annum for undergraduate students in England provides one particularly stark example of this) and where discourses of employability are widespread (Yorke 2004). More broadly we ask this question in a context where the dominant economic model is that of neo-liberalism, an ideology which stresses individual attainment (Harvey 2005) and which has seen models develop which view higher education as valuable only insofar as it enhances an individual's economic advancement. The idea of learning for its own sake or in order to cultivate responsible citizens has been overtaken by the idea of learning simply for economic gain.

We stress the need to understand the nature of the music industries not as an abstract idea but as a concrete (if fluid) reality which has implications for *all* musical careers whether that be as a classical or pop musician, a teacher, music industries employee or entrepreneur. We are interested in what it means to be a 'musician' in the current climate and what attributes are necessary to earn a living from this activity. We retain traditional Marxist ambivalence towards free market capitalism (it produces fantastic goods while simultaneously exploiting the majority of humanity) and believe that notions of employability *per se* have limited relevance in those industries – such as music – which are dominated by self-employment. However, we also believe that it is incumbent upon us as Music educators to provide

114 *Martin Cloonan and John Williamson*

dispassionate, research-informed, critical accounts of the music industries for our students. In fact, we want to go further and argue that higher education institutions (including Conservatoires) which claim to be teaching Music, but does not provide dedicated courses on the music industries are doing a disservice to students.

We do not expect this argument to win us many friends and have ourselves been accused of being government/business lackeys for making the sorts of arguments we make here. However, our intent is not to encourage students to fit themselves to existing economic models, but to critique them and develop alternative ways of thinking. We simply believe that in a context where many of our students wish to pursue careers in music and where the music industries are characterized by an over-supply of labour, insecure employment and low pay (DHA 2012) we question whether it is acceptable for students to graduate in Music without having any critical insight in to the industries in which they seek to work. We are, of course, aware that students enter Music degrees for myriad reasons and not all of them will be seeking a career in music. But we assume that the vast majority will wish to be involved in music – as performers, teachers and fans – and argue that such roles will be enriched by a critical understanding of the music industries.

We also suggest that even those students whose concerns focus on the musical text – whether that be via analysis, performance or composition – will have their education radically impoverished without consideration of the *con*text of such activities. As Martin (2015) notes, musicology has moved beyond the study of texts to look at areas such as social meaning. He suggests that this 'analytical reorientation necessarily leads musicologists to engage with issues that are also of fundamental concern to sociologists' (ibid: 98). This includes a concern with the music industries, the study of which has been a key concern of PMS scholars from a broadly sociological background from Adorno on and which we regard as essential to any well-educated music student.

The rest of this chapter falls in to three parts. We begin by outlining some recent developments in UK higher education and the place of Music within them, second we examine the nature of the music industries before moving on to questions of musical labour. Our premise is that – as Francis Bacon reportedly said – knowledge is power. We suggest that without knowledge of the music industries, Music students will be disempowered. We seek their empowerment.

Part 1: Higher education in contemporary Britain

It is important to note that here the teaching of Music within higher education obviously does not take place in a vacuum. Rather it occurs within material conditions which are shaped by the prevailing socio-economic climate and its concomitant political ideology. As Marx (1970, 64) explained in *The German Ideology*: 'The ideas of the ruling class are in every epoch the ruling ideas', and Harvey (2005) has illustrated how the dominant political ideology of recent years has been that of neoliberalism, serving the interests of a reconfigured ruling class. Space prevents a detailed analysis of neoliberalism here, but it is succinctly described by Harvey as

> ... a theory of political economic practices that proposes that human well-being can best be advanced by liberating individual entrepreneurial freedoms and skills within an institutional framework characterized by strong private property rights, free markets and free trade.
>
> (ibid., 2)

One manifestation of the dominance of neoliberal thinking has been the widespread erosion of free (as in fully state-funded) higher education and its replacement with a fee-based system. Students as consumers has become the norm. Within the UK the Browne report of 2010 on the funding of higher education (Browne et al. 2010) – and, in particular, the role that student fees should play – has often been seen as the apex of this sort of thinking. As leading educational commentator Stefan Collini has noted:

> Essentially Browne is contending that we should no longer think of higher education as the provision of a public good, articulated through educational judgement and largely financed by public funds... Instead, we should think of it as a lightly regulated market in which consumer demand, in the form of student choices, is sovereign in determining what is offered by service providers (i.e. the universities).
>
> (2012, 178–9)

Collini concedes that the present system in England is not a completely free market as the state is still heavily involved in providing student loans and other means of support for teaching. However, it is necessary to note that the current (2015) UK government sees the arts almost only in market terms[3] and as the arts are not prized in the job market then support for them should be sacrificed in favour of the so-called STEM (Science, Technology, Engineering and Maths) subjects. For example, UK Education Secretary, Nicky Morgan, expressed concern that school students choosing arts subjects were making decisions that would 'hold them back for the rest of their lives' (Vaughan 2014). Prior to this, the Browne Report had recommended that public support for teaching in higher education be targeted towards the STEM subjects (2010, 47) with the result that government support for the teaching of these subjects was to be ring-fenced, while the arts, humanities and social sciences were to be left to universities themselves. In effect the latter subjects were to be more marketized.[4] Students in Music programmes may wish to consider why their degrees do not attract the same level of public support as their STEM-subject peers.

We remain opposed to such developments and to moves which treat our students as consumers rather than co-investigators. We note that Scotland, where we are based, has not followed England's lead in introducing undergraduate fees and provision for Scottish domiciled students remains free at the point of delivery. This at least suggests that another way of doing things is possible in England, something which is confirmed by the German experience where an experiment with undergraduate fees has effectively been abandoned (Hotson 2014). We do, of course, support moves to restore funding to arts and humanities courses. However, we also want to empower students in ways which go beyond turning them into consumers.

We also write as non-musicians who have worked in and around Music departments for a number of years. Many academics in music departments primarily define themselves through their professional identity as musicians or composers, rather than as lecturers. Their students often share this orientation. Most would rather be out playing and composing and view the academic study of music as, at best, a means to end. While such observations constitute precisely the sort of generalizations which we discourage our students from making, we hope that readers will bear with us here for the sake of argument. We empathize with the aspirations of our colleagues and students (the two are not mutually exclusive) who wish to concentrate on making and performing. We suggest that the results of the widespread nature of such aspirations are not so much an indifference to the business of music, so much as a general feeling that its study is not a matter of urgency and perhaps best left to others.

In order to test our belief that the business of music is largely disregarded within Music Departments in the UK, we searched the University and Colleges Admission Service (UCAS) website in autumn 2015 for undergraduate Music degrees, restricting our analysis to *only* those programmes which were called Music – and *not*, for example, Music and Creativity, Music Performance, Music Technology, Popular Music etc. The survey was also limited to those offering full degrees (rather than other qualifications such as foundation degrees or a higher certificate or diploma). This resulted in the initial identification of 54 providers offering the sort of Music degree which matched our criteria.

Further details of what the degree Music programmes consisted of were then obtained. This was not always easy as websites often hid as much as they revealed. Our aim was to identify courses within Music degrees which could be classified as coming under "Music Business", "Professional Development/Practice" and "Placement". One of us has already noted problems of course and degree nomenclature with regard to PMS degrees and courses (Cloonan and Hulstedt 2012, 6) and similar problems arose here. Nevertheless, it is possible to make some generalizations.

The examination of the UCAS site showed that ten institutions running Music degrees had courses which under the broad ambit of "Music Business", eight had "Professional Development/Practice" courses and eight provided placements. A further two referred to Personal Development Plans.[5] Thus overall around 19 per cent of programmes can be said to have a dedicated Music Industries element, while around 15 per cent had placement and/or Professional Development/Practice options. It should also be noted that some programmes made some play of the professional practice elements. These included Coventry University which tells students that they 'will be treated as a professional musician at the start your career from the moment that you arrive on the course' (www.coventry.ac.uk/course-structure/arts-and-humanities/undergraduate-degree/2016–17/music-ba-hons/) and the Royal College of Music which stresses the availability of 'Career development support and advice from the renowned Creative Careers Centre' (www.rcm.ac.uk/life/beyondthercm/creativecareers/). While such provision does not necessarily meet our desire that music industries courses are taught, it does suggest that students need to be aware of a world beyond musical texts.

However, more generally it is salutary to compare the results previously found in UK-based PMS degrees (Cloonan and Hulstedt 2012) with those found with Music degrees. The results here suggest that at a somewhat crude level it can be said that the teaching of courses on the music industries is far more prevalent within PMS degrees than it is in more traditional Music degrees. As noted above, around 19 per cent of Music degrees included a Music Industries courses, something which is standard in PMS degrees. In addition, while only eight of the fifty-four Music degrees identified here offered placements, over 50 per cent (seventeen out of thirty-two) of PMS degrees were reported as offering these (Cloonan and Hulstedt 2012, 18). While it should be noted that eight of the institutions offering Music degrees had courses around professional development, it appears that within UK higher education, popular music is still conceived of as being commercial music (despite the fact that most of its practitioners are not commercially successful), while the majority of traditional Music degrees do not invite students to consider their relationship to the market. This imbalance strikes us as perverse, as *all* musical practices take place in market situations. In essence the economics of staging an orchestral performance and a rock band are not that different – costs have to be covered in various ways and thus the 'success' of each is not purely aesthetic. Moreover, we suggest that asking students to compare the staging of such events are potentially immensely empowering.

We note that in terms of gaining 'real word experience' the placement option is something which is obviously important. Examples from the survey, such as Kent and Huddersfield, offer students the opportunity of a year on placement, illustrating the provision of music industries experience as a substantial element of institutional thinking. However, it is necessary to add a note of caution here, as in order to maximize their effectiveness, placements need to take place within the context of programmes which also include a course on the nature of the music industries or face the risk of working in abstraction. A true understanding requires knowing the context in which new skills are being learned.

The analysis of the UCAS data suggests that music departments as a whole have emerged relatively unscathed from the employability agenda – or, put another way, are failing to engage with it. Our own view of employability is that it has limited cachet within those professions, such as music, wherein the dominant contractual arrangement is that of self-employment (DHA 2012). Once again, we suggest that institutions which do not contain courses where such issues are discussed and critically analyzed are doing their students a disservice. For us the fact that students who aspire to work in the music industries may be spending three years of their lives and £27,000 in fees for Music programmes which may leave them no wiser about the machinations of the music industries than when they started, this is a matter of some concern. We are aware that in some institutions, music industries' issues such as copyright and management may be addressed within modules whose prime focus lies elsewhere – for example in performance. However, while we welcome this, we do not believe that it goes far enough. If the tables were turned and aspects such as analysis, composition and performance were addressed only as aspects of courses on the music industries we doubt whether this would satisfy the justifiable concerns of our colleagues. If nothing else, dedicated courses on topics illustrate institutional recognition of their importance, while treating issues as aspects of broader courses illustrates a concomitant lowering of the importance attached to them.

Finally, it should be noted here that another contextualizing factor is that higher education academics are increasingly being encouraged to collaborate with industry via activities which fall under the general ambit of knowledge exchange. In brief, the idea here is that academics share their expertise with industry and vice versa to mutual benefit. One welcome aspect of this is the chance for student interaction with key industry figures, something which we would encourage. However, there is a need for academics to retain independence and we have warned previously of the dangers of academics being drawn into becoming advocates when their role should be one of dispassionate observers and critics (Williamson et al. 2011). We advocate not simply the teaching of courses on the music industries, but courses based on critical thinking, on questioning music industries' norms, rather than simply passing them on. This raises the question of what sorts of industries are being observed.

Part 2: The music industries from Adorno to Adele

The figure of Theodor Adorno still looms large within PMS. As the first major critic of 'the culture industry', his analysis that this industry was based on standardization and ultimately catered for false, rather than genuine, needs is still one which lays down a challenge to all theorists of what are now colloquially known as the creative industries. While many PMS theorists have challenged key Adornian concepts such as the passive audience and the extent of standardization, he remains important as someone who insists on presenting the *reality* of industrial practices and their effects and our work seeks to follow this example. While much of the development of PMS can be seen in terms of trying to counter Adorno with some optimism of the will (Frith 1983) his challenge remains.

Adorno's main concentration was on the recording industry, a characteristic shared by a number of subsequent PMS theorists. Whilst such an orientation might be understandable (popular music has often been understood in terms of the 'hits' of the day which were delivered by record companies), it has not always been helpful in that it occluded other parts of those industries working in and around music. In previous research, we have come to develop the concept of plural music industries, rather than a singular music industry. The origins of this can be dated to our survey of 'the music industry' in Scotland in 2002 (Williamson et al. 2003) which was produced in a context where previous academic (and other) accounts of that industry had conflated it with the recording industry and in particular the machinations of the major record companies. Our research in Scotland revealed a great deal of musical activity, but no major label presence. This experience led us to develop the concept of the music industries (plural) rather than music industry (singular) which had dominated previous accounts (Williamson and Cloonan 2007, 2012). Our aim here was to illustrate both diversity – in terms of the range of artistic and economic activity which occurs beyond the major record companies – and complexity, in terms of the dynamic interactions and interrelationships between the various strands of the music industries wherein the relative strengths of constituent parts are in constant evolution.

As part of our research into the music industries, we have also looked at the lives of musicians over a 120 year period through the prism of the UK's Musicians' Union (Williamson and Cloonan 2016). The results resonate with our practical experience of working in the music industries and confirm that, for the most part, the supply of labour exceeds demand, leading to low earnings and insecure employment. Degree programmes which are aimed at musicians and hide this reality from their students are doing them no favours. The reality should be portrayed. Many university Music Departments are clear that they are not attempting simply to produce musicians for the music industries. However, it seems likely that a majority of Music graduates will continue to interact with the music industries – in their broadest sense – post graduation. Here we are also keenly aware that students need to be able not simply to *understand* the nature of the music industries, but to *critique* them – i.e. to apply critical thinking to that understanding.

One recent example can be used to illustrate this. In November 2013, the UK implemented the European Union Directive 2011/77/EU which extended the period for which sound recordings remain in copyright from 50 to 70 years. The move followed fierce lobbying from a range of high profile organizations within the music industries and fierce resistance from a range of academics (see Williamson et al. 2011). The debate here centred on what a desirable period of copyright should be in a context where assignation of copyright by writers and performers is a primary mechanism through which money is made within the music industries. The longer compositions and recordings remain in copyright, the longer they can potentially make money for their copyright holders. However, the vast majority of compositions and recordings make little money and there is some public interest in allowing works of art to enter the public domain after a reasonable period. But what might that be?

Proponents of the new regulations argued that the moves would benefit aging musicians whose recordings from the 1960s were about to fall out of copyright (meaning that they could be commercially exploited without the performers being compensated). Opponents argued that comparatively few musicians would benefit and that the public good would be better served by limiting the copyright term and allowing public access to these old recordings. It was also noted that the moves towards term extension were happening at exactly the time when recordings made in the 'golden age' of British popular music – especially those of the Beatles – were about to fall out of copyright (Harkins 2012), which would have meant that record companies, to whom performers generally assign their copyright and which controlled the copyright in those recordings, would no longer be able to claim exclusive rights to be able to market them.

The rights and wrongs need not detain us further. What is important here is that fundamental questions were being raised about the proper remuneration of performing musicians. What value society places on musical composition and performance was being debated, disputed and decided. The decisions not only affected musicians' remuneration for playing on recordings, but the ability of composers to use such performances in their works (as, for example, in sampling). We suggest that students graduating from Music programmes should, at the very least be able to have an informed view of whether that extension was a good thing or not. If the answer to that (admittedly rhetorical) question is 'Yes', it seems that a number of things follow: the history of copyright should be taught, its development analyzed, its underpinning rationale questioned and its outcomes debated. As an abstract idea, copyright might not mean much to the student obsessed with Bach or Miles Davis or developing their performance or compositional prowess, but as a concrete reality it underpins the workings of the music industries and it is thus of vital importance to practitioners. We suggest that musicians should not only know about the musical texts which they produce, but also the industrial *contexts* into which their work is flowing. Students who are spending £27,000 in tuition fees as part of a process which they hope will facilitate employment in the music industries should surely not find themselves at the end of three years as ignorant of the workings of the music industries (within which we include the traditional 'music profession') as they were when they began their degrees.

We observe that the music industries exist in 'a constant state of flux'. This makes both understanding trends and seeking employment hazardous. For example, the recording sector can be seen as dominant for around forty-five years (circa 1963–2009), but has subsequently declined in the internet age where the fortunes of live music and music publishing have become increasingly important. Those seeking to work in the music industries *need* to understand these things and to think critically about their implications. If music theory is a key to the understanding of music, then theory also has much to teach about the music industries – not merely in abstraction but as *lived experience*. Here Adorno remains a key starting point not necessarily because he is right, but because he shows that it *matters*. It is not necessary to share his views of the culture industry to share his commitment to musical life and to trying to understand – and critique – the forces which underpin it. But we would also add key works by authors such as Becker (1982), Frith (1983), Peacock and Weir (1973) and, perhaps above all, Ehrlich (1985). What each of them contributes to is an understanding of the lives of musicians *as workers* (Williamson and Cloonan 2016), that is a people trying to make a living from their musical ability. It is surely incumbent upon higher education working in music to get students to reflect on how they intend to work.

Musicians need to be able to reflect on the factors which affect their chances of employment and their remuneration. Neither of us is a musician and we are aware that notions of what constitutes a musician remain contested. However, both of our experiences and the existing literature suggest that musical prowess is not enough (O'Neill 2003, 79). Of course, musical skills need to be developed and this is not an attack on performance-based courses or programmes *per se*. But musical skills alone are not, it seems, enough. If this is the case (and we have no doubt that it is), then it has implications which we spell out in the next section.

Part 3: Discussion: what is to be done?

It should now be clear that we regard degree programmes which are aimed at developing musicians in order to facilitate their working in the music industries, but which do not contain courses on those industries as doing a disservice to their students. Some of the few fortunate ones who find themselves working as full-time musicians may end up with managers who will take care of the business side of things, but the majority will need to attend to their own business. Doing so will be all the harder if they have not been taught how to critically evaluate the workings of the music industries.

This need not entail the making of detailed business plans (although it might), more the exploration of the relationship between the art and commerce and the factors which have mediated this relationship over the years. We cannot (or would rather not) imagine students who have no interest in exploring the factors which have shaped musical practice over the years and which will shape their own. The teaching of the music industries should not be the passing on of information, but the critical investigation of practices of music making and the exploitation (in all senses of the word) of musical compositions and performances.

122 *Martin Cloonan and John Williamson*

We have no doubt that such courses should be compulsory. Part of neo-liberalism has been the elevation of consumer (for which in higher education read 'student') choice to the status of the sacrosanct. However, choice is not necessarily a good thing, especially if there is too much choice (Scheibe-henne et al. 2009) or if that choice is not an informed one. In addition, there are subjects in which to leave the curriculum to student/consumer choice would be to tempt disaster (Medicine springs to mind). We suggest that for those wishing to enter the music industries, being able to choose not to be educated about those industries risks similar disasters. What is needed is less choice and more expertise. This may not engender more success in popularity contests such as the ridiculous National Student Survey, but it will engender more critical and empowered workers.

Some concluding thoughts for students

We are aware that the intended audience for this book might find some of our arguments a little abstract. However, we suggest that they are in fact fundamental. It is not necessary to buy into the rhetoric of students as customers (although we recognize that in some cases it might help) in order to believe that Music students *must* be taught about the music industries. This should not involve indoctrination, it should involve empowerment. Education has long involved processes of indoctrination as well as liberation. But the text is meaningless without the *context*.

Previous research has illustrated that a concern about the pernicious impact of vocationalism and teaching of music industries courses is not just restricted to those working within the classical music world. In fact, there is evidence that many popular music students simply wish to make music and have little interest in courses about the business of music (Cloonan and Hulstedt 2012). Furthermore, the employability agenda which occupies much time within UK higher education now, creates problems for those working within sectors where *self*-employment is the norm. We suggest that Music students need to think not so much about getting a job within music, as being able to develop the sorts of skills (personal as well as professional) which will allow them to cope in a business where self-employment is the norm. For us, being a musician necessitates being music business-savvy, at least in the sense of understanding how it works and one's location within it. Such knowledge is power.

As we end this chapter we are aware that it may jar with much of the rest of this book. However, we feel this supports, rather than undermines, our arguments. Nowhere else in the book is the thorny issue of the reality of working in the music industries raised. Moreover, as PMS specialists we note that while several chapters here mention popular music in passing, only this one comes from within PMS – i.e. from those academics concerned with the form of music which the majority of people listen to (whether by choice or not) day in and day out. We are aware of many music departments

The music industries   123

which have a single popular music expert, but none in which popular music dominates and classical music is restricted to just one expert. The fact that the latter scenario is almost impossible to imagine intrigues us. Meanwhile traditional music departments remain dominated by the western canon, with PMS largely the domain of the non-traditional, often less prestigious, universities (Cloonan and Hulstedt 2012).

Our aim was to ask what graduates of Music undergraduate degree programmes should be able to do at the end of their programmes. We suggest that they should be able to make important decisions about their careers in critically informed ways and that this requires critical engagement with the music industries during the course of their studies. It is incumbent upon all Music degree programmes to provide critical information on the state of the music industries that many students aspire to work in. This does not mean blind adherence to current ways of working and distributing profits, but subjecting such practices to scrutiny and challenging the rhetoric coming from both government and music industries' organizations. It means helping students to think through the implications of the business decisions they will make during their careers and to consider alternative ways of establishing musical careers. It does not mean avoiding criticism of the reality of the music industries, but it certainly *does* mean imparting knowledge of what that reality is. We fear that some would rather that this remained opaque, something which happens elsewhere, rather in the lived reality of musicians.

So, we suggest that undergraduate music students should demand Bach, Beethoven and Boulanger, as well as the Beatles, PJ Harvey and Nina Simone. They should by all means take the opportunity to improve their performance and/or compositional skills and given encouragement to understand as many different musical forms as possible and to be able to put them in a wider socio-historical context. But, those who are seeking a *career* in music then should also *demand* that their tutors help them to understand the workings and realities of the music industries. Only then will such tutors have truly assisted in empowering their students. Only then will a Music degree have shown its worth. Like it or not, music *is* a business, so music students should make it their business to understand it as such. Only by doing so will they ever be able to do what Public Enemy (and we) would have them do – Fight the Power.

Notes

1 John Williamson managed the Scottish band Belle and Sebastian, Martin Cloonan managed Glasgow act Zoey Van Goey (see Cloonan 2015).
2 The main representative body for musicians in the UK, the Musicians' Union, follows this approach and organizes different sections for Teachers, Orchestras, Writers, Live Performance etc. See www.musiciansunion.org.uk/Home/About-Us/How-the-Union-Works/MU-Sections, accessed 26 February 2016.
3 One example of this is that the current Secretary of State for Culture Media and Sport (effectively the UK's Minister for Culture), Sajid Javid, has described

124 *Martin Cloonan and John Williamson*

ticket touts as "classic entrepreneurs", seemingly endorsing a view that tickets for concerts should go simply to those with the deepest pockets.

4 See www.andyworthington.co.uk/2010/11/22/did-you-miss-this-100-percent-funding-cuts-to-arts-humanities-and-social-sciences-courses-at-uk-universities/.

5 It should be noted that some institutions provided more than one of a selection of a Music Business courses, placements and Personal Develop Plan. For example City has an optional Music Business course and provides placements, while Kent offers a year in industry as well as a Professional Practice module.

Bibliography

Adorno, Theodor W. 2001. *The Culture Industry: Selected Essays on Mass Culture* (ed. J. Bernstein). London: Routledge.

Becker, Harold. 1982. *Artworlds*. Berkeley: University of California Press.

Browne, John et al. 2010. *Securing a Sustainable Future for Higher Education: An Independent Review of Higher Education and Student Finance*. Department for Business, Innovation and Skills. www.gov.uk/government/publications/the-browne-report-higher-education-funding-and-student-finance. Accessed 26 February 2016.

Cahn, Meyer M. 1948. 'There Is No Music Business'. *Music Educators' Journal* 34/5: 38–40.

Cloonan, Martin. 2005. 'What Is Popular Music Studies? Some Observations'. *British Journal of Music Education* 22/1: 77–93.

———. 2007. *Popular Music and the State in the UK*. Aldershot, UK: Ashgate.

———. 2015. 'Managing the Zoeys: Some Reminiscences'. In *Organising Music: Theory, Practice, Performance*, edited by Nic Beech and Charlotte Gilmore, 226–35. Cambridge: Cambridge University Press.

Cloonan, Martin and Lauren Hulstedt. 2012. *Taking Notes: A Mapping of HE Popular Music and an Investigation into the Teaching of Theory and Analysis*. Edinburgh: Higher Education Academy.

Collini, Stefan. 2012. *What Are Universities For?* London: Penguin.

Department of Business, Innovation and Skills (BIS). 2009. *Higher Ambitions: The Future of Universities in a Knowledge Economy*. HMSO.

DHA Communications. 2012. *The Working Musician Report 2012*. Musicians' Union.

Ehrlich, Cyril. 1985. *The Music Profession in Britain since the Eighteenth Century*. Oxford: Clarendon.

Frith, Simon. 1983. *Sound Effects*. Constable. Oxford: Oxford University Press.

Griffiths, Dai. 1999. 'The High Analysis of Low Culture'. *Music Analysis* 18/3: 389–434.

Harkins, Paul. 2012. 'Extending the Term: The Gowers Review and the Campaign to Increase the Length of Copyright in Sound Recordings'. *Popular Music and Society* 35/5: 629–49.

Harvey, David. 2005. *A Brief History of Neoliberalism*. Oxford: Oxford University Press.

Harvie, Jen. 2013. *Fair Play: Art, Performance and Neoliberalism*. Basingstoke: Palgrave Macmillan.

Hotson, Howard. 2014. 'Germany's Great Tuition Fees U-turn', *Times Higher Education Supplement*, 13 February 2014. www.timeshighereducation.com/features/germanys-great-tuition-fees-u-turn/2011168.article. Accessed 26 February 2016.

Martin, Peter. 2015. 'Music and the Sociological Gaze'. In *The Routledge Reader on the Sociology of Music*, edited by John Shepherd and Kyle Devine, 97–104. Routledge.

Marx, Karl. 1970. *The German Ideology*. London: Lawrence and Wishart.

Negus, Keith. 1992. *Producing Pop*. London: Edward Arnold.

——— 1996. *Music Genres and Corporate Cultures*. London: Routledge.

O'Neill, Susan A. 2003. 'The Self-Identity of Young Musicians" in *Musical Identities*, edited by Raymond MacDonald, David Hargreaves and Dorothy Miell, 79–96. Oxford: Oxford University Press.

Peacock, Alan and Ronald Weir. 1975. *The Composer in the Marketplace*. London: Faber and Faber.

Scheibehenne, Benjamin, Rainer Greifeneder and Peter M. Todd, P. 2009. 'What Moderates the Too-Much-Choice Effect?'. *Psychology and Marketing* 26/3: 229–53.

Vaughan, Richard. 2014. 'Nicky Morgan Tells Pupils: Study STEM Subjects to Keep Your Options Open', *Times Educational Supplement,* 10 November 2014. www.tes.com/news/school-news/breaking-news/nicky-morgan-tells-pupils-study-stem-subjects-keep-your-options-open. Accessed 26 February 2016.

Williamson, John and Martin Cloonan. 2007. 'Rethinking the Music Industry'. *Popular Music* 26/2: 305–22.

———. 2012. 'Contextualising the Contemporary Recording Industry'. In *The International Recording Industries*, edited by Lee Marshall, 11–29. London: Routledge.

———. 2016. *Players' Work Time: A History of the British Musicians' Union*. Manchester: Manchester University Press.

Williamson, John, Martin Cloonan and Simon Frith. 2011. 'Having an Impact? Academics, the Music Industries and the Problem of Knowledge. *International Journal of Cultural Policy* 17/5: 459–74.

Yorke, Mantz. 2004. *Employability in Higher Education: What It Is and What It Is Not*. Edinburgh: Higher Education Academy.

6 Writing about music in the 21st century

Eva Moreda Rodríguez

Studying for a Music degree in a university setting – as opposed to, say, a conservatoire – is, to a great extent, about learning how to write about music. Music students at British and many other English-speaking universities write tens of thousands of words worth of essays, maybe even an undergraduate dissertation, over the course of the three or four years it takes them to get an undergraduate degree. They are assessed, to a very significant extent, on their ability to write about music – perhaps more so than they are on their ability to perform or compose, depending on the programme they are studying and their own course choices. Some of them might be looking further into the future, beyond assignment deadlines and assessment: they might be hoping that the ability to write clearly and convincingly will be a strong asset in their future careers, whether this involves writing specifically about music or not. In fact, these days, university prospectuses often name writing as one of the most valuable and marketable skills arts and humanities students will acquire during the course of their degrees. Beyond purely utilitarian approaches, though, those of us teaching in Music may have a number of reasons to give students written assignments: we would like our students to develop the ability to write critically and analytically about music. In doing so, we hope that our students will be developing an ability to *think* about music as well: in our academic culture, both processes seem to be inextricably linked. Maybe we would also like to expose our students to the very different ways in which music can be and is written about, inside and outside academia; we would like them to consider, and maybe practice, how each of these genres and styles differ, and where and when some modes of writing can be more useful and illuminating than others in making sense of music.

In this chapter, I illustrate how engagement with new modes and genres of writing developed in the last 15 years after the advent of Web 2.0 can help us and our students work towards those goals. I will also discuss how these new modes and genres have made it easier to cultivate a range of approaches to writing about music and to make sense of music through writing. I have chosen not to engage substantially with well-established genres of academic writing (namely the essay), as there is already considerable bibliography on

Writing about music in the 21st century   127

and help with those, and instead focus on less well-explored, ever-evolving genres of writing. This does not mean, however, that I uphold the view that traditional genres must be replaced with new media; on the contrary, I argue that it is the combination of traditional and new genres, rather than the focus on new genres per se, that can be particularly fruitful in helping us and students develop better writing skills.

Traditional writing genres and digital natives

In 2001, Mark Prensky influentially coined the terms 'digital natives'; this was rooted in the claim that technology had irremediably changed the brains of those born around 1980 affecting the ways in which they absorb and process information. Consequently, argued Prensky, 'digital natives' were fundamentally a linguistic and cultural community distinct from their teachers ('digital immigrants') and, to respond to the needs of digital natives, the education system needed to be revolutionized beyond recognition by technological change (Prensky 2001a). Prensky's views were enthusiastically embraced not only by some sectors in academia (Underwood 2007; Palfrey and Gasser 2011) but also, most notably, by popular journalism and educational policy. However, the concept of 'digital natives' also attracted well-founded criticism from its inception. Critics have pointed out that the divide between digital natives and digital immigrants is not actually a binary divide, but has to be thought of as a continuum or a spectrum which includes different ways and degrees of engaging with technology (Warschauer 2002); that being a digital native is not about being born after a certain year, but rather about engaging in certain practices (Helsper and Eynon 2009, 1); that Prensky's classification has ignored how diverse the younger population is, both in terms of access to technology and in terms of class, race etc. (Helsper 2008; Helsper and Eynon 2009, 3 and 14); and that the claim that digital natives 'learn differently' has little or no empirical support (Bennett et al. 2008, 779; Helsper and Eynon 2009, 3). It could also be argued that some of the older 'digital natives' (i.e. those born in the early- to mid-1980s) are now increasingly joining the other side as teaching staff – which does not mean that they are necessarily equipped to understand students better than digital immigrants.

Drawing on the above-mentioned criticisms to Prensky, in this chapter I will regard the new genres and media of writing about music made possible by Web 2.0 not as a revolution digital immigrants struggle to make sense of, but rather as extensions and developments – often unexpected and exciting – of traditional genres of writing. It is probably not uncommon nowadays for an undergraduate Music student to write about music more often than was the case only a generation ago – and in a more extensive number of genres and contexts too. Students express their views on a range of music in their Facebook and Twitter accounts, and in the process they often interact with others. Some of them might engage in more discursive kinds of writing – in blogs in which they write about the music they listen to, perform or compose, in isolation or combining it with other kinds of writing; in MySpace profiles or YouTube channels where they promote their music. Such facility to engage with music in writing – or at least the availability of this possibility, whether students make use of it or not – should be at the back of our minds when teaching students how to write about music. On the other hand, however, the problems our students are facing are not very different from those encountered by other people who, in different times and places, found themselves wanting or being asked to write about music: audience, genre, style, voice, argument, relevance, the problem of communicating about music solely through words – the same problems that we face when we try our hand at the traditional genres of academic writing.

Let us have a look, for example, at the essay, which many will probably regard as the traditional genre of undergraduate academic writing *par excellence.* (Here we could add the undergraduate dissertation as well, which can indeed be understood as an extended undergraduate essay in that they both focus to a great extent on the same abilities). Most definitions of 'essay' provided by essay-writing guides made available online by teaching and learning centres tend to emphasize the fact that it involves developing an argument, and they typically name two reasons why students should learn how to construct an argument and express it in writing: first, the essay is credited with instilling a sense of belonging to the scholarly or academic community, in which people communicate and advance their discipline typically through written argument (Gocsik 2005). Second, the ability to write convincingly and argumentatively is regarded a marketable skill which arguably will be highly valued even by those who are looking for jobs outside their discipline (Williams and McEnerney 2013).

We could think of these two reasons as two *problems* of writing about music – or of writing, more generally – that writers have faced over the centuries, and we could argue that, in the digital age, these two problems are more pressing than ever. In regards to the first point, developing an argument in an essay is, after all, about thinking in terms of connectedness and explicitness (Andrews 2003, 119). And it is already a common trope to state that, in the Information Age, our students, all of us, are bombarded with information at all times – whether textual, visual, aural or audio-visual. When could a tried-and-tested method, such as the essay, to establish connections between disparate bits of information be more necessary than now? Similarly, the idea of belonging to a scholarly community resonates with our students' experience of creating and developing an online presence: it is already a well-established notion in the academic study of internet practices and usage that the internet offers users the ability to craft and choose between a number of different online identities and to belong to a number of different online communities (see, for example, Palfrey and Gasser 2011, 25). In this regard, developing an academic, scholarly identity might not be too much of a leap for a student used to interacting with different types of people online

Writing about music in the 21st century   129

on a daily basis, presenting a slightly different version of her identity to each group of people.

I argue, therefore, that the potential of new media and genres of writing is best realized if combined with other forms of written assessment. By this, I do not mean just the essay or undergraduate dissertation. In fact, most – if not all – music departments have indeed used other forms of written assessment for years: the learning or listening diary, the reflective commentary on one's performance or composition, the ethnographic account. To this we could add the blog, the Twitter account, the wiki – all genres and modes of writing that have been made possible by Web 2.0 and with which the average student is more likely to be familiar with before he or she starts university. A carefully considered mix of these genres through the course of a degree can help to promote reflection about what writing about music is: how these modes of writing differ, what purposes they serve, why they exist in the first place, and why and how they are assessed. In other words, it is about not regarding the academic essay as the be-all and end-all of academic writing; instead, comparing it with other modes of writing might encourage students to see what may appear like inscrutable rules as socially constructed conventions which allow us to engage with our object of study in a particular way – all the while being aware that there are alternative writing genres which might be more appropriate if they wish to engage with music in different ways.

In the remainder of this chapter, I will discuss three new genres of writing about music and how working with them in the classroom can help us improve not only students' writing, but also their (and our) critical understanding of what writing is, and thus act as a bridge into academic writing on music. In the first section, I will focus on how social networking can help illustrate the question of audience or readership, and how such social networks can be used to introduce students to academic writing. In the second section, I will focus on blogs to discuss issues pertaining to the genres of academic writing about music, exploring the question of whether the essay, the dissertation and the reflective commentary are the main genres of writing we still want to use and how they can be complemented by new genres and whether all of these genres are means to an end or skills with a real market value in the digital economy. In the third and last section, focusing on the hypertext, I will discuss what it means to write about music – whether we are asking students to write about a score, about sound or about performance – and how the new genres of writing can help students become more aware of this.

Rethinking how our students write and respond to feedback

When reflecting about the ways in which technology has changed the way in which students think about writing, the initial reaction from some of us might be to say that the possibility of writing anywhere, all the time, to be

130   *Eva Moreda Rodríguez*

read by potentially everyone with an internet connection, has made students and other users of technology more careless about their writing, mainly in terms of grammar and spelling, but also in terms of argument and consistence. The alleged decline in the quality of written expression among younger generations is often accompanied by a wave of 'moral panic' (Bennett, Maton, and Kervin 2008, 782) and presented as tantamount to the 'decline of cultural standards' (Fitzpatrick 2012, 43), which is indicative of the central role of writing in our culture. Fitzpatrick (2012, 46), however, has rightly pointed out that these modes of writing (and the forms of reading which underpin them) need to be acknowledged by 'members of traditional literary culture', instead of being dismissed as 'inherently frivolous and degraded'.

The possibilities for receiving feedback on one's writing have changed as well. Not so long ago, teenage and young adults' writing (outside school assignments) was kept mostly private: one could silently write poetry or a novel and keep it secret from everyone except for a few trusted friends who wrote as well, or one could publish it in obscure literary journals. Now, one can upload one's completed work to numerous websites, have it beta-tested, have it read and commented on by similarly-minded people. The possibility of receiving feedback is almost constantly available, and feedback is usually received within a relative short span of time as well. Writers can also control to a certain extent the type of feedback they would like to receive and the channels through which they receive it; for example, it is possible to limit who is allowed to write on a blog, MySpace or Facebook profile, or to delete feedback selectively.

Of course, being able to receive feedback on a continuous basis does not mean that the writer is continuously critically evaluating, filtering and responding to that feedback, but this does not imply that the writer is completely immune to it either. Indeed, it could be argued that our students' experience of writing on social media is based, to a great extent, on dialogue: many of them will be doing a great deal of their writing on music informally in social networks. Traditional educational tasks, such as homework or essay writing, can therefore seem isolating to them (Ktisis 2008, 30). While I strongly advocate that university should encourage personal and private study and reflection, this does not mean that we cannot make peer-to-peer interaction work to our advantage.

Our students' familiarity with this kind of networked writing which prompts or allows immediate feedback could be used as an initial step to introduce them to academic writing in music. In the past, I have taught introductory courses in music studies to students of other subjects or potential students who had not made up their minds yet. Many of them cannot read a score, and so I usually advise them to simply 'write about what you hear' instead of focusing on the minutiae of notation. I must confess, though, that I am not completely satisfied with my own answer. On one hand, it is about being able to *describe* what they hear – and describing pitch, harmony, rhythm, form, is relatively easy to teach, even to people who cannot read music with any degree of fluency. But there is a second element students sometimes struggle with: why does it matter? Why write about this music in the first place? And yet students may be dealing with these two kinds of questions all the time when writing short, informal comments about music on YouTube, MySpace, Facebook or Twitter: they might express why they like or dislike a piece of music, why they think everybody (or nobody) should care about it, and they might be supporting their answer, to some extent, with reference to particular aspects of the music. Their short comment may also be part of a broader conversation between listeners. Writing about music online, in the informal context of social networks, can therefore be an attempt to answer the same questions we deal with when writing academically – who, what, why and how; engaging students in a short exercise or reflection of this kind may therefore make academic writing on music seem less intimidating.

Rethinking the genres of academic writing

My second example refers to the fact that the widespread use of technology and the ways in which it has impacted our students' writing habit can serve as an impulse to re-think current genres of academic writing, in the same way as, throughout history, social, economic and technological changes have caused new genres of writing about music to appear, sometimes filling in new niches – for example, concert reviews from the nineteenth century onwards – but also at the same time fulfilling and resonating with already existing concerns regarding music. This is why I prefer to think of new modes of writing as an *excuse*, rather than as the starting signal to do away with current writing practices of academic writing under the banner that writing crafted, continuous prose is allegedly becoming obsolete, or that digital natives do not possess the required attention span or discipline to engage with traditional ways of learning how to write (as suggested by Prensky 2001b). The former would be short-sighted, the latter patronizing. In this section, I explore one such genre, the blog, discussing how it can be integrated within existing academic genres of writing about music – increasing, in some cases, their potentialities – while also expanding in different directions.

There are two particular features of the blog which make it particularly interesting and valuable as a genre to be used alongside traditional academic genres: on one hand, it is content-focused (Miller and Shepherd 2004) and, more specifically, text-focused; it still requires a considerable effort from the student in terms of writing continuous, well-crafted prose, as opposed to Twitter or Facebook, where brevity is paramount or at least highly valued. On the other hand, it is an almost perfect metonymy for the Internet in that it is both public and intensely private at the same time (Miller and Shepherd 2004): the most successful blogs tend to be those in which the author, even if she is writing in a professional capacity, presents herself to us as a real person, with beliefs, preferences and biases; this might provide students with a

132   *Eva Moreda Rodríguez*

more relaxed environment than the traditional genres of academic writing, in that the possibility to express their own views, to 'be themselves' might be appealing and at the same time familiar.

Being such an intensely 'first-person' genre, blogging lends itself particularly well to reflective writing. In its most basic form, the use of blogging in undergraduate academic writing may simply involve students typing the entries of a learning diary into WordPress, Blogger or a similar platform and then posting them online, as opposed to typing them into a Word document. Granted, there are some adjustments which need to be made and which could be discussed collectively with students to illustrate the need to draw attention to the conventions of different genres. For example, unlike a printed learning diary, a blog can attract immediate written feedback (in the forms of comments) from a very large number of individuals, as opposed to just the member of staff marking a paper assignment. Will this type of feedback be allowed? Will it even be actively encouraged and assessed? Will the comments section be open to any internet user who can access the blog from any part of the world or just to other students in the course? Will there be rules for feedback comments, and what will happen if someone transgresses these rules?

A further area for discussion with students may focus on what will constitute the final, assessable product. When briefed about a learning diary-type assignment, students are usually reminded that the final submission must be edited; the expectation, therefore, is a finished and cohesive product which tells some sort of story, pretty much like an essay. But blogging is by definition about timing; a blog is a work-in-progress, so asking students to edit their blogs into a finished product, for the sake of assessment, could be seen to contravene the genre conventions and genre expectations (but, if we do away with the final edit, how do we assess the work?).

The potential of blogging, though, may extend beyond providing a Web 2.0 version of a classic assignment such as the learning diary, and a look into other humanities disciplines and their ways of integrating new genres within established writing practices may be productive for us in music as well. Let us consider, for example, the role of blogging in the teaching of English and Creative Writing: Kathleen Fitzpatrick (2002) has argued that the novel is not made obsolete by the new genres, but its writing and its study can actually be complemented by new genres such as blogging. Indeed, the first-person narrative of blogs can offer valuable insights into how to construct a first-person character and develop a distinct narrative voice (Fitzpatrick 2007, 169). Although I am not arguing that developing creative writing skills should be a central element when using blogging to teach our students how to write about music, these insights can arguably be valuable for music students as well: consider, for example, primary sources written in the first person, such as auto-biographies, memoirs, letters or diaries; students who have experience with blogging or a similar genre may find it easier to relate to historical forms of self-fashioning. Furthermore,

Writing about music in the 21st century   133

the 'time-based' construction of one's own creative personality through a number of discrete, time-bound utterances (i.e. blog posts) may be of value to those students aiming at developing their creative personality as a composer or performer.

Apart from being a useful tool for developing particular skills to be applied elsewhere, blogging also constitutes a potentially valuable professional skill from an employability perspective. I am not advocating that we renounce the other types of (less obviously marketable) writing skills, but we certainly should keep an eye on how skills in new writing genres can match the challenges posed by today's professional music world. Although it is relatively unlikely that a significant percentage of our students will be able to make a living as professional music bloggers, blog-writing or online writing skills are useful skills in a great variety of careers within and outside of music, including performing or composing, where building up and interacting with an audience base has to be regarded as an essential requirement.

What does it mean to write about music?

There is a third traditional difficulty faced by writers on music to which the modes of digital writing can be applied productively: the question of what it means to write about music and why it matters. It is already commonplace to cite the elusiveness of music or its non-representational nature as the reason why it is allegedly so difficult to write about music. An alternative and perhaps more truthful way to put it would be that, unlike in other humanities disciplines, writing about music can involve different things and can serve different purposes.

When I announce that I am going to write about music, what might I be writing about? We might write about a score as physical object, which would include comments on editorial matters. This is, of course, a very particular genre usually found in specialized publications, but which can be revisited in the classroom by making use of the possibilities offered by the Internet: there is a wealth of scores available for free (the Petrucci Music Library is perhaps the best-known example), and our students are already making use of them when they need a piece of music for performance or study; such free resources have often replaced library catalogues as the students' first point of call. And, although editorial concerns may not be on our students' minds when their main goal is to get a piece of music as quickly as possible, and possibly for free, we can turn the situation to our advantage and ask students to reflect in writing about their search for a score: what editions of the piece have they been able to find? How do they compare? What led them to choose one over the others?

Another possibility is writing as a means of reflection on music as an experience, which encompasses elements of performance and analysis but with a clear focus on the value or significance that the music has for the listener and the wider community. Integrating genres of online writing within the

134 *Eva Moreda Rodríguez*

classroom can help students to become more aware of the different components of 'the musical experience', and understand better what they are asked to write about – simply because these elements can now be displayed on a screen simultaneously, as opposed to being just apprehended abstractly. We can envisage, for instance, what a 'musical experience' could look like on MySpace: in relation to 'listening', there will be different items on display which relate to and inform, in one way or another, the listening experience. For example, an artist may use certain labels to identify herself; these determine how she turns up in searches, and also inform the listening experience to some extent. The 'Comments' section can also become part of the musical experience since any listener can read others' comments or contribute to them; these too can influence the listener's choice and expectations. The functionality 'Similar songs' suggests songs the user might like based on his browsing history; this puts each individual song in the context of a listening sequence – a more time-extensive musical experience – which is hardly imaginable before social networks came into being. This has its limitations, too: the possibility that one is hardly confronted with new musical experiences; the falsely neat cataloguing by 'genre', often based on commercial criteria rather than anything else. Or let us consider Spotify: here students can simulate or manipulate listening experiences simply by creating playlists, naming them or reordering the tracks in it. In both cases, writing may be used in a traditional way to record *a posteriori* reflection or in a more exploratory way, as a part of the user's interaction with these social networks.

Once we have decided what aspect of the musical experience should be focused on, this may have to be broken down into manageable components. This is a traditional approach for a lecturer teaching his or her students how to write about music, and a number of books and how-to online guides are written from that point of view: how to write about melody, rhythm, harmony, form, timbre. For some of these elements (rhythm or harmony, for instance) western music theory provides us with a relatively sophisticated descriptive vocabulary, which in some cases can even be borrowed or adapted to discuss popular or traditional music. But what about timbre, for example? Can we conceivably discuss critically in writing the range of timbric possibilities of an instrument, the range of timbres we have recently heard at a performance or recording, without heavily relying on 'the poorest of linguistic categories, the adjective', as Barthes (1977, 179) famously remarked in *The Grain of the Voice*? This is indeed not a new problem for writers on music, and I do not wish to uphold the idea that there is an easy solution for it hidden in the application of digital writing genres; yet they can certainly help us and our students articulate why it is important to discuss all these categories, why they matter and why music matters and why it is worth bothering to write about music in the first place. I will specifically focus on how hypertexts can help us answer some of these questions.

Although it might seem counterintuitive, I would like to start by discussing what hypertext is not good for. At first sight, nothing seems more

Writing about music in the 21st century 135

connective, and hence fit for academic writing in the new brave digital world, than a page of text (understood in its broadest sense) in which a simple mouse click can take us to any other text which the author of the hypertext thinks is connected to the primary text in any way (Landow 1989, 173). As has already been noted, however, hypertext is not so much a tool for analysis as it is a tool for *analogy* (Feustle 1997, 116). Pretty much as in Borges' 'The Garden of Forking Paths', hypertext can lead us to somewhere we had not planned to arrive, but each of the steps in our way is accidental – there is no reason why we had to end up exactly where we did. Academic writing and thinking, on the other hand, typically requires students to envisage the paths they want to take and establish a hierarchy between them, make a choice, establish which connections are fruitful and which are not, and give the reasons for it. This is a key feature of academic writing which hypertext does not quite promote. I therefore do not share the faith in hypertext as an almost revolutionary tool for teaching, something which was first purported almost twenty-five years ago (Landow 1989, 173; Katz 1996) and now seems highly dubious.

Where hypertext *is* useful, however, is in bringing together all the things we refer to when we talk about music (the performance, the score, the work as idea, the experience) in an explicit, graphic way which stimulates student reflection. This may start right from the moment in which we ask students to create a musical hypertext: the first question for them to consider would then be, in what way we can consider music as 'text'. Does this mean that we have to put the musical score, as the primary text from which all other secondary 'texts' will be linked, at the centre of it –-, and if so, what could be the problems of this approach? Which edition of the 'text' will be chosen, and how will we alert the reader of the existence of other editions and the significance or credibility we attach to each of them? Or could the primary text be, say, a spectrogram representing a piece or a performance, that is, a visual representation of sound which can be displayed simultaneously on screen?

Similar questions about what constitutes music and how to integrate these different practices in our writing about music could be raised when deciding what secondary texts will be linked to the main text. For example, a group of students might be working on a hypertext involving the analysis of a Schubert song. Hypertext gives them the opportunity to include hyperlinks to performances of that song, and this opportunity leads them to look in YouTube performances they may want to include. Among their findings, there are two particular recordings which are interesting: one from the 1910s, the other from the 1950s. Why do students find them interesting for the purposes of the task they are completing? Because these two different performances lead them to analyze the song differently, to understand the relation between the singer, the composer and the poetic voice differently.[1] This is, of course, something which could have been brought to the students' attention during a lecture, or something which some of them might have found by themselves without the need for a hypertext, but the multiplicity of

136   *Eva Moreda Rodríguez*

connections offered by the hypertext and the opportunity to see all of them physically in one space has the potential to trigger reflection about what it is that we need to focus on when writing about music.

Conclusion

Web 2.0 and the new writing genres emerging from it have changed the ways in which people write about music – but perhaps not that much. In the end, many of the questions students face when asked to write academically about music will be the same as the ones encountered by other writers on music at different moments in time: what to write about, how to write about it, for whom, how to exploit the characteristics of a genre. Lecturers and other teaching staff may be less familiar with technology and with Web 2.0 than our students are – although such claim must be taken with a pinch of salt – but most of us are definitely experts in writing about music: we are exposed on a daily basis to different genres and styles of writing about music on a daily basis, we write professionally in all or some of these genres and styles, and our own writing and research depends on our ability to critically evaluate and analyse other people's writings – on examining how these people approached the issues I have described before. Research-led teaching can therefore extend beyond content and be applied to the teaching of writing skills as well: when writing is historically considered, we are likely to find unexpected parallels between new and traditional forms of writing that can then be transformed into strategies for our students.

Note

1 For the original case study see Leech-Wilkinson (2009, 800).

Bibliography

Andrews, Richard. 2003. 'The End of the Essay?' *Teaching in Higher Education* 8 (1): 117–128.

Barthes, Roland. 1977. *Image – Music – Text*. Hill and Wang.

Bennett, Sue, Karl Maton, and Lisa Kervin. 2008. 'The "Digital Natives" Debate: A Critical Review of the Evidence'. *British Journal of Educational Technology* 39 (5): 775–786.

Feustle, Joseph A. 1997. 'Literature in Context: Hypertext and Teaching'. *Hispania* 80 (2) (May 1): 216–226.

Fitzpatrick, Kathleen. 2002. 'The Exhaustion of Literature: Novels, Computers, and the Threat of Obsolescence'. *Contemporary Literature* 43 (3) (October 1): 518–559.

———. 2007. 'The Pleasure of the Blog: The Early Novel, the Serial, and the Narrative Archive'. In *Blogtalks Reloaded: Social Software Research and Cases*, edited by Thomas N. Burg and Jan Schmidt, 167–186. Social Software Lab.

———. 2012. 'Reading (and Writing) Online, Rather Than on the Decline'. *Profession* (January 1): 41–52. doi:10.2307/41714136.

Gocsik, Karen. 2005. 'What Is an Academic Paper?' Dartmouth College. http://writing-speech.dartmouth.edu/learning/materials/materials-first-year-writers/what-academic-paper.

Helsper, Ellen. 2008. 'Digital Natives and Ostrich Tactics? The Possible Implications of Labelling Young People as Digital Experts'. Beyond Current Horizons. www.beyondcurrenthorizons.org.uk/digital-natives-and-ostrich-tactics-the-possible-implications-of-labelling-young-people-as-digital-experts/.

Helsper, Ellen, and Rebecca Eynon. 2009. 'Digital Natives: Where Is the Evidence?' *British Educational Research Journal* 36 (3): 1–18.

Katz, Seth R. 1996. 'Current Uses of Hypertext in Teaching Literature'. *Computers and the Humanities* 30 (2) (January 1): 139–148.

Ktisis, Stacey M. 2008. 'The Facebook Generation: Homework as Social Networking'. *The English Journal* 98 (2): 30–36.

Landow, George P. 1989. 'Hypertext in Literary Education, Criticism, and Scholarship'. *Computers and the Humanities* 23 (3) (June 1): 173–198.

Leech-Wilkinson, Daniel. 2009. 'Musicology and Performance'. In *Music's Intellectual History: Founders, Followers and Fads*, 791–803. RILM Perspectives I. RILM.

Miller, Carolyn R. and Dawn Shepherd. 2004. 'Blogging as Social Action: A Genre Analysis of the Weblog'. In *Into the Blogosphere. Rhetoric, Community, and Culture of Weblogs*, edited by Laura Gurak, Smiljana Antonijevic, Laurie Johnson, Clancy Ratliff, and Jessica Reyman. University of Minnesota. http://blog.lib.umn.edu/blogosphere/blogging_as_social_action_a_genre_analysis_of_the_weblog.html.

Palfrey, John, and Urs Gasser. 2011. *Born Digital: Understanding the First Generation of Digital Natives*. Basic Books.

Prensky, Mark. 2001a. 'Digital Natives, Digital Immigrants'. *On the Horizon* 9 (5): 1–6.

———. 2001b. 'Digital Natives, Digital Immigrants, Part II: Do They Really Think Differently?' *On the Horizon* 9 (6): 1–9.

Underwood, Jean D.M. 2007. 'Rethinking the Digital Divide: Impacts on Student-tutor Relationships'. *European Journal of Education* 42 (2): 213–222.

Warschauer, Mark. 2002. 'Reconceptualizing the Digital Divide'. *First Monday* 7 (7) (July 1). 1996–2002. http://firstmonday.org/ojs/index.php/fm/article/view/967.

Williams, Joseph M., and Lawrence McEnerney. 2013. 'Writing in College'. University of Chicago Writing Program. Accessed June 14. http://writing-program.uchicago.edu/resources/collegewriting/high_school_v_college.htm#_Toc431538572.

7 Assessing making and doing

Nick Fells

Introduction

Starting from personal reflections on formative experiences I gained as a student at the University of York and my later encounter with rather different structures at the University of Glasgow, in this chapter I develop the holistic notion of 'generative practice'. The term draws on phenomenological conceptions of space and place formulated by Tuan (1977) and Morris (2004), and is intended to address some of the problems associated with the idea of *creativity* in music-making.

I consider generative practice in relation to composition teaching at Glasgow, and in particular in relation to a course entitled Contemporary Music Ensemble, which attempts to nurture students' experience of music as sensory, spatial and social. I then go on to consider our approach to assessing such practice.

Background

Since its inception in the early 60s, the Music Department at the University of York became known for its innovation in music education. It was a maverick, reflecting something of the personality of its flamboyant founder, Wilfrid Mellers (see John Butt's contribution in this volume). Partly this was due to the way teaching was structured through a series of 'projects': an innovative system devised by Richard Orton whereby students were grouped together by mutual interest in a given topic rather than by year or skill level. Each project spanned four weeks, with teaching taking place over two full days each week; the topics offered each year reflected evolving staff interests and the ebb and flow of broader musical discourse, rather than any fixed notion of 'what should be taught'.

From our perspective as students, the project system comprised entire days of immersion in a workshop setting, exploring topics through a combination of discussion, critical and analytical study and creative practice. The days between were spent 'being musicians' and finding our way: reading, listening, hanging out, practising, rehearsing and composing. Scholarship was afforded no special status of its own, rather it was entwined with composition and performance: testament to Mellers's pioneering and inimitable musicianship, which was still felt strongly despite his retirement eight years before my arrival in 1989.

York at that time indulged the interests of those drawn toward what seemed to represent the new, exotic and experimental. The project system offered a very broad range of topics. Over the course of a degree, one's studies might range (as in my case) from North Indian rag to Mozart's operas, from community music to analytical studies of concerto form. Beyond classes, much of one's time could be spent composing, or working in the studio or participating in diverse performance activities; again taking my case as an example, these ranged from playing gamelan to learning shakuhachi to playing a great deal of contemporary music. The department's informal atmosphere was punctuated by vigorous critique and debate. The openness and flexibility of the project system was underpinned by a permeability between critical, intellectual endeavour and creative practice and experimentation. It was an environment that favoured the unconventional, and at that time (the late 80s and early 90s) it was still probably the only music department in Britain to admit such an eclectic range of study.

My experience there afforded some perspectives on music education that would later come to underpin my composition teaching at Glasgow. These were four fold: first, that repeated encounters with unfamiliar sound worlds form an important site of learning; second, that music experienced as a lived spatial, sonic and social phenomenon imbricates its tactile-physical and emotional-intellectual dimensions, deepening our understanding of music's significance as a cultural process; third, that creative production demands particular kinds of ethical and social responsibility that are significant to human behaviour more broadly, in other walks of life; and finally, that critical enquiry can be integral to creative practice, forming a kind of feedback loop for generating new lines of enquiry. Some of these ideas will be explored further later on.

In contrast to the wide-ranging environment at York, the ethos at Glasgow seemed more restrictive. When I arrived as a new lecturer in 1998, teaching was somewhat compartmentalized: music history comprised its own distinct strand in the curriculum and was taught almost entirely synchronically; composition was split into 'free', 'tonal' and 'twelve-tone' courses; and classes were atomized into weekly one-hour lectures and tutorials spread throughout the year, contrasting greatly with York's intensive full-day sessions. It was clear that reflecting the kind of immersive, dynamic practice-based approach to teaching I had experienced at York would not be straightforward.

Over time, though, I came to recognize that the Glasgow system had positive benefits. The fragmentation of class time was rooted in the long-standing cross-disciplinary nature of Scottish education and in particular,

140   *Nick Fells*

of the Glasgow undergraduate MA degree (a degree tracing a direct line back to the medieval *trivium/quadrivium*). Students on this four-year programme study in usually three different disciplines for the first two years, before specializing in years three and four. As a result, students in first and second year attend classes across three subject areas, often on the same day and certainly within each week. Whilst a direct translation of the York system could not work in that context, I came to realize that despite its limitations, the Glasgow approach had the advantage of enabling intensive cross-subject pollination. Students could learn alongside peers taking classes in very different fields, with contrasting and sometimes contradictory values and approaches. The resulting environment engendered a breadth of critical perspectives drawn from right across the arts and humanities and beyond.

Within this context, then, my colleagues and I gradually developed the learning environment. The edifice of music history began to break down, focusing more on instances of stylistic, cultural and critical phenomena; performance teaching opened up to a wider range of repertoires; and we began to take steps to transform composition teaching. Here, though, the problem remained that the practical constraints of the Glasgow cross-disciplinary timetable tended to impede the introduction of extended, immersive practical tasks that would help nurture a more experiential kind of learning.

Rethinking composition teaching and assessment

My personal motivation for introducing a more immersive, practical form of composition teaching came from those perspectives described above, gleaned from my time at York: enhancing students' encounters with unfamiliar materials; nurturing a view of music as lived spatial, social and sonic experience; experiencing creative production as an ethical, social practice; and embedding critical enquiry within creative practice. In the early 2000s, Bill Sweeney and I set about reviewing our composition teaching. We wanted the course to involve students more in active, practical exploration. To quote Janet Mills and John Paynter, we wanted to aim for 'education rather than instruction', drawing on students' own 'natural resources of wonder, imagination and inventiveness' (Mills and Paynter 2008: 1).

One obvious way to approach this seemed to be through ensemble devising: simply getting students making sound together in a space, mediated by social dynamics. So notwithstanding the constraints of the timetable, we established a weekly pattern of one-hour devising workshops, where in each session multiple parallel ensembles were given quick, straightforward processes for making and organizing sound together; with these processes we tried to avoid complicating factors such as any need for notation, or placing students under pressure to improvise as such. Rather, simple iterative procedures were used for building structures from tones, shapes and aggregates, all the while trying to encourage critical listening. These workshops were then repeated with the same group of students later the same year, and again the following year for the same group. In this way, despite the time pressures arising from the Glasgow cross-disciplinary timetable, we were able to establish something of a *culture* of devising over the longer term that nurtured an attentiveness to the basic social, sensory and spatial dimensions of the musical experience.

This attempt to grow a culture of devising threw up a number of phenomenological observations that are worthwhile exploring, particularly in that they had a bearing on the development of a sister course to composition – the Contemporary Music Ensemble.

Musicking and the sense of space

I have mentioned above the simple notion of devising as making sound together in a space. We could say that music is like walking, requiring us to interact spatially and bodily with the world. We can do this without thinking about it – it gets us from A to B, figuratively – or we can do it reflectively, listening, looking, and attending consciously to the richness of our sensations.

In *The Sense of Space* (2004), David Morris builds on Maurice Merleau-Ponty's work on spatial experience. He contends that 'the sense of space is the basis of all social experience and of perceptual experience in general' (Morris 2004: vii). Morris's wide-ranging analysis has direct relevance for music making, since it is concerned above all with the moving body, which is of course central to the act of performance. Morris is concerned not with measured, objective, or geometric space, but rather with 'perceived space as we experience it before objectifying it'. This he calls 'lived space' (ibid.), using this notion to focus his study on the interaction between the moving body and the world.

This seems fundamental in relation to the cultural practice of music. Christopher Small's 'musicking' can be viewed as rehearsing, establishing, and cementing relationships that are fundamentally social. Musicking is the practice of human culture through the articulation of sound – for Small, through musicking, we articulate complex relationships and hierarchies of relationships; it is a process that allows us to make non-verbal models and metaphors of human behaviour (Small 1998: 200).

Whatever form it takes, a fundamental feature of musicking is that it is at some level about bodies moving and practicing space – that might involve playing an instrument or singing; or it might be dancing, or listening in space, singing along, shouting and clapping in appreciation; or listening to and 'touching' sound in virtual spaces that intersect with our directly lived space, such as sonic spaces created in loudspeakers or headphones. In this way, musicking is inseparable from Morris's 'perceived space as we experience it'.

142   *Nick Fells*

Ethics and place

Morris links these issues of space and body to ethics:

> our sense of space arises in the intersection of movement and place, specifically developmental movement and social place. The intersection will have an ethical aspect, since a social, developmental body is a body placed in an ethical situation... our responsibility in face of others and in face of place inheres in our sense of space... our sense of space thus entwines with our sense of the ethical and of place.
>
> (Morris 2004: viii)

In this we find a parallel with Small's proposition that:

> musicking is about relationships, not so much about those that actually exist in our lives as about those that we desire to exist and long to experience ... during a musical performance ... desired relationships are brought into virtual existence so that those taking part are enabled to experience them as if they really did exist.
>
> (Small 1998: 183)

Again, there seems a parallel: Morris's ethics of place is imbricated with Small's bringing into virtual existence of desired relationships.

It is notable that Morris invokes *place* in relation to this discussion of ethics. Turning to Yi-Fu Tuan's 1977 book *Space and Place*, places are defined as 'centers of felt value where biological needs, such as those for food, water, rest, and procreation, are satisfied' (Tuan 1977: 4). Tuan goes on: 'What begins as undifferentiated space becomes place as we get to know it better and endow it with value ... furthermore, if we think of space as that which allows movement, then place is pause; each pause in movement makes it possible for location to be transformed into place' (ibid.: 6). For Tuan, then, place is space endowed with value, and partly at least this value arises from the combination of movement and pause. In this it seems there is a clear musical parallel – both actual, in terms of performing and making utterance – and metaphorical, through the narratives, gestures and metaphors for movement we find in the sonic art works we experience.

So these ethical and spatial dimensions are central to musicking. Making music becomes both a rehearsing of social relations deployed in the wider world, and a practising of space that imbues it with value, a way of constructing a sense of place, socially and physically. This might suggest that the situation we are trying to establish with our collective devising ensembles has a more profound potential significance for students than simply as a way to 'learn how to compose'.

Body and world

One of the key innovations in Morris's work is a crossing of body and world through movement. To introduce this idea, Morris discusses the problem of depth perception. He couches depth not in terms of Cartesian distance, but rather in terms of our sense of volume: 'we can treat depth as an objective dimension interchangeable with height and width. But before that we must have a more basic perceptual experience of voluminous things, and that is our focus: how do we first of all perceive things and ourselves as standing out in depth?' (Morris 2004: 2). Morris describes his experience of sitting on a bench outside Toronto city hall: 'I would seem to be part of the depths that I perceive. There is a problem though. I perceive things in depth as here or there, as near or far, in front or behind. But I do not perceive myself in this way' (ibid.). He distinguishes between the *ordinary* depth observed in the environment, by which he means the ordering of parts of the environment by depth (in other words, we observe things as in front of or behind other things), versus the *extra-ordinary* depth we perceive of the body, which seems not subject to that kind of ordering. With 'ordinary', he invokes an ordinal structure – first, second, third. But the sense of one's own body parts does not seem ordered in that way. For instance, we do not generally describe our left hand as distanced to the left of our body – rather, our left hand partly *defines* our sensation of left-ness, even when not positioned to the left. Morris's *crossing* refers to this interaction of our body with the world. He goes further, proposing that such a phrase presumes these already to be two independent separate things that subsequently interact. Rather, 'crossing' implies that the two are *mixed* – at once interdependent, arranged in a flowing threshold. Body and world cross one another. The body is not a separate sensing machine 'within which signs of depth are decoded' – rather it is 'in the depths of the world… through a flowing threshold that overlaps both body and world' (ibid.: 5). He reaffirms the point: 'our sense of space is not constituted by cognitive or neurobiological structures that are merely on our side of things; our sense of space is enfolded in an outside, in a world that crosses our body,' (ibid.: 6)

The idea that our sense of space might arise from a continuous flow of body with world seems to have implications for musicking. If we layer this idea with, say, Salomé Voegelin's *sonic sensibility* (Voegelin 2010: xiii) and her description of listening to recordings of Merleau-Ponty's voice as 'being honeyed' (ibid.: 6) as a kind of touching of sound with our ears, we start to regard ourselves as sounding, listening, practicing bodies less bounded, less separate, less geometric, and less self-oriented than hitherto. Such thoughts challenge our perception of our behaviour. Perhaps, socially, ethically, such a viewpoint enables us to loosen our grip on the need to assert *self*, if the experience of physical self is rather more fluid and intertwined with the world and others than we may assume.

144 *Nick Fells*

The HEI context

The introduction of devising ensembles to our composition courses enabled us to some extent to introduce students directly, experientially, to these issues of body-world crossing, sense of place and ethics. These ideas even point toward a rethinking for students of what it means to play in an ensemble, something in itself that might uncover a rich source of musical innovation.

In order to explore these issues fully, however, it was clear we needed to do this in a way that was more direct and not related necessarily to composition teaching per se, but that it was a practice-in-itself: a kind of musical creative practice that imbricates composition and performance, but that is not necessarily improvisation. However, I see an issue with the word creative.

Creative: generative?

I have already mentioned the notion of 'generative' practice. When we say creative, perhaps what we really mean is generative. We need to be careful because of course 'generative music' and 'generative art' are already used in relation to algorithmic computer-generated art. But for our purposes here, the word generative might be worth some consideration. Generative and creative are close in meaning. *Oxford English Dictionary* defines the verb 'create' as 'to bring into existence something which has not existed before; to cause, occasion, produce' (2016); whereas to generate is 'to bring into existence; to produce from other substances or as the result of some process or action; to cause, give rise to; (mathematics) to produce by specified operations or by the repeated application of rules to some initial items' (ibid.).

Though both refer to production – a bringing into existence – 'create' seems bound to the ineffable, to the idea of something that cannot be described. Aside from obvious divine overtones, it suggests something is created that has never existed before, as if from nothing, mysteriously, inexplicably – to create is to originate. 'Generate', however, suggests *re*production: a conversion of things into other things, a coming together of processes and substances, the repetition of actions. We might argue that musicking is on the whole more *generative* than creative. We might ask if it is even possible for music making to involve the creation of something from scratch, where *nothing* existed before. The term generative practice, then, might be useful in emphasizing the synthesis of practice from multifarious other sources: materials, sounds, works, personal histories, motivations and repeated or repeatable processes and operations. It enables us to distance ourselves from the pressure to create as if from nothing – to originate, in that sense. In the learning situation, it allows us to focus on a developmental practice, building on what came before or on what we witness others doing.

Improvising, composing and utterance

Related to this of course is the question of improvisation. I started thinking about *generative* musical practice as a continuum or line, with so-called 'free' improvisation at one end, and maybe automated computer based algorithmic processes, perhaps involving little human agency, at the other. Everything else in between seemed to be some form of 'composing', 'interpreting', or 'improvising'. Such linearity though seems to oversimplify the relations between different kinds of practice, which often overlap, merge or collide; perhaps generative practice is more of a multidimensional *field,* in which utterance arises in different forms and from different motivations.

Peter Kivy's work discusses the relationship between music and other forms of human utterance (Kivy 1990). Irrespective of how we make it, of where it sits in the generative field, musicking is perceived in the ear of the beholder as the result of a process of utterance. Such utterance made in a musical context we could consider a kind of abstract proposition. By making a musical utterance, I propose that my sound relates to this other sound, or relates to me, or to you, or to some memory of something or other in the past. If I play the shakuhachi for instance, it immediately proposes a physical relation between me and the instrument, constituted as a visual image witnessed or imagined; it proposes too an audible relation between my blowing action and the resulting sound. At a further level of abstraction, it proposes a relation between the sound event and my relationship to the tradition of shakuhachi playing, even the zen notion of emptiness, and my breath. Perhaps the audience or fellow players perceive some, all, or none of these, or perhaps they perceive other relations that I do not.

Whether these propositions are made as a result of composing, improvising, or interpreting is in a sense neither here nor there in the witnessing ear. My contention, then, is that there are not hard boundaries between *how* music arises, but rather a fluid continuum of approaches.

Utterance, learning and being critical

What is it then to 'learn composition', or to 'learn to perform'? We could say that we learn through a generative practice, a productive doing. Generative practice produces – it gives rise to artefacts, experiential foci: events, performances, showings. In music, if we take Small's line, this productivity centres on the rehearsing and representation of idealized forms of human relationships through heard utterance. We can think of learning, then, as undertaking this productivity, this 'doing', but with a self-critical frame of mind. If we accept that musical utterance can be an abstract form of proposition, then that self-critical frame of mind might be constituted in us testing or challenging our own propositions or utterances as we make them.

But utterances in a musical context are not language elements – they do not signify directly, through words. At best, any subject invokes intersubjective

146　*Nick Fells*

relations, and any object, any sound produced, is fleeting, ephemeral and ambiguous. But in this context subject-object relations are anyway in a continuous state of enfolding in the sensory-motor act of listening, as Voegelin explores, for instance (Voegelin 2010: 36). A sound utterance in a musical context is not a proposition in the way that 'the dog is barking' is a proposition. Rather it renders into utterance a fluid set of potential significations. It might share aspects of the *form* of a proposition. By making sound in a musical context, we might *always* be saying effectively 'here is a sound; it has potential significations for you; it affords certain ways of hearing it, or listening to it. Take it or leave it'.

Returning to learning, then, perhaps challenging or testing our own musical propositions is more to do with testing those potential significations, those affordances. On the whole, the affordances of a sonic utterance in a musical context will take the form of suggestions of further relationships: relationships to other sounds; to the source of the sound, or an implicit source; to memory, or our culturally-acquired knowledge of other comparable sounds; to the physical context or the space in which the sound propagates; to my body, to your body, to the score, the player...

This then is what I would contend is being self-critical in musicking – it is about testing and challenging the capacity of our musical utterances to afford relationships to be perceived. The building of such self-criticality, then, to me, is the mainstay of teaching in this field – whether in 'composition', 'performance', 'music technology', 'sonic arts', 'improvisation' or any domain in which broadly speaking a generative musical practice is the mode of activity in question.

Reconciliation: generative practice and assessment

In teaching in the domain of 'generative making', then, learning is achieved through experiencing, doing – essentially a form of constructivism. The environment has to afford a multitude of possibilities for doing – a multitude of possible directions, pathways and outcomes, in order to lead to rich learning experience.

In general, though, the dominance of objective based education in national education systems tends to favour *limiting* the available pathways; it places the emphasis on narrowness or particularity of outcomes, in order that these outcomes might be straightforwardly measured. Learning is packaged into commodities ('outcomes', 'modules', 'degrees'), and experience is bought and sold like so many pairs of shoes. Music education has struggled to reconcile its intersubjective processes of generative utterance with the public requirement to create such packages.

On one hand, we can complain, and wring our hands. On the other, we can work with it and these days often do, essentially subverting and repurposing the model and opening up space for multiple possibilities and unforeseen outcomes. In the context of institutional ILOs (Intended Learning

Outcomes), John Butt often talks about '*un*intended learning outcomes' – John's point being that the most valuable experiences are often those that happen *despite* the structure or formalized intent of the class, course or institution – through *ad hoc* experience, knowledge uncovered or synthesized in unforeseen or unpredictable ways. But in an institutional context, achieving such richness or flexibility, and importantly maintaining it over the long term, needs a rigorous and well-reasoned critical approach. It needs carefully formulated criteria for assessment, and careful thinking about what it is we want those criteria to do.

The trick we need to master is to create an environment that affords the unforeseen – as so many music departments do very successfully – and in teaching generative practice (composing, performing), we *both* point students toward articulable, measurable outcomes, *and* take a subversive approach to the design of those outcomes, assimilating the unpredictable.

Duchamp's anti-art comes to mind. In presenting the urinal as art, Duchamp led us to view both in a new, dissonant, relationship. The gallery suddenly extends outward to the everyday, and the visceral everyday encroaches on the gallery. This new point of view destroyed the gallery no more than it destroyed the urinal. Rather the dissonance affords a taking to task of our experience of both. Similarly, we can undertake our complex process of generative musical utterance within the institutional game of assessment without destroying either. They can co-exist, arguably to mutual benefit.

Virtuosity and excellence

In music, perhaps more than in the other arts, historical notions of technical excellence and virtuosity have persisted as benchmarks for student achievement. Musical performance, and not just in 'classical' music, has been valued in terms of technical brilliance and its adherence to accepted aesthetic norms. Often this has resulted in repetitious, uncritical acceptance of those norms, or even the construction of new norms where there were none (for example, in lazy assumptions about tradition, without recourse to historical evidence). In other words, performance is assessed in relation to how others performed in the recent past based on the presumption that 'same is best' – that is, don't create dissonance between the urinal and the gallery; don't generate new affordances; just repeat the ones we're used to.

But the notion of excellence can be applied in a more critically informed way. To excel is, by definition, relational. It means 'to be superior', 'to surpass others' (OED 2016). Excellence means going beyond where others might, perhaps even beyond what we ourselves had previously conceived. The notion of technique also is relational, since techniques are deployed in the pursuit of aesthetic goals: some techniques will be useful for some goals, others for different goals. So any evaluation of 'technique' presupposes understanding those goals, which might be different to our own, and certainly

148　*Nick Fells*

different for different individuals and cultural contexts. We might find excellence, then, residing in the relation between techniques and aesthetics.

I am simply outlining here how the assessment of a productive practice need not rely on technical fixities, but can be open to a field of technical competencies applied in relation to aesthetic goals. The focus of such assessment might lie in the qualitative evaluation of the sophistication of a student's process of exploring the *relations* between technical, mechanical, sensory–motor factors and the affordance of sonic–formal possibilities.

A contemporary music ensemble

So how might such assessment work in practice? Alongside the revision of composition teaching in the early 2000s, we took a fresh look at our Contemporary Music Ensemble course. This had focused on performing twentieth-century chamber music, but it struggled given that its instrumentation and size changed radically each year. It made sense to rethink the course, and given the introduction of devising ensembles in our composition teaching, it made sense to orient the contemporary music ensemble toward making its own music through devising and realising open-form and indeterminate works. Around the same time, I was involved in the formation of the Glasgow Improvisers Orchestra at Glasgow's Centre for Contemporary Arts, which brought together a wide range of musicians from the city's contemporary jazz, classical and pop scenes. It was a melting pot of musical personalities and of strategies for performing and devising. Discussions with members of the group, particularly with composer and guitarist Neil Davidson, had a significant impact on the course's new shape and direction.

Embracing open forms, indeterminacy, devising and improvising meant some careful thought was needed about assessment. A starting point was to re-examine our criteria for the composition and performance courses, to see what might be adopted or adapted for this new generative ensemble situation.

Assessing composition

In composition, we had wanted to make explicit the integration of critical thought and creative practice. We adopted a criterion that had long been used in the department in respect of critical writing, one that looks for 'evidence of insight and originality, independent thought and judgement'. Immediately, of course, questions are raised around these terms in respect of composition. What does 'insight' mean in the context of practice? How is it made evident? What about 'originality', discussed already in relation to creative versus generative practice? To an extent these are clarified in the notion of 'independent thought and judgement', which calls on students to seek out their own means to generate, through their own intellectual and practical labour. Partly, then, we see insight and originality evidenced by students taking initiative: reaching out beyond accepted wisdoms to find their own way of making, based on their own capacity for self-criticism.

On the other hand, we might consider that 'insight and originality' in respect of composition warrant a little more discussion. Martin Parker-Dixon, in a paper produced for the Royal Musical Association's Practice as Research network (2015), argues in support of the notion that composition can be research. He contends it is possible to formulate a 'cognitively significant claim' about composition, and that a cognitively significant claim is a 'non-trivial, contentious, falsifiable proposition or thesis which necessarily entails development, activity and discussion'. In composition teaching, we could consider as cognitively significant claims those questions and problems we ask students to address in their composition projects. The necessary development, activity and discussion that entails might comprise first the processes that underpin the making of the work; rehearsing, realizing or workshopping the work; making test pieces, demos, experiments, sketches; and coming and discussing their work, individually with us, or as a group, or to their peers. Such discursive, sharing environments enable the development, expression and exchange of insights, revealing otherwise hidden properties or characteristics of the materials, sounds or processes in the work under development. Assuming we as teachers are also there as assessors, we can judge the extent to which those insights arising during the development of work is accounted for in the outcome. So insight can be folded back into the work as part of the development process, and we can evaluate the extent to which that 'folding back' is evident.

Originality too is problematic. Parker-Dixon asks 'can one thing be more original than another? "More original" might just mean older and the "most original" will be whatever has the largest set of heirs. But I don't see how this could easily be seen as a value'. I would challenge this. I think we *can* use original as a value, but perhaps not quite in the way we might expect. Originality can mean 'novel or fresh in character or style' (OED 2016). So the word need not be used only in the literal sense of an absolute origin, the first of its type – a musical performance is still just a musical performance, after all. It may mean 'fresh', in other words 'refreshing' or perhaps 'surprising'. This is where we find substance in the distinction between 'creative' and 'generative'. In the 'creative', we might seek originality in the spontaneous production of something completely new – never before known or witnessed. In the context of undergraduate composition, this is clearly unreasonable. In the 'generative', we could conceivably seek originality in the *synthesis* of elements – in other words, we might find refreshing or surprising elements somewhere within a range of resources (intellectual, stylistic, material, methodological, sonic) upon which the work draws. In this way, originality is not absolute, but relational, arising from the relations between elements from which the work is synthesized.

Our criteria go on to seek 'understanding of key concepts'. This is dependent on context. For instance, it could refer simply to the methods and

150   *Nick Fells*

practices we have shown the students in the course. Alternatively, concepts might relate to a student's own aesthetic goals, and in that sense students have an opportunity to define the context for the evaluation of their work. They might, for instance, choose to build a work by making sustained instrumental textures from large numbers of short sounds; in this case, we might evaluate how that texture is evidenced aurally, by considering the extent to which its defining characteristics are heard – in a sense, evaluating how clearly or fully someone has articulated their own concept.

The last of our revised criteria for composition seeks 'formal structure and stylistic consistency'. We aren't interested in 'stylistic composition', particularly. By 'stylistic consistency' we do not mean composing using generic conventions, though it does not preclude that. Rather, it is meant in the sense of a consistent manner or mode of expression – consistency in the organization of elements, and continuity in the resulting aesthetic characteristics (keeping in mind, of course, that *dis*continuity can itself be an important aesthetic characteristic).

Assessing performance

In performance, assessment criteria had tended historically to focus on classical interpretation. More recently, with the arrival of David McGuinness as performance coordinator, came a broader approach. There was more openness to a wide range of genres, styles and repertoire, and a greater emphasis on imaginative and critical thinking. Assessment still assumes an interpretative basis – that the task in hand is the realization of existing notated works. However, as with composition, the revised criteria for performance are open enough to apply across a broad range of practices, including 'generative' practice.

The first of the performance criteria calls for 'projection of musical ideas'. This expands to include clarity, expressive quality, sensitivity and character. *Projection* implies a dynamic spatiality: travelling outwards from the source, throwing forwards – making something audible at a distance. So we can think of this criterion as evaluating the perceived clarity of 'expressive character' *at the listening position*: in other words, an evaluation of how well changes in the spectral envelope of the performed sound (what we might think of as the 'carrier' of 'expressive information') are perceived at a distance.

This is straightforward where we can agree about what 'expressive character' means, in relation to generic norms or expectation. But for works which are less determinate in 'expressive character', or perhaps that embody aesthetic qualities that tend to counter generic conventions of musical expression – for example, works not designed for 'projection' in the conventional sense – this criterion affords an interesting opportunity to explore relational thinking between 'source' (player), and 'receiver' (listener) at a distance. For example, in a score such as <*boundary music*> by the *Group*

Ongaku composer Mieko Shiomi (1963), players are invited to make sound as the 'faintest possible to a boundary condition whether the sound is given birth to as sound or not'. This establishes and then questions the relation between player and audience. At what point *in space* is the 'boundary condition' found, at any given playing dynamic? At what distance from the performers does it occur? To what extent does the boundary need to be made explicit to the audience, or is it sufficient only for the player to experience it? There is a world of possible responses to such a score that relate directly to the notion of *projection* without recourse to notions of 'expression' or 'character'. In the context of assessment for the contemporary music ensemble, we want each player to consider such questions, and we expect their critical response to the score or process to be evident through the sensitivity of their performance.

After *projection*, the next criterion looked for 'understanding of style, idiom and structure'. Again, despite its orientation toward stylistic interpretation, we can consider how such a criterion might be applied in improvising or in approaching open form or indeterminate scores, the kind of activities we undertake in the contemporary music ensemble. In these contexts, we seek out evidence of students' ability to *construct* style. We think of this as students building sonic forms in which we recognize common features or elements that persist through the performance – in other words, a consistent application of features of sound materials that together comprise what we might call an 'idiom'. The students' materials might form *their own* idiom: one not relating to any particular generic convention, but one derived and developed through the consistent exploration of specific types of sound and sound forms. Students here can really 'own' the idiom, taking a composing role.

There is reference here also to *structure* – a term that often seems to confuse students, in my experience. In interpretation, it implies that as performers we understand where phrases are heading and how phrases can be grouped together in structural/formal units, and making sure we don't play in a way that undermines the audible identity of those formal units. In the context of our contemporary music ensemble, where students might be improvising or following more process-oriented or relational scores, we can think of structure in terms of Cage's 'division of the whole into parts' (Cage 1961: 35). This implies a relationship: that we can relate parts to the whole through aural recognition of features that repeat or recur. Through recurrence and variation in playing, students can create formal units of sound that signify a relation to the whole, that enable us to recognize structure. Through this mutual recognition of sound forms arranged in patterns and structures, the relationship between player and listener develops.

In assessing performances by the ensemble, structure might also refer to the patterns of organization that result from procedures or instructions outlined in text or process-based scores. For instance, in pieces such as Christian Wolff's *Exercises*, structure might refer to the rules and processes that

152   *Nick Fells*

govern the progression of listening and responding across the ensemble – and therefore we might evaluate students' ability to realise those rules and processes effectively.

The next criterion for assessing performance focuses on 'technique/intonation and use of range of sound/tone'. This is a contentious issue in relation to the broad range of contemporary musical practices. 'Technique', as discussed already, in classical music invokes the notion of virtuosity. In evaluating a Mozart performance, we might listen out for speed and dexterity, the extent to which the student has trained their muscles to realize the piece in a way we consider aesthetically and stylistically satisfying. We have knowledge of the historical and stylistic context, and base our evaluation on that. This raises a question of 'appropriate observers'. Byrne et al. (2003: 280) argue that assessment of creative activity needs to be grounded in a *consensual definition* of creativity. They suggest that observers need to have contextual knowledge about the creative activity happening before them, so that they understand its aesthetic goals appropriately. In order to evaluate 'technique', then, observers need knowledge of the likely range of possible performances of that work, given its particular stylistic, aesthetic, cultural and historical context. Importantly, 'appropriate observer' does not necessarily equate to 'specialist' on a particular instrument, or in a particular style. A specialist's contextual knowledge might be deep, but it could also be narrow; unfamiliar or innovative aesthetic goals may then appear to be *inappropriate*, simply because they do not fit with commonly accepted norms, traditions or conventions. In assessing performance, we try to avoid this by focusing on a critically argued, evidence-based approach to style and technique in relation to the aesthetic, historical and cultural contexts of the works being performed.

Considering technique in relation to virtuosity throws up some problems in the context of our contemporary music ensemble course. In improvising, or realizing open-form or indeterminate works, decisions in playing can be made in relation to organizational processes – the decision *not* to play can be as important as anything to do with dexterity or control. Avoiding overt gestures or 'shapes' can be central to aesthetic goals, more than any conventional sense of 'expression'. In our criterion, the phrase 'use of a range of sound/tone' allows us to rethink technique. It admits *timbre* as musically significant. It admits the creation of sounds that are fragile, unusual, or differently-shaped to those we might expect in (for instance) classical music performance. Also, the exploration of sound/tone can become a *process*, relating for instance to Andy Keep's 'instrumentalizing' (Keep 2009) – a process of uncovering the sonic palette inherent in an object. Although Keep's discussion centres on non-instrumental sound and 'creative abuse' of objects, it could apply also in the context of instrumental or vocal performance as an exploratory process. The notions of 'extended technique' and 'creative abuse' converge; we might think of the 'musique concrète instrumentale' of many of Helmut Lachenmann's works in this context also.

In assessment terms, then, we can make judgements about the technical processes deployed in the exploration of sound, and their appropriateness in the context of the piece being played.

Our last criterion for performance seeks 'awareness and projection of ensemble skills' and 'evidence of collaborative practice'. In the contemporary music ensemble context, many of those ensemble skills are no different to any other ensemble playing – ability to balance; ability to project; ability to synchronize or coordinate. What distinguishes a generative ensemble such as the contemporary music ensemble, though, is the layering of performance with higher-level decision-making about the organization of sounds and materials in relation to what others in the ensemble are doing – what we might think of as compositional responsibility. For instance, in improvisation, a key ability might be to *recognize opportunities,* as they arise in the moment: opportunities for shaping, for creating surprising or idiomatic sound forms, or for blending with a prevailing texture or aggregation. In playing an open form work, a key ability might be to judge the 'placement' of events in time, or to judge when to proceed to the next instruction or next part of the score.

These kinds of decisions involve balancing *continuity* and *change* – essentially, judging musical *form.* This is really where our criteria for assessing performance and composition converge. In improvising and playing open-form works, students encounter performance issues: sound production, physical control, projection, balance. But they also encounter problems of composing: when to change; how to generate and shape materials; when to place material; when to be silent; whether to occupy foreground or background; whether to lead or follow; or how to decode the aesthetic goals implied by instructions or scores that may be ambiguous in their specification of particular sonic outcomes.

So the contemporary music ensemble engages students in a form of collaborative practice we can genuinely describe as generative; a practice that involves the domains of performing and composing but is exclusively neither.

Concluding remarks

In practice, this hybridization of criteria from composition and performance works well for the generative ensemble context. Assessing such activity, though, is still not an easy task. The ensemble's performances require substantial unpicking and critical analysis and that can be challenging. We have been operating this assessment scheme since the mid-2000s, and in that time have built up considerable experience, particularly in holding the kind of intersubjective negotiations between 'appropriate observers' necessary to establish a consensus about the quality of the work. The key, in addition to having precise but open criteria, is the rigorous application of a multi-staged process. There are clear steps we go through to build up an assessment gradually. We evaluate the whole group, as it realizes each piece or project; then we consider contributions from individuals in performance. We then look at

154 *Nick Fells*

the written critical reflection from each individual student, evaluating that in relation to the notes we each made during the performance. We always use two markers, who calibrate their marks at two stages: once immediately after the performance, in general terms; and then again, after each reading the reflective commentaries submitted by each student. The process, then, is necessarily intersubjective – it comprises a consensus, and takes into account the students' own reflection and evaluation of their work.

The scheme of assessment outlined here has enabled us to nurture our contemporary music ensemble as an instance of generative practice. It has facilitated a kind of experiential learning through students encountering their peers, as fellow imaginative musicians, through the social, sensory and spatial experience of musicking, and it has enabled us to account for that learning in an objective-based educational context. More broadly, and personally more importantly for me, the openness of the process goes some way to bringing to the Glasgow undergraduate experience something of the richness of open exploration, the space for imagination and the deep engagement with the 'stuff' of musicking that I gained in my own undergraduate days at York.

Bibliography

Byrne, Charles, MacDonald, Raymond & Carlton, Lana. 2003. 'Assessing creativity in musical compositions: flow as an assessment tool'. *British Journal of Music Education* 20 (3): 277–290.

Cage, John. 1961. *Silence*. Middletown, CT: Wesleyan University Press.

Keep, Andy. 2009. 'Instrumentalizing: Approaches to Improvising with Sounding Objects in Experimental Music'. In *The Ashgate Research Companion to Experimental Music, edited by* James Saunders, 113–30. Farnham, UK: Ashgate.

Kivy, Peter. 1990. *Music Alone: Philosophical Reflections on the Purely Musical Experience*. Ithaca, NY: Cornell University Press.

Mills, Janet and Paynter, John, eds. 2008. *Thinking and Making: Selections from the Writings of John Paynter*. Oxford: Oxford University Press.

Morris, David. 2004. *The Sense of Space*. Albany, NY: SUNY Press.

Oxford University Press, 2016. *Oxford English Dictionary Online*. www.oed.com. Accessed 24 May 2016.

Parker-Dixon, Martin. 2015. 'Composition *can* be Research'. Unpublished discussion paper for the Royal Musical Association Symposium on Practice as Research, University of Manchester, June 24, 2015.

Small, Christopher. 1998. *Musicking: The Meanings of Performing and Listening*. Vol. Music/culture. Middletown, CT: Wesleyan University Press. http://GLA.eblib.com/patron/FullRecord.aspx?p=776766.

Tuan, Yi Fu. 1977. *Space and Place: The Perspective of Experience*. 2nd edition, 2001. Minneapolis: University of Minnesota Press.

Voegelin, Salomé. 2010. *Listening to Noise and Silence*. New York: Continuum.

8 The teaching of creative practice within higher music education

Guerrilla Learning Outcomes (GLOs) and the importance of negotiation

Louise Harris and David McGuinness

This is an edited transcript of a conversation between Louise Harris and David McGuinness on the teaching of creative practice in a university environment. Harris teaches courses in Sonic Arts at both undergraduate and postgraduate levels, and McGuinness co-ordinates the undergraduate Performance programme. The initial point of departure for their conversation was a checklist for teaching in the arts by the writer Michael Rosen (2014), but most of the discussion considers the challenges of encouraging creativity within what can, at times, be a rigid institutional framework.

The conversation covers a number of a specific areas, including how artists learn and forms of creative knowledge, the presence or absence of a historical canon, the limitations of assessment, developing a freelance mentality, a co-researcher relationship with students and the impact of an institution's mindset and culture. It ends with a consideration of what elements are required for the successful teaching of creative practice across a range of subject areas.

Forms of knowledge – constructivist learning and 'facts'

DMcG – I think one of the important questions to ask is how artists learn in the first place, and there's already a considerable body of work on this,[1] but what we can be sure of is that artists don't simply follow systematic courses of study! They get curious and interested and explore things that they find interesting and helpful.

LH – Yes. In *Lighting from the Side*, Nyrnes's 'rhetorically based model for developing and analysing artistic research' (2006, 15) asks some interesting questions about how we both conduct and discuss arts research and offers some intriguing perspectives which can be applied to the nature of research-led teaching in the arts. Indeed, she suggests that

156 *Louise Harris and David McGuinness*

one may question whether this talk about the research process in strategic and linear terms helps us to obtain a clearer view and understanding of artistic research. Does artistic research proceed in a linear manner towards a goal? Or does it resemble more closely the production of a picture, a composition in space? According to Anna Pakes: 'Even if art is a rule-governed activity, in the broad, Wittgenstein sense, it is not a straightforward means-end process, each step of which is guided by clearly defined norms' (Pakes 2005:3)

(Nyrnes 2006, 7).

I think that is often what the vast majority of university degree courses are geared around; the linear transmission of particular forms of knowledge and fact. And I think 'fact' is a big problem (or perhaps opportunity) for creative practice, because there is no 'fact', and there is no linearity to the knowledge as such. Which always, inevitably, leads to questions from students such as 'how do you assess this?' and 'how do you know what's good and not good?', and that's something that I struggle with. One of my ways of dealing with it is to spend time looking at and reviewing pieces of work with students – either past pieces of work or pieces that have nothing to do with the course (often, in fact, suggestions from students themselves). Through asking them questions such as 'what's good about this?', 'what's less good about this?', 'what would you give this if you were assessing it?' and so on, you can start to elicit the kind of critical and analytical thinking you want them to apply to all the work they come into contact with. Also, what always surprises them is how much we agree on things, even if it is not necessarily something they would choose to listen to, look at, watch, read: they still have the ability to recognize value and to appreciate my, and other students' responses to it. So one of the skills that they develop is the ability to respond critically to material.

DMcG – Apart from anything else, this idea of knowledge not being communicated linearly is the reason we are having a conversation, and not each writing a chapter in this book. Scientists, I guess, communicate with one another through the medium of the academic paper, and it can be an exciting way to present something you've been working on for a long time. But artists don't: even in a relatively scholarly field such as so-called historically-informed performance, you come across few if any scholarly papers in general circulation amongst artists, and when you do, it's still at the more studious fringes of the community. And this is because there are other, less linear ways for musicians to communicate: even the early music world is based far more on oral or aural tradition than it is on scholarly work.

The difficulty here is that we have to try to work within a university context, which is built not around creative practice, but much more fundamentally around how the sciences work. The framework is very linear, and we are expected to teach using constructive alignment,

The teaching of creative practice   157

where each unit of learning is built upon a previous one.[2] But what happens in creative practice is that you try something out and then you try something else out, and rather than building constructively, you might decide to kick most of it over and go somewhere else. It's not necessarily a constructivist process; it is more likely to be messy and chaotic, and so a more flexible model is required in order to teach creative practice in a meaningful way. The challenge is finding ways to do this within a formal structure with all its attendant self-perpetuating administration, often looking for opportunities to bend that structure.

LH – I think you are right. And I think what is interesting about what you're saying in terms of artists not communicating through academic papers is that at the moment I am trying to write a research paper for a conference in which I am going to talk about my own practice. But what I have found that I've ended up doing is talking about the process, not the work. I have been doing a lot of reading about liveness, agency and so on, often written by practitioners,[3] but usually they are still talking about the process underlying the work as opposed to the work itself. I supposed one of the reasons for this is that the process is more tangible and, perhaps, easier to discuss than the work itself, so we can talk about the things that go into the work, like the context surrounding it or the technology involved, or how it is mediated, with relative ease. It can also help to illuminate the work, I feel, and this is what the critical commentary we ask for in Sonic Arts courses is for – it's to illuminate the creative process underlying the work itself, and to demonstrate that awareness of what has gone into it, not just in terms of the person making the work but also the context surrounding it, the technology mediating it and so on. I think that's an important part of developing a student's individual creative identity (Hugill 2008); getting them to address, consider, critique and reflect on their processes, not just hand in a creative work in isolation.

DMcG – It is similar to what we do on the Performance course in asking students to write a commentary explaining why their work is the way it is: it's a separate thing from the performance itself. We don't get them to write a programme note to go along with it. It seems weird to me to invite an audience to come to a performance, and then to begin by selling them something to read in case they get bored with what is happening on the stage. I now try not to read programme notes until afterwards, as I want to be entertained by what is happening in front of me, not by what I can read to try and explain it.

The delightful absence of canons

DMcG – One of the challenges of encouraging creative work to happen is that there has to be openness in what we allow students to produce as assessed work: the brief has to be sufficiently open to allow them to bring

158   *Louise Harris and David McGuinness*

their own interests to the table. This comes back to the Michael Rosen article in which he talks about students needing to 'feel they are working in an environment that welcomes their home cultures, backgrounds, heritages and languages'. He is also making a political point there, but what is important for us is that we're not saying 'This body of work is more valuable than that one', but rather giving students tools to explore what they find most interesting, engaging and exciting.

If our students are from a classical music background, I often have to deal with the expectations of 'classical training' and the canon. Usually these are quite unhelpful, unless that's a culture that the student particularly wants to explore, in which case they've got a great start if they have a grounding in it already.

LH – I think that is what I find most liberating about teaching what I do: there isn't really a canon. Well, it depends on who you talk to – some of my colleagues would disagree with me, I'm sure. But for me, there isn't really this sense of 'these things are important, these things aren't' – students can bring a piece of work they've found that's fifty years old and we can talk about it on a relatively level playing field with one that was made last week. There isn't that sense of value judgment or 'this is important, this isn't' – that just doesn't have relevance in my field; or rather, for me it doesn't. There are problems and opportunities there, of course – it is great to have such a massive pool of work for students to draw from, and of course that's just increasing all the time as technology becomes more accessible and affordable. But you also get stuck into these questions of 'should' – so 'what should I be looking at', 'what should I be doing to get an A', 'which of these is better than the other' and so on. And so you have to try very hard to break them out of this binary should/shouldn't, good/bad perspective and structure a more equitable approach to dealing with contemporary practice.[4]

The limitations of assessment

DMcG – It is a very difficult question to deal with, that one: 'What do I need to do to get an A?' At some point we have to articulate that the business of getting a degree is, to some extent, an artificial construct: it's not real life. In order to get a degree, you have to satisfy the university authorities that you have accomplished a set list of achievements, but some of the music I love the most just wouldn't get a good mark as part of a music degree. That does not mean that I value it any less.

If assessing work as part of a degree were simply about what we as assessors like, then that would create all sorts of problems: assessment criteria are there to make it clear that everyone's work is treated in the same way, and that there is a level of impartiality, but those institutionalized criteria are not the same as our own artistic

The teaching of creative practice 159

assessment criteria in real life. Having said that, I would hope that they are at least related, otherwise the assessment process would be pretty meaningless!

It is particularly important in performance teaching to make it clear that assessment is not a personal judgement, because performing is at its heart an intensely personal activity and performers are often very shy and vulnerable. What is good about having completely clear and very explicit criteria for assessment is that we can try and make it clear that getting a particular grade is not a judgment on a performer as a person. I didn't realize when I started teaching just how important that is – being able to say 'That's what that mark meant, and it's all that mark meant', that it didn't mean anything else.

For a student, it may be that a process that got a really rubbish mark might end up including a very valuable learning experience, and be much more useful in the long run than getting an A. I think it is important to say that out loud to students: that getting a degree is just getting a degree, and what is more important are the experiences that go along with it.

LH – And equally, for example, I received an interesting comment on a course evaluation this summer after a semester of teaching MaxMSP which, let's just say, there are often mixed responses to! But there was a comment from a student who felt that they had done very badly and hadn't got on at all with the technology, but that they really 'loved their new way of listening to the world'. For me, this is exactly what teaching at university is all about – that you might not engage with everything you are taught, or indeed feel that you have done well at something, but that you are broadening your experiences and you're opening your mind to new things and new ways of engaging with the world. I think that's really valuable and exactly what I would want. It's about the things you learn around those targeted, summative assessments just as much as fulfilling a particular set of requirements.

Negotiation, freelance mentality and Guerrilla Learning Outcomes (GLOs)

DMcG – It's also like the difference between ILOs (Intended Learning Outcomes) and Unintended Learning Outcomes, which can be the most interesting aspects of teaching.[5] One of the things I have found rewarding in teaching performance is getting students to perform in groups, preparing a 10- or 15- minute performance over a few weeks alongside musicians they may have very little in common with. Initially there was a lot of student resistance to this, as they, understandably, didn't want to put even a small proportion of their degree result in the hands of anyone else. But the word that keeps coming out of this process is 'negotiation': if you are put into a group of five or six diverse people, with

160　*Louise Harris and David McGuinness*

an open assessment framework (the only stipulation being the duration of the performance and the involvement of every member of the group) you have to be open to negotiation, because if everyone sticks to a rigid idea about the nature of their own involvement, the group just will not function. That process of starting either with very strong ideas, or no ideas at all, and gradually developing the work with other people, can often mean doing a lot of internal negotiation with yourself too.

It also develops a sort of freelancers' mentality. There tends to be an emphasis in universities on employability (where success is defined as 'getting a job'), but I'm more interested in encouraging independent adaptive individuals who are not always dependent on someone else giving them work to do; instead, they can be self-sufficient to a greater or lesser extent based on the skills and creativity they've developed. Of course there are negotiations involved in having a job, but the creative end of music and of the arts in general is dominated by freelancers, and there's a massive amount of negotiation involved in that sort of life from day to day.

LH – I think negotiation is a good term generally, and we have talked a lot about the structures we work in and trying to fit the teaching of creative practice into these structures; and that's not often an easy fit. So you do spend a lot of time negotiating what is most fruitful and useful for you and for the students and attempting to reconcile this within the structures in place. Which is why I like this term 'unintended learning outcomes'. I think in my case, they are always intended by me; they just aren't necessarily explicitly stated on course descriptors because there isn't necessarily a place for them. In fact, they are more 'guerrilla learning outcomes'!

The co-researcher relationship

DMcG – I really like the idea that you have written about of developing a co-researcher framework (Harris 2016), but my question about it is how you get to the point where that is possible, because you can't come in at level one and expect students immediately to be experts in a particular field. How do we get to that co-researcher stage, what is the groundwork you have to do?

LH – I think for me, research doesn't necessarily imply a certain amount of knowledge or specialism; it is something that happens all the way along in a lot of different ways. So in undergraduate teaching we have three levels of Sonic Arts and if they take all three levels then by the time they get to the third they will have a totally different perspective and set of experiences, hopefully, than they did at the first level. But I think what I try to do throughout is to get rid of the idea that research is what you do for writing essays; instead, we spend a lot of time talking about various forms of creative practice and people who are doing interesting

The teaching of creative practice   161

things and trying to point them towards this world of things that are happening that they might be interested in. And that is research for both them and me, because I have to spend a lot of time looking at and listening to work in a range of contexts just to try and keep up to some extent with what is happening in the broader world of contemporary practice in the arts, not necessarily just in the Sonic Arts. And so it is a co-researcher relationship, because very often they're showing me things I am unfamiliar with just as much as I am trying to show them things they're unfamiliar with, and it becomes quite an interesting reciprocal relationship. For me, developing that framework is also about devoting time to it – so allocating time in class not just to teaching skills and demonstrating technologies, but also to listening and looking and thinking and talking about a whole range of creative practice, so I'm not this authority figure who is imparting wisdom to them but we are on a much more equivalent level and we are exploring and transferring knowledge between each other. I am also very lucky with teaching here that the class sizes are small enough for me to able to do that in a small group context, which is obviously hugely helpful for developing that kind of openness and freedom to discuss ideas and share perspectives.

DMcG – I am trying to work out from my own teenage years whether there was a point when it felt like, rather than simply acquiring skills, I was able to take the skills I had and start exploring. Maybe there wasn't a clear dividing line between the two: if you are a curious person, then the two of those are always going to go hand in hand with one another.

LH – I think the advantage that my field could be argued to have over yours, too, is that it is relatively easy to get to a state of proficiency whereby you can make what you want to make without having to put in years and years of groundwork. For example, if you want to play the piano to Grade 8 standard, that might take years to achieve. But if you want to make a piece of electroacoustic music, that will of course take some time to develop the necessary skills, but you are usually coming from a background of working with computers and of listening to the world, then have put a certain amount of the core skills are already in place. So, in some ways, you can start to get some sort of creative autonomy with the tools a little sooner. It's a steep learning curve, but it does allow the co-researcher relationship to develop a little more quickly. And I think what is interesting about that, as a consequence, is that it allows students to begin to take ownership over their own creative identity a little more readily, and hopefully to be able to think of the work they do with me as something that exists outside of classes and is integral to them as a creative individual, not just a means to an end to satisfy an assignment brief. And equally, there are skills that I am still developing too and I think it is important to communicate that to students as well: that I'm not some sort of godlike authority figure, but that I'm an artist who works out in the field that they're engaging with. I'm someone who is researching through practice and who is hopefully making some of that practice a little more accessible to them. This is related to Stoller's (2014) ideas about creative knowledge being, to some extent, an emergent property of experience – that 'learning is ... an act of making which takes artistic production as its paradigmatic case' (2014, 55). For me, that's central to the co-researcher relationship.

DMcG – The difficulty with being an artist, though, is that there is a large amount of self-doubt involved. It's good in some ways to be aware of that and let it inform how you work with students, so that they know it's OK to doubt that what they are doing is right or even 'good'. Not being like everyone else can in fact be very positive: imposter syndrome comes with the job.

Having openness of repertoire when teaching performance can open up great opportunities, but the difficulty is that every genre and sub-genre of music has its accepted practices, body of history, stylistic conventions, performance conventions and so on, and we want the students to demonstrate that they have engaged with all of that. That's a big ask in itself, but then we also want them to be creative, and that's really quite a lot! It is like saying 'Learn all of these bespoke rules and conventions, and then once you have assimilated all of those, find an interesting way to break them'.

The openness also means that there is another negotiation to be had with each student regarding how versatile they are, addressing the breadth of music they are interested in and capable of dealing with. The days of habitually performing a baroque, a classical and a twentieth-century piece in a student recital are long gone, and quite right too. But once that comforting canon and sense of what is accepted as a 'classical training' are gone, you have to find some way to define what's there instead. I think you are in a better position to do that than I am, because you haven't got the weight of 200 years of conservatory tradition bearing down on you, nor the fact that there are thousands of music students in conservatoire-like places around the world all learning much the same thing, which may or may not have much useful application outside the learning environment.

It can be quite difficult to escape from the university, and having an academic post means there are always countless things that the university can give you to do. But it is vitally important to get away, to spend time exploring who your audiences are and where they are, and to get out there and talk to them.

Of course, it is now built into university strategies in terms of Knowledge Exchange and Impact that we get out and engage with those audiences, but besides that, from a more selfish point of view, it is important to spend time with people who are at your own artistic level or above it, in order to inform your teaching and feed that creative bit of yourself. And no matter what it is that you do, those people are few and far between, and it takes effort to spend time with them. But without it, your teaching and research will go dry pretty quickly and start to run out.

Structural limitations and time constraints

LH – On the topic of time, though, one of the limitations of a degree structure, particularly for the development of creative practice, can be the time implications. It can be problematic to put a time limit on a creative process. For example, I can struggle to make a piece I know I need to do by a certain time. I can usually get it done, but it sometimes becomes something that you force through and that you have to do by a certain time as opposed to fulfilling some sort of creative process and letting it unfold as you would without that time limit. When you have the time to properly think through ideas and let it happen organically, things are usually more satisfying and often much better pieces of work as a consequence. So in our case, trying to delimit that within a semester can be somewhat problematic.

DMcG – The thing about teaching performance is that it is audience-focused: the audience (and the examiners) are going to be there at a certain place at a certain time, so it's an immutable deadline. It is a fact of creative life that if you are going to meet an audience, you have to show up when they show up. With other kinds of work, it's not the same, but for performance-based work the existence of that deadline means you will not always necessarily be most satisfied with the work, but because of the deadline you will have produced something.

I have recently been hiding in a cottage editing a record, and it is very instructive listening back to recording sessions, because when you revisit the recording process, you come up against all the decisions you would like to have made differently. At the time, you just needed to get it done, and the lessons are learnt for the next time. To be honest, I think those 'Oh, I wish I'd done that differently' lessons are more important for our students than what grade they get.

LH – I think that is one of the advantages that performance has over things like composition and Sonic Art – especially when dealing with students – because there is always an implied 'public-ness' to it: it will be in front of an audience, even if it is just your mum and dad and assessors. Someone is going to watch it. By contrast, it's really difficult to get students to exhibit their work when it is something like a composition or even something that is intended for installation – they will hand it in to you but are quite wary of showing it to someone else. This is why I like to have a lot of 'show and tell' sessions as part of my courses, during the process and at the end of it, because I want them to think about how they are going to feel about the work being in front of an audience and not just being something that gets handed in at the end of semester and then it is done.

To some extent, I am trying to create a community of practice (Lave and Wenger 1991) – a safe place where they can show their work and get

164 *Louise Harris and David McGuinness*

feedback on it from a group of like-minded individuals with a common goal. But trying to get students to submit things for festivals and open calls for work is also really difficult, because they don't see it as valid for public consumption – it is just something they do for assessment. Which is why trying to get them to develop and have ownership over their creative identity is so important; to try and give students the confidence to put their work out into the world and see what happens to it. The trouble with assessment generally is it is very insular and in house and becomes something that happens one day and is over, which can be quite a limiting thing in a creative process.

DMcG – Developing a creative identity can happen at lots of different paces, and being confident about your creative output is rarely going to synchronize with the end of a degree!

LH – Yes, or the end of a semester when you are handing work in.

DMcG – I think with all of these things, we have to be really careful to make it clear that they are just staging posts and not the most important things. Students individually have to figure out what the most valuable experiences and aspects of the process are for them, and it often isn't the assessed aspect. Because, fundamentally, the vast majority of people will not care what class of degree you get, but they will care about what experiences shaped you and what you learnt while you were earning that degree. If you are not staying in institutional academia, a first-class degree isn't a whole lot of use to you: it's not even a guarantee of funding if you are staying! It demonstrates that you have a certain kind of ability, but other than that it doesn't say an awful lot about you.

Mindset and culture

LH – I think there are things to get out of university that aren't grades – that are experiences and – what was a big thing for me – a change in mindset. For me, it changed how I thought about things, which was really important.

DMcG – Do you think the culture of the university and the students you are surrounded by could be the biggest thing you take away?

LH – I think it can be, though it depends on the institution and of course your responses to it. I think, for me, I rebelled quite violently against the way in which things were done at my institution and sought out things that were deliberately contrary to that ethos, which meant that I approached my masters and my PhD in perhaps a more open and a very different way to how I might have done otherwise. It is certainly very formative, in a load of different ways, most of which you don't really comprehend at the time.

DMcG – I think the temptation, especially in a research-led university where we are often hired on the basis of our specialist interests, can be to teach in a 'Be like me, do what I do' kind of way; after all, we got the gig

The teaching of creative practice   165

because of who we are, and who we are also helps to define what the institution is like. Although he is guarding against exactly this, Fred Frith says 'The only thing you can be in front of students is yourself' (Andriessen 2014, 7'52"):[6] you cannot pretend to have experience or expertise you haven't got. However, that's not the same as expecting students to share your interests; in fact, it can be quite alarming when they are interested in the same things! My immediate thought is usually 'Are they just saying that to get on my good side?'

LH – Tied into that is something which we discussed earlier, which is allowing students, and it being OK for students, to explore things that aren't what you are interested in and to have their own perspectives on the things that you are interested in. I always say to my students 'it's OK if you don't like this, but you have to be able to tell me why' – you have to be able to articulate what it is about it that doesn't work, just like when something does work you need to be able to tell me what about it does work for you. And I think that is part of what university teaches us: critical and analytical thinking about things instead of just reaching snap judgments and sticking with them. You start to think in more detail about things.

DMcG – Yes, and I am still surprised by how some students will say 'I don't want to analyse this because then I won't like it any more'. It is sometimes difficult to get them to realize that you can pull the thing to bits and then stick it back together and still think it is brilliant, and that the process isn't going to take away that excitement or mystery or whatever the magic thing was that made it interesting in the first place. If our teaching removes that, then we have really failed spectacularly.

Summary of principles

LH – I think one of the things that we've come to realize during the course of these conversations is that regardless of what area of creative practice you teach, there are similarities in terms of approach and the things we value across these various teaching and learning environments. And often those similarities are there, or perhaps need to be there, regardless of course content or structure or the way in which things are assessed. We feel they need to be there for effective learning within the context of creative practice to take place.

DMcG – The challenge is figuring out how to make them possible: we have talked about GLOs or what we might call 'unassessables', but we still have to have a course, and that course has to enable the GLOs and the unassessables. So the trick is to design the course in such a way that there is room for these unassessables to happen. I think that is what Michael Rosen was talking about in the article that started this conversation.

LH – Tied into this, I came up with this almost Rosen-style 'checklist' of criteria for effective practice-based, research-led teaching

166   *Louise Harris and David McGuinness*

and it is clear that there are a lot of parallels between it and what we have been talking about. Perhaps it's just worth taking a look at that?

1   *Students should feel actively involved in their learning and feel part of a collaborative learning community.*

For me this is something that should be difficult to escape when being involved in creative practice, but I know from experience it often isn't. On occasion, educators can be tempted to try and teach creative practice in a very dictatorial, authoritative way, trying to get students to replicate their own ways of working.

DMcG – Or they only try to teach one person at a time, which can obviously be useful in certain circumstances, but perhaps isn't ideal for fostering that sense of community and collaboration.

LH – Yes, and tied into that is:

2   *Students should have frequent opportunities to receive feedback on their work and provide feedback to others.*

This is one of the reasons I do so many 'show and tells' – it is part of developing a collaborative learning community and also encourages them to be much more open about sharing their work. I suppose with performance this is something that happens all the time?

DMcG – Actually, it doesn't happen as much as we would like, as the students are quite reluctant to get up and play in front of each other. We try to make space for that as much as possible, but getting them to take the plunge is difficult, because it is such a personal thing to do.

LH – But part of creating the space for that comes, I think, from:

3   *The community of practice should spend time reviewing and critiquing existing work and articulating and reflecting upon their responses to it.*

That is something we have discussed extensively, but I think it's really important. It is often difficult to get students to recognize that things are happening out in the wider world that they are, essentially, a part of, and to try to have them engage with it and situate themselves in relationship to it is essential for a lot of things. One of those is developing the freelancers' mentality we discussed earlier: taking ownership over their own work in a more professional capacity.

DMcG – Related to that, one thing that we have tried to do recently is getting students to critique concerts, not just from the perspective of critiquing the work and the performer, but also from the perspective of figuring out what you can learn as a performer from watching others perform – to try and find the lesson in each performance.

The teaching of creative practice 167

LH – So the next principle is:

4   *Students should feel that their individual perspective is valuable.*
      For me that is very important, and very much tied into a lot of the points that Michael Rosen was making. And following on from this is that:

5   *Students should feel that their individual creative work is valuable, is contributing to an ongoing professional portfolio, and has longevity outside of assessment within the university context.*
      I think is this something that I struggle with and I wonder if perhaps it is less of an issue for performance students? That they perhaps see what they are doing as by implication a more public and outward-facing thing?

DMcG – Well, when you get up on stage you are the physical embodiment of your work, so to some extent you're carrying it around with you all the time.

LH – And I think that's one of the reasons that we've started to include performance in the Sonic Arts courses in the final undergraduate year. Once they have got to the stage of being competent enough to do things live we try to encourage them to do so, because it is a totally different way of working. It is really important for them to challenge themselves and develop a different kind of skill, outside of the apparent safe haven of submitting a fixed, delimited piece of work that you can carefully craft out of real time. Which brings me to the final principle of:

6   *Students should ideally develop a co-researcher relationship with their tutor/lecturer.*
      What all these things have in common is that student and lecturer need to have a good, functional, open and collaborative relationship. This is probably essential across any kind of teaching across higher education, but it is particularly important when you're trying to teach creativity, which is often very personal. It needs to feel like a safe place where they can work without feeling that they're being judged.

DMcG – You cannot encourage someone to be creative unless you have figured out where they are to begin with, and let them know that that's OK: they have to feel secure about where they currently are. Then really all you can do is suggest to them possible places they might go next, and, to quote Fred Frith again, let them get on with it (Andriessen 2014, 9'00").

LH – And I think that is difficult, because it can be very tempting (and it's not just students who do this!) to compare yourself to other people around

168 *Louise Harris and David McGuinness*

you, rather than being concerned about what you are doing and what your personal creative voice is.

DMcG – Perhaps self-doubt is a sort of friendly adversary. We step away from it from time to time to get some work done, then sidle up to it again to keep ourselves self-critical!

Notes

1 Kaufman and Sternberg (2010) is a useful introduction to many perspectives on creativity.
2 A key text on constructive alignment is Biggs and Tang (2007).
3 The *Contemporary Music Review* issue on 'Resistant Materials in Musical Creativity', particularly the papers by Ferguson (2013), Peters (2013) and Norman (2013) is useful here, as is Auslander (2012).
4 To clarify this further, what I'm trying to convey here is that of course there are works and composers/artists that we consider important and historically significant, and of course this is acknowledged and discussed in class. What I mean by the lack of a canon is that I try not to put all the emphasis in class on addressing these particular pieces/composers/trends but rather allow students to explore both historic and contemporary practice without an emphasis on what is/isn't important and what they should/shouldn't be engaging with.
5 There is a similarity here with the hidden curriculum, as explored in Margolis (2001).
6 This YouTube clip includes an interview with Frith about the teaching of improvisation, in which he rejects the notion of being able to 'teach something', but rather aims to 'provide tools for people to be critical, and stimulated and curious and open-minded and engaged in the process of discovery, and then you leave them to get on with it' (9'00").

Bibliography

Andriessen, Bas. 2014. *Fred Frith 'Gravity' Extra*. Nijmegen, Holland. https://youtu.be/Clx8MBFnQxw.

Auslander, Philip. 2012. 'Digital Liveness: A Historico-Philosophical Perspective.' *PAJ: A Journal of Performance and Art* 34, no. 3: 3–11.

Biggs, John B., and Catherine So-kum Tang. 2007. *Teaching for Quality Learning at University: What the Student Does*. 3rd ed. Maidenhead: Society for Research into Higher Education/Open University.

Ferguson, John Robert. 2013. 'Imagined Agency: Technology, Unpredictability, and Ambiguity.' *Contemporary Music Review* 32, no. 2–3: 135–149.

Harris, Louise. 2016. Thinking, Making, Doing: Perspectives on Practice-Based, Research-Led Teaching in Higher Music Education. In Burnard, Pamela and Haddon, Elizabeth eds., *Creative Teaching for Creative Learning in Higher Music Education*, 1st ed. Oxford: Routledge.

Hugill, Andrew. 2008. *The Digital Musician*. New York: Routledge.

Kaufman, James C., and Robert J. Sternberg, eds. 2010. *The Cambridge Handbook of Creativity. Cambridge Handbooks in Psychology*. Cambridge, New York: Cambridge University Press.

Lave, Jean, and Etienne Wenger. 1991. *Situated Learning: Legitimate Peripheral Participation*. Cambridge: Cambridge University Press.

The teaching of creative practice   169

Margolis, Eric, ed. 2001. *The Hidden Curriculum in Higher Education*. New York: Routledge.

Norman, Sally Jane. 2013. 'Contexts of/as Resistance.' *Contemporary Music Review* 32, no. 2–3: 275–288.

Nyrnes, Aslaug. 2006. *Lighting from the Side: Rhetoric and Artistic Research*. Bergen: Kunsthøgskolen i Bergen.

Peters, Deniz. 2013. 'Haptic Illusions and Imagined Agency: Felt Resistances in Sonic Experience.' *Contemporary Music Review* 32, no. 2–3: 151–164.

Rosen, Michael. 2014. 'How We Teach the Arts Is as Important as the Fact We're Doing It'. *The Guardian*, June 4. www.theguardian.com/teacher-network/zurich-school-competition/teach-arts-michael-rosen-education-worthwhile-students.

Stoller, Aaron. 2014. *Knowing and Learning as Creative Action*. New York: Palgrave.

9 On teaching composition

Why it can be taught and why that matters

Bill Sweeney

THE LITTLE ROSE.....

The little rose, oh how should it be listed?
Suddenly dark red and young and near?
Oh we never knew that it existed
Then we came, and saw that it was there.

Unexpected till we came and saw it
Unbelievable as soon as seen
Hit the mark, despite not aiming for it:
Isn't that how things have always been?
     Bertolt Brecht, trans. John Willett (1976, 447)

Higher Education Institutions in the UK love ILOs (Intended Learning Outcomes). Students mostly think that we should have them (though perhaps seldom read, or think, about them): but they love model answers. However, teachers of composing know that a fixation with outcomes often defeats the process, and that it is immersion in process that unlocks artistry.

A sense of comfort in the presence of paradox is helpful here, perhaps suggesting the pedagogical subterfuge of offering the student a clearly laid out, conscious pathway while ensuring that the route map to Parnassus leads to uncertainty, reflection and the embrace of the unexpected.

Modelling: modelling results v. modelling behaviour

In compositional analyses, whether delivered as a lecture or by directing students to published sources, we are all too often offering the assurance of a model result which can be achieved through the operation of a set of technical procedures. The danger comes if we ignore the fact that analysis is inevitably post hoc: it can often be difficult to disentangle those features which become apparent simply through observing the work from those which have resulted from the composer's intentions (which may be implicit or explicit). Analysis also tends to stress interconnection and coherence (what Tovey might have recognized as 'normality') at the expense of unexpected,

On teaching composition 171

even disruptive events (what Kerman might read as 'the uncanny'): these can often contain the most significant features of a work (Tovey 1949; Kerman 1979, 2001–2002). The key quality, which can be difficult to identify and transmit, is how the composer has *behaved* with the materials and techniques at their disposal.

We may speculate about behaviour, and that speculation may either be based on our own direct experience of dealing with similar situations, or on clues derived from the composer's own statements or known behaviours, but speculation is not knowledge. However, this is not necessarily an impasse. If we follow Stravinsky's lead in including concepts such as 'appetite' and 'speculation' amongst the necessary conditions from which composers must suffer, then the deployment of speculation, so long as it is accompanied by a degree of scepticism, can be beneficial in the development of the concept of compositional behaviour (Stravinsky 1970, 51, 27, 49). Speculation can reveal productive uncertainties, possibilities which go beyond the already known and predictable. It is a situation rather than a procedure and one in which the interaction of conscious and unconscious processes can be promoted, but it is best achieved by modelling behaviour rather than by modelling results.

Stravinsky (1970, 28–31) indicated that after the initial, necessary and conscious decisions about the limitations of a particular work, he found that, working at the piano, he had to find the right tempo in order to make progress. Elliott Carter would work with a set of intervals until he reached the point at which he could improvise with them. As he described the process to Jonathan Bernard (1990, 205):

> Very often, in recent years, I have started my pieces by deciding that I would take a certain chord and use that as a basis of a composition. And then I fool around, turn it around and discover what its elements are... but then I really don't know what the next step is. [...] The sketches don't show this, because there's an awful lot of mental work that's never put on paper.

Janáček was observed repetitively pounding out the same terse motifs on the piano in the initial stages of new work (Vogel 1981, 26–27). Apparently so different and idiosyncratic, these activities have in common a disregard for planning and objectives and a sense of infiltration: infiltration of the self into the physicality of the material (as well as the more familiar interpretation of a process of absorption of the material into the self). To model this behaviour demands a sense of trust in the process, a joy in the act of experience through experiment, and coolness in subsequent observation and evaluation.

One of the problems for the teacher of composition, after assessing the aptitude and experience of the individual student and the nature of their initial ambitions for a particular new piece, is to design and encourage activities

172   *Bill Sweeney*

which are exploratory and open-ended. Activities which involve (as well as mental imagery and the employment of a pencil) engagement with the physical presence of the material whether through improvisations or through repetitive play-back of cells and variants. Which parameter (pitch, rhythm, timbre, gesture etc.) is to be approached first is not, in general, important: experience will teach that this will vary from work to work and from time to time and a playful practice in choosing the initial activity will encourage ease in switching from one to another in the process of discovering the idiosyncratic language which will allow the new work to flow.

Feedback and assessment inevitably deal with the credit-bearing commodity (the student's submission) and while attention can be paid to features which bear, or lack, the imprint of the kinds of behaviours already noted, it will tend to focus on the result (cross-referenced to the ILOs). This can conflict with the principal reason for the inclusion of the practice-based study of composition in higher education, which must be the development of the students' engagement with 'thinking in (or with) music' rather than the production of new repertoire or even the training of new professional composers: these should be by-products of a successful school of composition rather than its aim. Already some activities can balance assessment between the success of the end performance and the individual student's ability to demonstrate a reflective understanding of the processes. (Often in workshop projects through which groups of students devise musical narratives by exploring the interactions between fixed elements and improvisation, individual negotiation and collective collaboration: in these practices speculation has to be brought out of its ghetto of the un-, or semi-conscious and shared with the community). Perhaps we are guilty of allowing the prestige of the finished, well-presented musical score to overwhelm the educational value of accomplished engagement with process, of performative exploration. If so, we need to reflect further on the content and nature of student submissions and the weighting of the different elements of the development process, and of the 'product' itself.

In other words, pedagogy in musical composition should concern itself more with, for example, the design of activities which proliferate material and encourage evaluation and selection rather than the illustration of the already known – activities which aim at drawing out the nature of the musical materials and only then exploring the formal narratives which can bring them to fruition.

Conscious action and unconscious awareness

The creative mind should not be locked into a single mode of thought or a single state of consciousness, but should move backward and forward (or upward and downward) through different stages of activity and states of mind. Thus the conscious mind, by designing the appropriate activity, can stimulate the capacity of the unconscious to produce imagery, while

On teaching composition   173

the unconscious brings forward practical tasks and problems for the wakened intellect. This latter phenomenon often manifests itself as a kind of irritation – the awareness that some important, but as yet unformulated question needs to be addressed.

The table below, while not exhaustive, gives an outline of modes of thought, types of activity and stages of development characteristic of creative work. The sequence should be read, in general, from left to right and from top to bottom, i.e. more than one "mode of thought" can be employed in each type of activity and similarly more than one type of activity may be appropriate at any particular stage of development. (The over-neatness of the tripartite presentation should be overcome by re-combination, layering and ... failure to complete a set of categories.) A tabular representation of stages of conscious and unconscious activity might be misleading: there are many more than two or three distinct states of consciousness or sensuous reaction and their interaction is even more fluid.

Modes of Thought		
Empathy	*interconnection*	*Projection*
Types of Activity		
origination	*elaboration*	*realisation*
Stages of Development		
Material	Texture	Form
generation	*investigation*	*relation*
proportion	*characterisation*	*succession*
speculation	*extension*	*progression*

In this scheme, the absence of 'inspiration' might be noted, mostly to avoid the unfortunate associations of that word with the various semi-demonic or supernatural popular representations of the creative mind. But in its sense of a seed, germ or metaphor, it can grow in the condition of empathy and be nurtured by interconnection around the stage of origination, while its other sense of 'in-the-moment' decision-making lies in the permeable border areas of conscious and unconscious action.

The concept of empathy as a starting condition for artistic work arises out of the way in which musical activities are bound up in the realization and recreation of a sense of human-ness. The enactment of a live performance is only possible through a collective and vivid sense of the interaction of the self and the other: the projection of one's own sense of gestural purpose while relying on a response which recognizes that purpose, and in formulating the gesture through imagining oneself in the place of the other. These relationships are fluid, variable and can be more or less successful. With the addition of an

174   *Bill Sweeney*

audience, the variant receptions, projections and interpretations multiply, but these simultaneous truths, misconceptions, even collective self-deceptions do not undermine the essentially human nature of the phenomenon. We are not in search of a single, monolithic revelation of 'the truth', but rather it is our engagement in the flow of musical, ideological, social and emotional stimuli that celebrates the central function of human empathy as a bridge out of solipsism and celebrates music as a powerful sensory focus for our journey.

The composer, as distinct from the technical executant or designer, thus has to find their place in these events, modelling the self (at least temporarily) according to the sense of the other, interacting not only with the tones, but with the possibilities for human discourse which the formal design and all its intricate, interconnected materials might realize.

Why style doesn't matter, except when it does

Composition students are usually obsessed with style: 'What style are you/ they (the examiners) looking for?' 'How can I develop my own style?' Composition teachers may often detect the unspoken/unspeakable questions: 'What is the "correct" style?' 'What is the currently acceptable style?' lurking behind many student enquiries.

Apart from student anxieties, there is the critics' obsession with the identification of style, often negating the possibility, or obscuring the evaluation, of a particular work's expressive quality. Both perspectives are characteristic of marketplace negotiation: the commodity to be 'sold' as an academic or socio-professional product or 'possessed' (even negatively) through a process of classification and labeling.

Grove online defines style as '(a) term denoting manner of discourse, mode of expression; more particularly the manner in which a work of art is executed' (Pascall n. d.). This historically neutral definition provides a useful basis, particularly in what it leaves unsaid: that the degree of alignment of any work of art with the mode of expression of any particular style is not a measure of its artistic, expressive quality (although it may well have an impact on its reception history). My personal experience of searching for appropriate styles for creative work seems to bear this out; at various times, specific styles would be self-characterized as 'not possible', only to have this ideological fervour confounded by the infiltration of specific works, written in proscribed styles, into one's consciousness. These moments of cognitive dissonance could be deflected for a while by creating a category of exceptions, but in the longer term the concern for style has had to be relocated to a critical outpost dealing with the evaluation of appropriate technique. It is quite possible – and intellectually respectable – to be engaged, moved, inspired and have our consciousness broadened to significant extents, by the works of as various composers as, for instance, Xenakis, Poulenc or John Adams. (It is also possible to experience mediocre work written in the mature manner of any of these composers.)

What is it that really counts? A reasonable pedagogic strategy exposes students to a range of styles (or at least to the techniques associated with them and to their cultural allusiveness and characteristic affects and interpretations) and can encourage experimentation with pastiche. However, the ultimate aim must be that the artistic work is not simply coloured by the stylistic tropes of any particular style, but should deliver a sense of embodiment: that the musical personality speaks authentically through stylistic norms, that the work is produced through empathetic sublimation rather than affectation.

The commodification of culture has accelerated and promoted some immanent trends in attributing or acquiring value through style. The adoption of new stylistic tropes as signifying the acquisition of a new and distinctive culture almost certainly predates the wave of troubadours who spread the ethos of sophisticated Arabic cultures through mediaeval Europe, but as production and dissemination have become progressively capitalized, the process of the extraction of value from the mass market has seen the identification with style mutate from a mark of social, intellectual or artistic distinctiveness to a form of consumer fetishism. In the modern era, popular music styles are now ingrained in generational culture and ruthlessly rotated to create a constant illusion of distinctiveness, with a commercially useful sense of neediness. As the human personality and sense of identity is crucially formed in the years approaching adulthood, the aspiring composition student can find it difficult to distinguish between the engagement with style on the one hand as a conversation between the unconscious and the volitional, and on the other its adoption as a mannerism satisfying educational or commercial market forces. From this vantage point, the eighteenth century's ease with the sincere irony of stylistic allusion seems all the more attractive.

On the other hand, a sense of appropriate style is necessary both for the creation of coherent musical communication and for informed reception. Scientistic approaches that seek to neutralize, or on the other hand universalize, some of the elements of musical language tend to rob the aural surface of associative power, or can create unintended, bathetic affects when the outcome of combinatorial procedures produces events laden with incongruous stylistic associations.

The important question is not 'Which style?' but rather 'Can I speak authentically – or ironically – through this style?'

A footnote on style, in the form of an interlude

In the course of his incisive lecture on the poetry of Hugh MacDiarmid, Seamus Heaney (1995, 107) remarks that 'this sense of a nascent truth, of a something not quite clearly apprehended, but very definitely experienced, is exactly what is embodied in "The Watergaw". Its real subject is the uncanny'. Heaney (1995, 106) has already described how the writer Christopher Murray Grieve transformed himself into Hugh MacDiarmid 'as a fully developed

176 *Bill Sweeney*

phenomenon, one who both produced and was produced by the language he wrote in' [Synthetic Scots]. The sense that style comes about, not just as a result of formally identifiable technical procedures, vocabularies and gestural habits, but as a web through which these conscious markers are interwoven with embodied intentionality, may perhaps be useful in relieving the anxieties of musicians and composers over questions of stylistic consistency.

Claire Taylor-Jay (2009) reviews a number of critical attempts to cope with the evaluation of style. In teasing out the limitations of value-laden approaches, such as 'High Art' v. 'commerce' (central to the contention that there are 'two Weills') and those of the opposing 'unifiers' (attempts to identify and confirm unity of 'voice' through the persistence of micro-elements such as 'added-sixth chords' or 'prevalence of the fifth'), the debate is certainly clarified. She seems to suggest that we simply accept and let such multiplicities be, which is an advance on judgemental approaches, but still does not find a way to define 'voice' in terms of composers. Even if we extend the 'micro' trace elements to include the broader and less data-bound stylistic fingerprints of, say, harmonic voicing and characteristic utterance or musical rhetoric, the 'problem' seems to remain. Perhaps if we follow Heaney's train of thought we may be able to propose that an individual artistic 'voice' might be best described as a situation rather than an object, a companion to the concept that 'meaning' in music is not in the score, nor is it simply a projection of the audience, but is rather a phenomenon which can only exist in the moment of performance: it is the ever-shifting perspective of realization produced in the dialectic between what we hear and what we know, our openness to the uncanny in dialogue with our instinct for taxonomy.

John Berger (1993, 34–40) also seems to indicate this approach in his discussion of the roots and nature of Picasso's discontinuity (even more distressing to the prevailing Euro-centric critical view than the examples of Weill or Stravinsky, in that he not only had diachronic changes of style – 'blue period', 'cubist period' – but was capable of synchronic discontinuity, producing works in markedly diverse styles within the same short time-span). In particular, Berger (1993, 38) invokes Lorca's explanation of the *duende* as 'a kind of undiabolic demon': not an angel or a muse, but

> ...the *duende* likes a straight fight with the creator on the edge of the well. While angel and muse are content with violin or measured rhythm, the *duende* wounds, and in the healing of this wound which never closes is the prodigious, the original in the work of man.

Who are the students and what are we trying to encourage in them?

For today's students, growing up under the dictatorship of consumerism and the monetization of style, discourse and identity, it takes considerable courage and perseverance to turn away from the tyranny of the product

On teaching composition 177

and embrace the art of musical communication for the sake of its human ethos. But the purpose of composition as part of a musical education must be about learning to think in tones, gestures and textures in the service of social, emotional, physical and intellectual human interactions. I have referred above to 'a sense of trust in the process, a joy in the act of experience through experiment' as the objective of studies in composition. The struggle for this is by no means new. The Scottish poet Hugh MacDiarmid (1995, 404) sought to promote his new definition of the Scots' creative psychology in an article in the *Scottish Educational Journal* of November 1926. He says (using the term Dadaist to denote the whole modern movement):

> The difference between a Dadaist and a respectable product of the Scottish Educational System is that the latter likes something he can understand and the former something he can't. It is obvious that the Dadaist must carry a process of elimination a good distance before he arrives at a point at which he can derive any satisfaction, whereas the R.P.S.E.S. needn't move off the bit. It is also obvious that liking something you can understand means throwing bouquets at your powers of comprehension all the time, while the Dadaist, on the other hand, is looking for *culs-de-sac* to bat his head against. The latter is, of course, a comparatively religious process. From the point of view of Education, the R.P.S.E.S. has little, if any, use for more than the minimum of it he can't evade – the minimum he can practically apply – while the Dadaist doesn't become one till, in some direction or other, he has learned all that can be taught and entered into unexplored territory for himself. Pedagogic interest, therefore – on a long view – lies with the latter. Apart from that it is surely a matter of personal honour. This stupid insistence on mere meaning, on values that, however idealistic at first glance, are all at best in the last analysis utilitarian, this disinclination for the incomprehensible, for what is beyond us ... are all dishonourings of our minds, panderings to what is commonest and basest in us, sloth, the fear to be different from other people.

Nearly a century on this is, in the language of some in academe, 'relevant, aspirational, inspirational' – and utterly transparent in its identification of our central problem.

Bibliography

Berger, John. 1993. *The Success and Failure of Picasso*. New York: Vintage International.

Bernard, Jonathan W. 1990. 'An Interview with Elliott Carter'. *Perspectives of New Music* 28/2: 180–214.

Brecht, Bertolt. 1976. *Poems*. Edited by John Willett and Ralph Manheim with the co-operation of Erich Fried. London: Eyre Methuen.

178 *Bill Sweeney*

Heaney, Seamus. 1995. *The Redress of Poetry*. London: Faber and Faber.

Kerman, Joseph. 1979. *The Beethoven Quartets*. New York: Norton, 325–326.

Kerman, Joseph. 2001–2002. 'Beethoven's Opus 131 and the Uncanny'. *19th-Century Music* 25/2–3, Fall/Spring: 155–164.

MacDiarmid, Hugh. 1995. *Contemporary Scottish Studies*. Edited by Alan Riach. Manchester: Carcanet.

Pascall, Robert (n.d.). 'Style'. *Grove Music Online. Oxford Music Online*. www.oxford musiconline.com/subscriber/article/grove/music/27041. accessed 17 Mar. 2014.

Stravinsky, Igor. 1970. *Poetics of Music in the Form of Six Lessons*. Cambridge, MA: Harvard University Press.

Taylor-Jay, Claire. 2009. 'The Composers's Voice? Compositional Style and Criteria of Value in Weill, Krenek and Stravinsky'. *Journal of the Royal Musical Society* 134: 85–111.

Tovey, Donald Francis. 1949. *Essays and Lectures on Music*. London

Vogel, Jaroslav. 1981. *Leoš Janáček: A Biography*. London: Orbis.

10 A reflective dialogue on teaching composition

Drew Hammond and Jane Stanley

This chapter takes the form of an edited dialogue between Drew Hammond and Jane Stanley who teach composition at the University of Glasgow. We will address a number of questions relating to composition pedagogy: what is the relevance of teaching music composition to students in a general undergraduate music degree? In what ways are we equipping our students with generalizable tools that may be applied in their various future careers? If students are engaging increasingly with technology in the process of creation (whether this be notation-based software or sound-editing programmes), should we be continuing to teach notation-based composition at all? What are the merits of notation? Are our assumptions concerning knowledge of repertoire valid in the context of the students we teach today, or should we adapt our syllabi to take into greater account the repertoire with which our students engage in their listening outside the classroom?

We reflect upon our individual pedagogical approaches to teaching undergraduate students. At a more fundamental level we consider *who* we are teaching: who are our students? Where are they coming from? To what extent might they intend to apply the skills we teach in their future endeavours? We consider some of the challenges we face in the context of teaching notation-based composition. These include different degrees of students' notational acuity, the influence of technology in their creative process and variable levels of familiarity with the repertoire to which we refer in the course of our teaching. We argue that student attributes including notational fluency, technical ability, aural imagination and repertoire awareness are interlinked and required in order to enable students to engage fully with our composition courses. In the course of interrogating the foundations of our respective teaching philosophies, we will consider the extent to which received wisdom continues to be valid in today's educational climate, as well as exploring the influence of our personal research areas on our teaching.

The majority of the students we teach at undergraduate level will not pursue composition to a specialist level. Indeed, many of them opt to take just one year-long module of the subject. This being the case, we ask to what extent students who engage with a year or two of composition are instilled with useful skills and knowledge. We argue that one of the main benefits of teaching notation-based composition to students is to provide them with crucial insight into the inherent difficulty of creating a musical work, replete with the full range of questions and choices that are entailed in the experience of making a notated piece. This knowledge may then inform students' study in a range of areas including performance and analysis. We explore the idea that notated composition may ultimately do something artistically, which no other music can do, and that its worth to students is inherent and self-justified.

What are the principles that underpin our approaches to teaching undergraduate composition?

JS – A key principle underpinning my approach to teaching composition is to enable our students to draw connections between practice, theory, listening and general music-making experience as well as to develop technical facility. It is important to me that students be encouraged to generate their own strategies, their own language. To that end, I teach through models and examples, providing insight into selected pieces through analysis and critical listening.

DH – My principles include a commitment to the value of studying music composition to a wide array of potential applications both in music and elsewhere, a belief in the importance of developing the students' individual approaches to composition and a recognition that the skills needed for music composition are diverse and may potentially overlap with all areas of practical and critical/scholarly approaches to music.

I wonder, are you talking more specifically about the kind of skills that you think we should teach?

JS – Certainly I am thinking about how what I teach will benefit students in the future, beyond their degree and regardless of whether they pursue composition to a more advanced level or not.

DH – I think that contextual knowledge is very important, and this connects to my own views. For instance, understanding performance in the context of being a composer is critical.

JS – And conversely, how might the experience and confidence gained as a composer make someone a better performer or listener? How might this knowledge enable learners to appreciate the processes involved in making these musical artefacts provide insight into that?

DH – I am conscious of teaching within the context of a broad humanities degree. Our degrees are not vocational, but rather are centred upon the rounded education of musicians. Composition might be considered as just one perspective from which our students explore music.

JS – To that I would add that I am very influenced by my own training as a student. I remember my peers and I were encouraged from the start

A reflective dialogue   181

of our degree (a Bachelor of Music degree in Australia) to develop an individual compositional identity. We were encouraged to be quite independent in carrying out research to scaffold our development. Key to this was having one-to-one tutorials from our first year, which is of course different to our provision here. In addition to the study of free composition, we received training in eighteenth-century harmony and counterpoint, and we also had a course in stylistic composition from the twentieth century in which we imitated the styles of Stravinsky, Messiaen, Debussy and Britten. I found that to be a particularly useful course. The experience of absorbing this range of styles, whilst at the same time being encouraged to develop my own, was fruitful.

Singing in a chamber choir was important as well, because having a practical music-making experience, whether it is playing an instrument or singing in a choir, was vital. I was simultaneously absorbing music from the canon whilst attempting to construct my own compositional language. This brings to mind a point made by John Harbison in his *Tanglewood Talks* (1985). He argues that 'we must study and learn "the classics" on faith. Not to do so means that our eventual, personal history will be too parochial to be useful' (1985, 14).

Without a sufficient range of reference points students will be faced with reinventing the wheel and falling back on a limited range of patterns. Courses fostering repertoire awareness are a key part of our provision.

DH – Yes, definitely. Broadly speaking I suppose we could say we are talking about the principle of 'being educated'. An awareness of reference points is a key part of this, but I think our ultimate goal is to facilitate students' personal responses to repertoire — to cultivate the individual. But are we teaching the right repertoire? Are we being culturally insensitive in some ways that are difficult for us to see, by privileging this Western canon?

JS – Yes, I feel quite troubled by that as well. I am very conscious in questioning this, because it would be wrong to develop an approach based simply on the way I was taught. I do see the value in being familiar with the canon and I would not want to discard this aspect of our provision. But how can we at the same time effectively support students in generating their own techniques and stylistic approaches? Do we place too much emphasis on imitation and pastiche? Exposure to unfamiliar repertoire can be very off-putting and alienating to students. It is vital that we question the assumptions underpinning our approach of teaching composition through familiarisation with models.

DH – I wonder if perhaps this is about communication and awareness on our part. I think it is important to explain to our students that we are presenting examples to them, and that our particular selections will be informed by our own backgrounds and experiences. We invite our students to examine these works and concepts with us, but whilst doing so we should

182 *Drew Hammond and Jane Stanley*

impress upon them that we are not holding these up as models to be imitated. We want to avoid a prescriptive approach that I think occurred a lot in the past, the notion that *this* is the tradition and *this* is how it should be done. It is vital that we allow space for students to reflect on how what is presented in class might be related to their own experience.

JS – Yes, it is all about forming connections. William Cronon (1998) invokes the phrase 'only connect' from *Howard's End* in the context of writing about liberal education. I like the principle that no information that we take on board is redundant... it is just a matter of working out how it connects with your existing knowledge. I think it is still valuable to teach the canon to equip students with reference points. I think we have both found that Messiaen's *Quartet for the End of Time* is usually a new experience for our first-year students. I would be reluctant to cut that from my syllabus. The more you can add into the mix, the richer the experience will be. But are there ways for students to take more of a lead in the directions they want to explore and learn? I am aware that we are currently Euro-centric in the repertoire that we present to our students.

DH – I think there is a distinction to be drawn between the way that we approach teaching between *mode* of inquiry and the *content* of the inquiry. There is no reason why the skills that you acquire studying one kind of music cannot be applied to another.

JS – I think you start with serialism in your second-year course, is that right?

DH – Yes, although the way I'd put it is that I start with a dismantling of 'assumed tonality' or 'assumed modality', and I wouldn't actually call it serialism because I don't ever get deep enough into integral serialism. It's more a case of trying to unlock the students' ability to think about harmony outside of a tonal framework, whatever that new way of thinking about it might be. But it seems to be that serialism and atonality are terms that get used as catch-alls for any harmonic approach that is not key-based. Tonality is so ingrained in our training throughout our childhood years. For example, my young son is currently learning the Kodály method which deals with solfege syllables, and this is fundamentally a tonal idea. I'm not necessarily saying that it's wrong to take this approach because you have to start somewhere...

JS – We teach by example. My lectures will cover in some depth examples of practice drawn from contemporary classical music. This semester I will be teaching a unit on spectralism and closely related styles to all of our students, and that will feature works by Grisey, Murail, Fineberg and Saariaho. And last year I taught a unit on the music of Ruth Crawford Seeger. This reminds me that one of my values in teaching is trying wherever possible to incorporate female role models. Because that is something that troubles me very deeply — that the canon is basically male. It's a terrible dilemma.

A *reflective dialogue*   183

DH – Certainly. We are dealing with a diverse group of individuals and we need to be conscious of the discrepancy between the canon, which can be reduced to a list of white males from the past, and our student body which typically consists of at least 50 per cent women. I agree that we have a responsibility to highlight potential role models.

Originality and teaching from models

JS – Within the context of teaching through an analytical lens, I tend to look to extrapolate techniques that students may wish to experiment with themselves. It can be easy to fall into the trap of talking very analytically about a piece without really focusing on concrete ways that students might apply that information. There is a fine balance between making composition look doable whilst fostering appreciation for complexity.

DH – And also I think to recognise the extent to which it is impossible to account for all of the levels of creativity that go into something like this. You can be extremely sharp and demonstrate a lot of technique, but the difference between a *good* composition, and something that is really great, innovative and exciting can often be attributed to quite subtle differences. It may have to do with some sort of spark that is very difficult to put your finger on.

I used to start just with reducing everything to numbers, but my launch pad for three or four years now has been the 1913 flute solo *Syrinx* by Debussy. As a piece, it is both very expressive and easy to analyse – you can identify the motifs for example. So I think you are right that probably doing a bit of both analysing work and introducing abstract principles and concepts is productive. But there is another consideration we should address here, which is that students have diverse learning styles. Some students are going to be excited about approaching a new piece from an analytical perspective, and others will want to be much more intuitive.

JS – Yes, I have found this to be the case as well in traditional harmony and counterpoint. Some students find rules to be very useful, whereas others approach exercises (e.g. in four-part harmony) in a more instinctive way.

In assessing work by students in our composition courses we do not prescribe or require that particular techniques be used in an assignment. We do, though, have an expectation that students will show an engagement with music of the last one hundred years or so. If they are writing pastiche of Romanticism, then it's not really part of this particular course.

DH – The way I look at it from my second-year teaching is slightly different from how we do things at Honours level, when we do not want our students to be engaging in pastiche, whether it be in the style of

Haydn, Messiaen or Reich. And I do find myself having to keep my own subconscious biases in check... a well-crafted and convincing imitation of a contemporary composer would be no more suitable in this course than a pastiche of Beethoven. Originality is an important criterion for assessment. We look to see whether the student reflected on what they have learned and tried to come up with an original take on it.

JS – I've had similar thoughts myself about potential subconscious biases in terms of musical style. It does happen occasionally that a student might compose quite a compelling imitation of, say, Steve Reich. When it comes to assessing a piece like this there will be much to commend on a technical level, but there will be little evidence of originality.

Originality really is the key distinguishing factor between a free composition course and a course in stylistic composition (e.g. of the eighteenth century). I am conscious that John Harbison might question the priority that we place on originality at an undergraduate level though. In one of his *Tanglewood Talks* (1985, 15) he argues that early on students should develop their skills through the process of imitation, leaving the pursuit of an original voice until later.

DH – I think there are different models to work from. I understand Harbison's point though. It is deeply embedded in the tradition too, because Schoenberg was not concerned with teaching atonality, but relied on foundational eighteenth-century tonal traditions (Schoenberg, 1991). However, that approach does not resonate with my own experience of music. In my high school years, before I became really aware of particular models to imitate, I would say I was creative as a composer. I composed what I would consider original but naïve music. Then as an early undergraduate I learned about tonality and I wrote very detailed but totally *un*original music, basically trying to imitate the styles of Debussy, and then later, Beethoven. It was not until I was able to fully absorb this and then leave it aside that I was able to return to my pursuit of the originality of my high school years. So I don't think the progression towards an original voice is a simple linear process. We are creative from the start, as very small children.

JS – This makes me think that in our early years we are encouraged to be creative in all sorts of ways visually, but perhaps less so with sound. In pre-school and primary school students are encouraged to play, but I'm not sure that as much encouragement is given to improvisation and composition-based activities.

DH – I think we could do a better job at encouraging early years' musicians simply to *make sound*.

JS – Even though I continue to advocate the benefit of teaching from examples, another aspect of learning we should highlight here is the importance of providing opportunities for our students to learn from their own experiments. We do this already by arranging annual workshops with professional performers. But so much can be gained by students playing their own and each others' music.

DH – Yes, and this something I have been developing in my own teaching over the last few years. When I started teaching here it was all quite abstract and paper-based. But more recently the concept of the composer-performer has become central to my pedagogical approach. If you challenge the students to get out their instruments I have found the majority of them rise to that challenge. But we have to be careful. We are dealing with students who come to us with a relatively diverse range of performance experience, and we do not want to alienate anyone. Many of our students will have achieved Associate Board of the Royal Schools of Music (ABRSM) grade 8 (or higher) on their instrument, but an equal number will not have attained this same level of experience. So I don't insist that everyone participates in class-based performance exercises, but I'm continually trying to think of ways to incorporate performance as part of the learning process. I should clarify that here of course I am talking about notation-based composition and performance. We already require all of our students to participate in-group improvisation workshops.

Who are our students? where are they coming from?

JS – Students entering our degrees are very diverse in terms of their levels of attainment both in performance and theory. We offer three different degrees at this University, a Bachelor of Music, a Master of Arts, and a Bachelor of Engineering (Electronics with Music). How many students come to us wanting to be composers from the outset, I wonder? In all three degrees that we offer, it is not until second year that students are offered courses in what we have been calling 'free composition'.

DH – Yes, this is a big challenge in our context. These three degrees present differing types of focus, from being entirely about music (B.Mus), to being about studying music alongside other subjects (MA), to studying music in conjunction with electronics (B.Eng). However, students studying on each of these degrees will all be taking the same composition courses, if they end up taking them. This means that our broader questions about how and why to teach composition must acknowledge the diversity in our students' ultimate goals.

Speaking personally however, I have to say that the idea of specialising in composition, or indeed the concept of studying music to the exclusion of all other subjects is very difficult to relate to given that I received my undergraduate education from a liberal arts college. I did not decide to major in music until the end of my second year. Alongside my college training I was playing music in a variety of contexts, and I

186 *Drew Hammond and Jane Stanley*

learned as much in the few years following my degree as I did during it. I am therefore very sympathetic with the broad-based arts degree and what studying composition might mean within it.

JS – The B.Mus degree that I undertook was a bit different from the one here too. During my first year we took a language and one other course (I chose psychology) alongside music courses. In second year we dropped one of those subjects, and in years three and four we concentrated solely on music. So to some extent my degree was akin to the MA that we offer here.

To what extent might our students intend to apply the skills that they teach to their future endeavours?

JS – I think composition at its best can be a way to develop lateral thinking, problem-solving, abstract thinking and organisation. These are all transferable skills.

DH – The skills that students acquire through studying composition are broadly generalizable. It is important for a performer to understand something of the process of composition just as a composer should understand something of performance. Taking just this year's lectures as an example, students who attended your lectures on spectralism will have learned something about the physics of sound, which broadens their education more generally. And students studying Charles Ives with me will have learned something about American history in the late nineteenth century, because Ives's music dwells on that so much. The point is that even for a student who may not pursue composition following their time with us, there will still be something in there that is worth holding on to.

If students become professional composers, the diversity of approaches inherent in our teaching should indicate that learning composition is not a prescriptive process, but rather the coming-together of an individual's awareness of:

- the innovations of previous composers;
- stylistic trends of Western art music;
- modernity in general and artistic modernism;
- contemporary concerns in music;
- technology and its effects;
- globalism and musical diversity.

Add to this the individual's sense of self *as individual* within their social group, artistic endeavour, industry, etc.

So I would argue that we provide training that can be considered vocational to those who purse composition further, but also generalizable

A *reflective dialogue* 187

knowledge and skills to people who might do any number of other things following their degree.

JS – To what extent do students in their senior Honours year have ambitions to pursue composition following graduation? Only a small proportion of students who study composition with us will take composition further. Some students do stay on to take composition at postgraduate level, or study further at a different institution. Many of our students go on to complete teacher training programmes to become secondary school teachers. Every year I write a number of references for students wanting to apply to these programmes. Students have also gone on to do arts administration, either staying here in Scotland or going down to London to work for one of the big arts organisations, perhaps with an ensemble, or with artist representation, or working with organisations like PRS. Arts administration is quite a common destination. So bearing in mind that we have a sense of where our students go, how do we think they intend to proceed?

DH – Students may continue to professional activities that include some forms of composition and composition-based skills, without ever clearly identifying as composers. For instance, a musical director must be able to engage in orchestration and arrangement at short notice; they must have a keen sense of harmony, in order to reduce, or 'explode' harmonic materials to fit a given situation; they must be a good reader with a strong understanding of notation; they must have a wide general knowledge of musical instruments; they must have a sensitive ear. In a sense, we cannot really worry about what our students go on to do with the broad, mix-and-match skill set, as well as the widened perspective on and appreciation for music. That is up to them. They decide.

In looking at the current professional lives of past students, which is really all we can do in determining where our students go, I am struck by the diversity of activity. Performers have continued to law degrees, non-performers have become professional, gigging musicians and artists, etc. The unpredictability of our students' futures suggests that I turn my attention to the education of the individual thinker, as a person, and not toward a restricted notion of a career path. This approach, however, poses some danger in the culture of accountability that now dominates higher education, which insists that we answer the question; do we achieve what we set out to do? If we believe that we are training people to be professional composers, then we must recognise that we are failing by and large to do that, not because of the value of our composition courses *as training,* but due rather to the simple fact that being a composer as an exclusive profession is an extremely rare prospect. However, if we believe that we are using the study of music to engender a skillset that is potentially useful across a wide array of professional activity in music and elsewhere, while at the same time enhancing the

188 *Drew Hammond and Jane Stanley*

cultural and professional perspectives of our students, then we may feel like we are doing what we set out to do.

JS – We might consider how these skills and perspectives might fit into the professional concerns of a secondary school teaching career. Even though our students will not acquire specific classroom training at the undergraduate level, they will develop valuable abilities, including critical thinking, using evidence to support their assertions, presentation skills, communication skills, an ability to collaborate, awareness of repertoire, contextual awareness, all of which may potentially be passed on to their future students if they become teachers. Skills that are specific to classroom teaching may be acquired in a postgraduate teaching certificate.

DH – As far as classroom teaching is concerned, we might consider the mode by which we enable students to acquire these skills. For comparison, classical 'behavioural' teaching and learning requires students to obtain knowledge and skills, and then judges them according to their ability to demonstrate them in standardised, accountable situations (tests). This methodology still dominates standardised testing at the secondary level and elsewhere. We, on the other hand, largely leave this methodology aside, requiring that our students engage in more cognitive, constructive and social problem solving that will result in the acquisition and cross-pollination of a wide array of skills, while at the same time realigning the perspectives of the individual students: so-called *transformative* learning. We must however recognise that the skills acquired are provisional, fluid and negotiated; they are part and parcel of the larger complex machinery of personhood. The perspective is illustrated excellently by John Cage's famous response to Schoenberg, upon being told that he had no feeling for harmony, and that he would therefore encounter a wall that he could not pass. Cage said, 'In that case I will devote my life to beating my head against that wall' (1968, 261). In this exchange, Schoenberg represents the classical conditioning approach to teaching, the notion that one must possess certain attributes (a feeling for harmony) in order to proceed. Cage, on the other hand, represents the essence of a constructivist approach that places the human activity of composing above specific attributes. One of the ways that we attend to a more gestalt assessment of a student's achievement is by providing specific assessment criteria that refer to 'individuality' or 'spark' in their compositions. We are partly asking students to surprise us, to show us something we were not aware that we wanted to see.

JS – We do teach and assess that way, yes. I anticipate that those who have studied composition with us would feel confident to teach composition themselves at secondary level. On the other hand, if they have never experienced hands-on the nonlinear way that composition works, or

A reflective dialogue 189

encountered some of the stumbling blocks that composers face, then they will not be able to fully empathise with their own students' compositional efforts.

DH – To that I would add that empathy is exceptionally important to learning and teaching. A more comprehensive, practical and holistic version of 'knowing how' to do something would be 'knowing how it feels' to do something. If a teacher understands traditional harmony and counterpoint, form, tonal and post tonal technique, notation; if a teacher has acquired aural skills, sight reading skills, historical perspectives on music and a broad knowledge of repertoire, then this still will not be enough if the teacher does not know how it feels to try to utilise these skills and perspectives to create something that is simultaneously technically robust, but also a kind of expression of oneself, of one's own identity, how they feel and how they perceive themselves in the world. Evidence of a lack of empathy in teaching composition can be found in many of the students who arrive at our doors in their first year, when the attitude of 'getting it right' dominates all considerations of self-reflection and the forging of an individual perspective.

JS – Relating this back to our underlying principles of teaching composition, I believe strongly in teaching students not to fall back on remembered patterns. By this I am referring both to patterns in sound as well as patterns of physical motion that we absorb through the experience of learning an instrument (an Alberti bass accompaniment is a simple example, or a particular harmonic progression). Learning about processes that sever this connection with memory play a valuable role in suggesting fresh ideas to a composer, which they are then free to intervene upon. This is a principle that I learned as an undergraduate. It could be any number of processes of course... algorithmic, serial, or the chance procedures of John Cage. These all come with historical associations of course, and will yield very different results.

DH – Perhaps there is an underlying principle that relates to objectivity. A truly creative and reflective compositional practice requires one to objectify their own approach, and be aware of their own subjective limitations. If one is able to achieve this, then they may start to recognise where these patterns are helpful and where they are perhaps not. Understanding myself, I know that I can never step aside dispassionately and entirely rearrange my compositional approaches. Yet at the same time, I have to know where to be flexible and allow for change.

JS – This relates to the justification for teaching systems, like algorithms in your case, or other scaffolding systems that force one to go down a different route and create a different musical organisation than if they were to base it purely on what was learned from previously encountered repertoire, like the catalogue of works in the ABRSM graded syllabi, as is the experience of many of our students. This relates to the idea of 'only connect' which I mentioned earlier.

190   *Drew Hammond and Jane Stanley*

Is it important to teach notation-based composition?

DH – Yes, it is important. Notation's durable five hundred-plus year history does not become irrelevant because of evolving technological approaches to music. In the last century, the inherently transient nature of 'live' performance has been identified and highlighted by the emergence of fixed recorded media, which has in turn suggested to us that notation-based composition is now less about a necessity to record musical ideas for dissemination, and more about an entirely unique musical practice, which has inherent value as practice. A score, as opposed to a recording, will be new in some respect every time someone comes to it; therefore it presents a unique catalyst for musical action, rather than an object for passive observation and appreciation. In a sense, notation is now free to become the focus of a philosophical reconstitution of musical practice, as is the case with the emergence of 'new complexity' in the 1980s. Musical practice for these composers was not about the production of ideal performances, but rather about the emergent quality found when performers come to terms with complex notation. And I should stress that the value of notation is not *as opposed* to fixed media. Some of the most exciting new music brings together the 'fixed' and the 'live' experiences, whether that be in the realms live electronics, laptop music, sound installation – what we call 'art music' – or in popular music practices ranging from Jamaican sound systems, to hip hop, to a modern dance D.J. mixing and live editing Motown recordings. All of this may profitably interact with notational practices that are founded in much older traditions. This is a good thing.

JS – I would add that there is an inherent value in notation that relates to equipping students with skills for a wide variety of musical inquiry. Simply, music notation gives us a unique way of conceiving of music. An obvious example would be the music of J.S. Bach: he could not have made the music that he made without notation, because he would have had to rely on memory alone. Polyphony and the complex counterpoint of the Baroque period could only be created and captured if one is able to plan it out on paper.

DH – That is an important point, and one that I have tried to make to students in numerous contexts. Notation is actually a way of thinking about music, rather than only a mechanism for communicating musical ideas from a composer to a performer.

JS – Conversely, it is also important to be able to improvise, and we encourage students to develop pieces without notation and to not be constrained by what the notation might look like on the page. Computer based sonic arts are important as well, where one has that immediate engagement with the sound object, and where one may mould and process the sounds directly. It also provides a different way of thinking, so I would want to ensure that students engage in these practices as well as notation. They all foster ways of thinking and problem solving that are of general benefit. When one engages in notated composition, they train their brains to process ideas, to visualise things in the abstract, interpret them and transcribe them onto the page. These skills apply directly to other areas such as musicology, where students must be able to access a range of repertoire for analysis – music that may have little other texts associated with it. In our composition course we do assess according to a certain level of rudimentary ability in notation, and by fourth year, we expect them to be creating professional level scores, with excellent presentation and a page layout, clear rhythmic and harmonic spelling, among other issues.

What are some of the challenges we face in the context of teaching notation-based composition? how variable are our students' notational acuities?

DH – Technology has by now eliminated notational music literacy as a main-stay of education. We see this in the diverse range of musician types in our student body; some are classical musicians, like in the case of the majority of our B.Mus students, and others are not, like some B.Eng with Music or MA in Music students. This has meant that our students' levels of notational awareness are varied as well, so to some extent in first and second year courses we attempt to level out this variation. No-tation software can help in some ways, but it also has risks. First of all, software audio playback mimics what occurs in fixed media 'concrete' music composition by giving the student immediate aural feedback on what they are creating. This can be useful, but should be approached with extreme caution, simply because the student may be tricked into thinking that what they are creating is ultimately the audio playback, and it certainly is not. When it comes to the audible results of instru-mental composition, a score itself is a concrete document that presents abstract ideas, not concrete 'sound objects' in the way that a recording does, no matter how detailed the notation, and no matter how seemingly realistic the audio playback. For this and other reasons I believe we must present notational software as one of a large number of potential tools for composition.

JS – Yes, the software has strengths and weaknesses. One of its major strengths is the way that it may be more flexible than pen and paper. Cutting and copying material, removing bars, inserting bars, mass ed-iting and filtering of notes, are all a bit of a nightmare if you are using paper. Yet at the same time it is much easier not to have bars on paper – to sketch things out, or to quickly scrawl musical ideas. Paper also ena-bles us to write down pitches without duration, and vice versa – to mix and match the harmonic and temporal elements. But it is important not to present one or the other as a better way of working, but that both are valuable tools when used productively.

The emergence of Sibelius in secondary schools provides one of our biggest challenges. Students arrive with a certain mentality because I do not think that they are encouraged to use pencil and paper as a conceptual method. Automated composing tools (plug-ins) are a particular concern, as they have the potential to remove a great deal of skill and decision-making from the composer. Voice leading is an example of a skill that I fear is being eroded by certain plug-ins in this software. A student need only insert a row of chord symbols and the computer will produce a fully voice-led four-part arrangement for keyboard.

DH – Problems with transposition often become evident when students are making transposing parts for chromatic music that was written at concert pitch. You end up with lots of nonsensical enharmonic spellings, which are usually present due to a lack of understanding and an overreliance on the automated computer process of transposition. The problem is also found in a lack of comprehension of the difference between a part written in the key of concert C major or A minor, and a part written in no key at all, which may initially look the same on the page, but is in fact different when transcribed.

JS – I am not certain how to face this challenge. Having more of an influence with schoolteachers on how the software should be used may be of benefit, but that is quite a big challenge. Certainly it is important to remember this when thinking of our composition students as future educators, and that a sea change in the way that secondary education uses notation software will necessarily be slow. From this perspective, we should police the way we recommend this equipment to our students. I understand that you require your first assignment to be handwritten?

DH – Yes, the decision to require second year composition students to submit their first assignment hand-written was taken with these things in mind. I get the sense that for many of my students it may be the only opportunity to truly experience making the score by hand.

Notation software also presents slightly more hidden issues to me as well. There are certain ways in which the software will always work. For example, vertical alignment will be perfect all of the time, and I also stress the importance of vertical alignment in all of the hand-written work I assess. However, recently I was looking at some seventeenth-century manuscripts. Generally, things matched up according to bar lines – a convention that was at that point fairly new – but within individual beats, things were only very loosely aligned. It makes me realise the degree to which the ideal use of notation is historically situated and dependent upon both the technologies that we use to produce it, and the contemporary performance practices.

A reflective dialogue 193

JS – Yes, not to mention the fact that the partitura, or compiled score, has not always been present in historical practices. Generally speaking, then, what is the influence of technology on our students' creative processes? Students are increasingly engaging with technology, and I am interested in the damaging influence of technology, and the problems caused by things already mentioned, such as the 'composing tools' in notation software. The worst thing that can happen is that the software prescribes patterns for the user, as in the case where a teacher might require students to write a four-bar passage using a particular set of chords, and then the students simply use a software feature to create an accompaniment pattern. That really does erode the creative, out-of-the-box thinking that we are looking for in our students.

DH – I would say that it is a challenge all about how we present those tools, because I do not think the technology itself is ever really the problem. We need to demonstrate how to use the technologies in productive ways, exciting ways, creative ways, rather than allowing them to become tools for the dumbing down of musical thinking. It is interesting to note along the way where anxieties always accompanied the emergence of new technologies, and to think about how we negotiate those anxieties. You are correct; it is all about teaching people how to use those technologies productively.

JS – Sound editing is an important technology and should be taught in tandem with notation-based composition. This is not only because it is likely to be a skill that may be used later on, depending on what students do in the future, but it also opens up a way to work with material that compliments notation. It is a very hands-on way to sculpt, mould and process sound, and ideally learning and appreciating fixed media sonic arts can influence aesthetic approaches to notation-based music. There may be a constant dialogue between that direct manipulation and notation. Both are important.

To what extent does this received wisdom continue to be valid in today's educational climate?

JS – I acknowledge that received wisdom does play a large part, but I am always keeping in check the extent to which unconscious things are creeping in, always being aware of them and reflecting on them. We are not asking students to reinvent the wheel, but to try and build upon what has come before.

DH – It is important for me to pull apart a question like this. I worry that today's educational climate has become very mechanistic. I feel strongly that what is valid to the educational environment must be up to the people who are engaged in that environment: students, teachers, scholars, performers, artists and so on. Education as a mechanism for aspects of society that do not first and foremost uphold the inherent value of knowledge and understanding will always only be 'training for something else'. All the things we have been referring to in our discussion about music in higher education go beyond training in the strictest sense, and into the constructive and transformative education of the individual musician. It is not to say that training is not important to what we do, but specific vocation is not the end target in our educational context.

JS – I see, so it is about being active and involved in what 'educational climate' actually means. In our research-intensive university context, this leads us to think about how our own areas of research affect our teaching. My personal research as a composer is certainly relevant, and I try to incorporate it as much as possible. The most successful lectures I have given involve me talking about my own music, and how my pieces relate to the wider context of influences. This makes the whole process more illuminating and engaging, as well as making composition seem more realistic, practical and achievable, as opposed to something out of a textbook. Through our own research, it becomes real for the students.

DH – That is certainly true. I will add that we are teaching something that is hard to outline in Intended Learning Outcomes, but absolutely essential: we are teaching people to care. And demonstrating our care and attention to our particular areas of focus does that very well. This is not a prescriptive way of teaching. In your case, for instance, a concern with female composers says something important about your investment as a woman in composition, and about what you value and how you choose to express your values as an artist. It does not make the claim that the models you choose in your teaching offer the only valid way forward, but rather that, regardless of the examples chosen, we must all truly invest in them, at a deeply personal level. And this is best demonstrated rather than 'told', or indicated rather than explained.

Bibliography

Cage, John. 1968. *Silence*. London: Marion Boyars.

Cronon, William. 1998. '"Only Connect": The Goals of a Liberal Education'. *The American Scholar,* Vol. 67, No. 4, Autumn: 73–80.

Harbison, John. 1985. 'Six Tanglewood Talks'. *Perspectives of New Music*, Vol. 23, No. 2, Spring – Summer: 12–22.

Schoenberg, Arnold. 1991. *Correspondence: A Collection of Translated and Annotated Letters Exchanged with Guido Alder, Pablo Casals, Emanuel Feuermann and Olin Downes*. Metuchen, NJ: Scarecrow Press.

Afterword

Nicholas Cook

There is no need to explain the situation out of which this book arises. That is because it is so clearly set out by Björn Heile in his introduction: the exponential expansion of the scope of music in contemporary society, driven by – and equally an expression of – such factors as the collapse in certain respects of traditional ethnic and class hierarchies, the growth of multiculturalism and cultural omnivorism and technological change. These powerful forces, coupled with changes that have taken place in the teaching of music at secondary level, have placed tertiary music education in a situation where options seem to range from an unacceptable narrowness and cultural irrelevance on the one hand to an unacceptable superficiality and dumbing down on the other – with the intermediate points on the scale being equally unacceptable. It is an extreme case of trying to fit a quart into a pint pot.

Before the apocalyptic hand-wringing gets into its stride, however, it is important to remember that what I have just described is the flip side of a strikingly positive transformation of music studies over the past generation. In place of the taken-for-granted Eurocentricity, the translation into repertory of rigid class and gender divisions, and the ubiquitous whiteness that characterized music education and research up to the 1970s, we now have a multiplicity of repertorial, generic, geographical, technical and methodological approaches, an openness to both the new and the old and a focus on the people in the music that has turned music studies into a particularly vibrant cross-disciplinary field, one that has contributed in its own modest way towards making the world a better place. At the level of professional research the story has been one of matched disciplinary and personal growth: my generation of musicologists (a term I use in the broadest possible way) trained under a narrow though deeply rooted music-educational system, and we have spent the rest of our lives extending our interests, knowledge and skills into terrains the very existence of which some of us had not suspected. The same could probably be said of many of the authors represented in this book.

But that kind of lifelong learning represents a completely different situation from that of today's school leavers who, through taking a three- or four-year music degree, are supposed to gain both breadth and depth in the

196   *Nicholas Cook*

understanding of a musical universe in which big bang has become steady state, as well as gaining a diversity of transferable and employability skills hardly heard of a generation ago – while at the same time quite possibly holding down a job in a local bar. The challenge is as real as it sounds, and perhaps as real as in any other discipline or career path, but at least – as the opening chapter by John Butt explains – it is not as if today's pressures represent the sudden collapse of a previous, enduring golden age. What many think of as traditional music education – what Butt calls the 'Kapellmeister' model – is an invented tradition, and like other invented traditions, it is not nearly as old as you might think.

To make the point, at the time of writing I hold the 1684 Professorship at the University of Cambridge, named after the year when the chair was set up – but the Cambridge Faculty of Music dates from the late 1940s and in any recognisably modern sense, music education at Cambridge goes back no further than that. (Until then holders of the chair performed, composed and took a few pupils.) Not only is traditional music education quite recent, then, but in its relatively short history it has gone through several transformations prior to, or leading up to, the present-day situation. Major landmarks are the 1963 Robbins report, which epitomized the post-war view of university education as a process of induction into elite civilization and habits of thought, and the revised QAA subject statement of 2008, with its radical commitment to inclusion (as Butt observes, the one strand that was excluded was the traditional 'Kapellmeister' model). The motor behind this change was the inexorable increase of student numbers across British higher education as a whole, which transformed an elite educational system into a mass one and left teachers wondering how to respond.

Butt provides both a historical context and a reality check for the central question of the book: as Heile formulates it, 'What, then, should university study of music include?' But there is another presence behind this book. It is haunted by the spectre of what might be described as the neoliberal university, as embodied in the report that stands most clearly at the opposite pole from Robbins: the Browne report of 2010, discussed in Martin Cloonan and John Williamson's chapter. In effect a rationale for getting as much as possible of the costs of a rapidly expanding higher education system off the public purse, the report defined university education in terms of maximising graduate employability and hence earning power. That turned university education into an investment opportunity for the individual, and universities into service providers. Completing this thumbnail sketch of the neoliberal university is a sometimes toxic combination of American management theory (which, ironically, was never applied to American universities) and Thatcherian accountability culture. Symptoms of this include the jargon that leaves its traces in this book, a favourite example being the specification of 'intended learning outcomes' (ILOs).

Given the intimate link between the neoliberal university and fees regimes, there is something ironic about its brooding presence in a book that

Afterword   197

emanates from Scotland – where, at the time of writing, universities do not charge fees, or at least not to Scottish students. Authors subvert its jargon: the idea of 'unintended learning objectives', it appears, comes from Butt, and is taken up by many of his colleagues, particularly composers (Louise Harris and David McGuinness turn it into GLOs, or 'Guerrilla learning outcomes'). But more importantly, they seek to subvert or resist the basic values that inform the neoliberal university, among which is the belief in the autonomy of the bounded individual that the political philosopher C. B. MacPherson called 'possessive individualism'. This resistance takes many forms. One is the ubiquitous emphasis on the values of interpersonal relationships, the opposite not only of the ideology of possessive individualism but also of the reifying regimes in which objectives are specified, outcomes quantified and performance measured. A term that reappears through the book is 'learning community', the point being that teaching is not a one-way process of imparting information or providing a service, but rather one of facilitation, a bilateral transaction in which staff and students act as co-researchers, participating in joint exploration. Such thinking has indeed become quite widespread in higher education in music, particularly in the conservatories, where basic aims, methods and values of practitioner education are currently the subject of vigorous debate (Rink et al. 2017).

Nick Fells builds this relational approach into his conception of composition itself. 'Music making becomes a rehearsing of social relations,' he writes, meaning that composition becomes an inherently ethical practice. Bill Sweeney agrees: the sense of humanness and of interaction between self and other is fundamental to both composition and performance, he says, so that what matters is not the assessable compositional product but rather the social process that gives rise to it. And other composer-authors concur, in terms that hark back to Robbins rather than Browne. Drew Hammond and Jane Stanley conclude their conversation by emphasising the need to resist the mechanization of education and the specification of vocational targets: instead, they say, we must uphold 'the inherent value of knowledge and understanding', and the most important thing is teaching people to care. That throws down a gauntlet to the values of the neoliberal university, but perhaps the most direct assault comes from another conversation between practitioners, this time Harris and McGuinness. The most important things you learn often have nothing to do with institutionalized assessment, they say, and it's the experience, the opening of the mind, that matters, not the qualification: who cares what class of degree you get? One wonders how that would go down with University of Glasgow students if – like their compatriots south of the border – they were paying £9,500 a year.

In terms of this book, however, one might say that the ideologue of resistance to the neoliberal university is Martin Parker-Dixon. His chapter is entitled 'The learning community, a _quodlibet_' and is strategically placed immediately after Butt's, so creating a conceptual grounding on which

198   *Nicholas Cook*

other chapters frequently draw. Parker-Dixon means 'quodlibet' in the sense of medieval disputation, and – setting out his argument according to categories of rigorous argumentation derived from Spinoza – he conveys a sense of the university as a community of scholars that Lord Robbins might have recognised (and that Lord Browne, one suspects, might simply not understand). The relational thinking I have mentioned derives directly from the idea of the university as a community defined by mutual respect and openness, by dispassionate reason rather than personal prejudice, and by a commitment to answer questions and share knowledge. These are obligations entailed in membership of the community, and as such a source of the ethical dimension that Fells, and other composer-authors, see as integral to composition.

The inherent values of learning experience rather than assessable outcomes, and more broadly of critical questioning as opposed to passive adherence to norms – both important elements in this book – are also integral to Parker-Dixon's argument, but at its core is what might be called a cognitive approach to the practical understanding of music. Drawing on the philosopher Robert Brandon, Parker-Dixon defines understanding in terms of concept acquisition, the clearest symptom of which is the ability to explain. You don't understand simple addition, he says, if you just reel off answers in the hope that one of them will turn out to be right: for someone who understands it, $7 + 5 = 12$ is a claim, not a hope, and 'claiming means that we should be prepared to stick up for our claim'. Translated into terms of music this means, for example, that to play a piece in a certain way is implicitly to claim that there are reasons that could be explained and debated as to why it should be played that way, and even as to why the composition is the way it is: 'A committed performance is one that implicitly defends the belief that the work is arguably as it ought to be'. That fits into Parker-Dixon's overall claim that, as taught in university departments (rather than conservatories, for example), 'music must be treated as an object of serious intellectual enquiry'. Indeed, to the extent that it involves meaning and intelligibility, he argues, there is no essential difference between music and the linguistic reasoning central to other disciplines.

As Parker-Dixon mentions in a footnote, there are parallels between this and the debate around practice as research (PAR). Indeed his argument that the performance of music in an academic context invites explanation and debate resonates strongly with a statement in the Criteria and Working Methods drawn up for the 2001 Research Assessment Exercise by the Dance, Drama, and Performing Arts panel:

> any practice in dance, drama or performing arts may qualify as research when it can be shown to interrogate itself; to be located in a research context; and to... achieve a wider significance for research in dance, drama and performing arts.

(RAE 1999, paragraph 3.57.7)

Afterword   199

Nevertheless it might be argued that to define music so tightly in terms of 'reasoned justification and intellectual enquiry,' as Parker-Dixon puts it, is to sacrifice too much of what music in particular can offer the academy, and in so doing to distort some of its most distinctive qualities. To take these in turn, music serves as a classic demonstration of the limits of reason. By this I do not mean to rehabilitate long discredited ideas of music as a product of nature rather than of culture. I mean that, if only because of its sheer complexity, working effectively with music – as performer, composer, or musicologist – means deploying rigorously logical approaches for as long as they are useful, but being ready to throw them over, whether in favour of some other, perhaps equally logical approach, or simply of intuition. Just as Butt argues that the apparently arbitrary, rule-based study of harmony and counterpoint promotes 'flexibility and adaptability to face unexpected challenges', so music promotes the pragmatic and contextual approach to rational argumentation that is a necessary part of practical understanding in many spheres, both within and beyond the academy. Parker-Dixon does make a gesture in this direction when he speaks of a danger that rigorous reasoning may 'close off the possibilities of alternatives, of play', but it is hard to reconcile that with his basic definition of music for the academy.

As for the distortion of distinctive qualities, I will cite one example that can be generalized to other spheres of musical practice, most obviously composition. There is an obvious precedent for the claim that performance – if it is to be more than mere entertainment and hence worthy of a place in the academy – must be supported, or at least supportable, by rational argumentation. This is the claim made by American music theorists, such as Wallace Berry (1989, x), that the illumination of structural relationships exposed in analysis is the basis of 'edifying' performance (where 'edifying' presumably means worthy of a place in the academy). Bluntly, you analyse the music, and then you translate your analytical outcomes into performance. Like ideas of music's naturalness, this highly rationalized approach – which I have elsewhere called the 'page to stage' approach – is nowadays largely discredited, not least for the way in which it sets dialogue between theorist and performer firmly on the theorist's turf. Parker-Dixon does something similar when he stipulates what performers need to do in order to be admitted into the academy, rather than asking how the academy's patterns of thought might be reconsidered to accommodate performance. But in retrospect, the principal flaw of the approach to performance analysis represented by Berry was its uncritical adherence to the values of explicit or declarative knowledge. One of the principal ways in which the field of musical performance studies has advanced since the 1980s is through a much-enhanced recognition of the role in performance of procedural or tacit knowledge, of which one – but only one – example is the embodied knowledge that derives from the interaction between the performing body and the material affordances of musical instruments. Satisfactory accommodation of performance and composition within Parker-Dixon's community of learning, I would suggest,

200 *Nicholas Cook*

depends on a well-developed understanding of the sometimes complex relationships between these two fundamentally distinct kinds of knowledge.

As I said, many colleagues draw on Parker-Dixon's thinking, in particular composers. Fells, for example, says it doesn't matter whether students like something; what matters is that they can give reasons for their likes or dislikes. In other words, they should think critically and analytically rather than making snap judgements. Similarly, he cites Parker-Dixon's idea that compositions can embody 'cognitively significant claims', and develops it into a model of composition as research that is reminiscent of the RAE panel's: 'discursive, sharing environments enable the development, expression and exchange of insights,' Fells writes, 'revealing otherwise hidden properties or characteristic of the materials, sounds or processes in the work under development'. Linking critique and composition, theory and practice, and developing a pedagogical perspective shared among colleagues: this is the approach that Heile refers to when, in his Introduction, he writes that 'we regard practical skills, such as performance, composition and sonic arts, scholarly approaches, such as musicology and critical reflection as interlinked and we seek to engage in a constant dialogue across these domains'.

That is not the only way in which the book evidences an ethos shared across diverse subdisciplinary specialisms. In his chapter, Heile emphasizes the transformation of listening habits attributable to mobile listening technology and download culture: old habits of monostylistic listening, he says, have all but disappeared. (In music, as much as in food, we might borrow Nathan Glazer's (1997) title and say 'We are all multiculturalists now'.) Heile's contribution focuses on the implications of this transformation for the writing of music history, but a profound belief in musical pluralism permeates the book, in particular – again – the composers' contributions. Authors repeatedly refer to the very different backgrounds of students whose experience may equally well be in classical or popular music, and their basic approach is to veer away from the idea of approved stylistic norms and instead emphasize students' personal aesthetic or expressive goals. Fells argues that technique should be evaluated not in relation to established norms, but in terms of the individual student's goals (and in this context the ability to discursively articulate those goals becomes an assessable component of composition). Sweeney agrees: the problem, he complains, is that students are obsessed with the idea of style as some kind of marketable commodity, when they ought to be pursuing their own ideas. There is a very obvious resonance here with Schoenberg's concepts of style and idea, and there is an equally obvious resonance with Adorno when Sweeney goes on to speak of style mutating 'from a mark of social, intellectual or artistic distinctiveness to a form of consumer fetishism', and of popular musical styles being 'ruthlessly rotated to create a constant illusion of distinctiveness'.

There is no harm in being influenced by Schoenberg or Adorno. My point, however, is that the highly inclusive approach enjoined by these authors is built on a foundation of high modernist ideology that is not itself exposed

Afterword 201

to critique. The same foundations are exposed when, in her conversation with Hammond, Stanley says, 'I believe strongly in teaching students not to fall back on remembered patterns'. It is true that she is speaking specifically of composition, and while composition has historically been overwhelmingly based on falling back on remembered patterns, that does not apply in the same way to modernist styles from Schoenberg through Ferneyhough. But then, the point was meant to be that we no longer take the modernist mainstream for granted or define composition in terms of style. And more importantly, while the ethos of questioning received wisdom expounded by Parker-Dixon resonates at least with modernist composition, it fits very badly with performance in anything but the most self-consciously experimental idioms. Falling back on remembered patterns is almost a definition of performers' tacit knowledge.

There is a telling passage in the other practitioner conversation, where McGuinness – an early music specialist who coordinates performance teaching within the Glasgow department – tells sonic artist Harris that he really likes the idea of teaching as a co-researcher relationship, but wonders 'how you get to the point where that is possible'. Harris explains what she means by it in terms of her own teaching, but then admits that it's easy in sonic arts because achieving proficiency doesn't require 'years and years of groundwork'. McGuinness replies, 'I think you are in a better position to do that than I am, because you haven't got the weight of two hundred years of conservatory tradition bearing down on you'. More than that, he says, 'every genre and sub-genre of music has its accepted practices and bodies of history and its stylistic conventions and performance conventions and so on'. (Another way to express that would be that each has its own remembered patterns that you fall back on in performance; that is how you manage to keep going in real time.) And McGuinness continues, 'We want the students to demonstrate that they have engaged with all of that. That's a big ask in itself, but then we also want them to be creative'.

It is arguably the idea of creativity that is causing the trouble. Fells objects to the word on the grounds that it is spuriously mystifying, suggesting something created out of nothing. It is not obvious that in music there can be creation out of nothing, he says, and so it is better to speak of 'generation', which emphasizes 'the synthesis of practice from multifarious other sources'. But I would argue that the problems lie just as much in other ideas associated with creativity: personal expression and authenticity, the breaking of rules and innovation. To take these in turn, I have already mentioned the emphasis on student composers' personal aesthetic or expressive aesthetic goals, while Sweeney writes that 'the important question is not "Which style?" but rather "Can I speak authentically... through this style?"': This is part of the unspoken modernism of which I spoke. Similarly, Fells speaks of breaking out of the constraints of traditional concepts of virtuosity, while McGuinness glosses his reference to creativity by adding that students are in effect being told, 'Learn all of these bespoke rules and conventions, and then once you have assimilated all of those, find an interesting way to break them'. But – as Emily Payne (2016) has recently argued in an article entitled 'Creativity beyond innovation' – such valorization of the new and different, though well-established in the discourses of the creative industries, is not a very productive way to think about creativity in performance, which not only involves embodiment, materiality and tacit knowledge but also operates within the framework of stylistic norms: indeed one might say that performance is at root a culture of repetition. Following Payne's lead, I have recently argued that a more appropriate model of musical creativity is to be found in what Tim Ingold and Elizabeth Hallam refer to as the 'creativity of improvisation', a social and forward-looking process of continuous accommodation to the other that is maximally opposed to the traditional 'creativity of innovation'.[1]

An advantage of Ingold and Hallam's version of creativity beyond innovation is that it sets what are generally called the creative and academic components of music studies on a more level playing field, leading to the realization that not only can academic work be creative, but there are close affinities between creativity in the various forms of performance, composition and research. Humanities scholars sometimes contrast their messy research processes with the logically conditioned stages of scientific research – so ignoring the distinction drawn by the molecular biologist François Jacob between 'Day science', which 'employs reasoning that meshes like gears.... One walks about it as in a French formal garden', and 'Night science', which 'wanders blindly. It hesitates, stumbles, falls back, sweats, wakes with a start... where thought proceeds along sensuous paths, tortuous streets, most often blind alleys' (quoted in Boden 2004, 126). In the present book, creative practitioners – to stick with this absurd but traditional term – see themselves as night scientists by comparison with the day science of their academic colleagues. Musicological work is described as based on the transmission of fact, proceeding 'in a linear manner towards a goal', with each layer of knowledge building consecutively on the previous one – in contrast to 'creative practice', where 'you try something out and then you try something else out'. As a musicologist I do not suppose I am unusual in finding my own ways of working better reflected in night science and 'creative practice' thus described: I am constantly trying something out and then something else. A more flexible concept of creativity will pay dividends in terms of a better understanding of music studies as a variegated but coherent community of practice, and indeed of the university as a community of learning.

In this way the book reveals not only the areas of agreement between author-colleagues, but their disagreements too: it would have been much less valuable to readers had a policy of editorial intervention sought to eliminate the dissonances. In this respect the joker in the pack is the chapter by Cloonan and Williamson, the core of which is the unexceptionable claim that all students should have the opportunity to learn about the music industries (a field in which Cloonan and Williamson are leading experts), and not just in how-do terms but in terms of critical understanding. With the broadening of musicology in the wake of the 'New' musicology of the 1990s, there is a much more general acknowledgement of the crucial role of economic, business and institutional structures in the shaping of musical practices, and as Cloonan and Williamson say, this is as much the case of classical as of popular music. But they sharpen the claim when they insist that these courses are essential and should therefore be compulsory for all students, in the same way that medical students are not allowed to pick just the courses that appeal to them: 'What is needed', they say, 'is less choice and more expertise'. And they up the ante still further when they say that any music department whose programme does not include such compulsory courses (which includes Glasgow) is doing its students a disservice.

Cloonan and Williamson's justification of these claims isn't on the grounds that you can't be said to really understand any musical practice if you don't understand the economic circumstances that give rise to it. It is rather on the grounds that 'the vast majority' of students who enter music courses do so with the aim of getting a job within the field of music, and that without an understanding of the music industries, they are simply not being equipped to do so. And the problem is that much more acute, they say, because – even when you include self-employment, which is widespread in music – there is work available for far fewer people than the combined output of the UK music education system. Again, institutions that 'hide this reality from their students are doing them no favours'.

These are undeniably important issues, but there are some problems with Cloonan and Williamson's arguments. You might say that employment figures for music graduates bear out their claims: the official statistics are hard to interpret because of the categories employed, but if we assume that the figures for 'Teaching and educational professionals' and 'Artistic, literary and media occupations' predominantly represent graduates working in music, then at the time of writing some 40 per cent of graduates from the Glasgow undergraduate programmes find jobs in music. But this begs the question of whether all those students really chose to go to Glasgow University with the aim of a career in music (implying that there is a 60 per cent failure rate). As Cloonan and Williamson indicate, their chapter draws in part on Cloonan's 2005 article 'What is popular music studies?', written at a time when Cloonan worked in the University's Department of Adult and Continuing Education. In that article Cloonan stated 'it is probable that many PMS [Popular Music Studies] students undertake their studies in the (often mistaken) belief that this will be a route into the music industries'. In its original context, this was a plausible claim: Cloonan quoted publicity material from the Commercial Music degree at the University of Paisley (now University of the West of Scotland) that clearly implied that was the purpose of their programme. But whether it is reasonable to generalize that claim to the university sector as a whole is another matter. On their websites, many, if not all, university music departments make a virtue

204   *Nicholas Cook*

of the variety of career paths to which their graduates proceed. Glasgow, for example, says of its BMus (single-subject) degree that it 'provides a sound foundation for careers in music administration, journalism, publishing, performance, composition, librarianship, research and teaching. It also provides strong transferable skills applicable to a wide range of careers outside music' (University of Glasgow 2016).

Transferable skills are, of course, key to the argument: in terms of employability you can only justify degrees in areas where there are insufficient jobs if you can demonstrate that they also provide essential skills for a range of other career paths. One of the strengths of humanities education in the UK since the 1990s has been the general acceptance of this argument – which is not the case of some other countries – and an article in *The Guardian* by Harry Slater (2013) reinforced it: two years earlier the CBI (Confederation of British Industry) had identified seven skills that define employability, Slater explained, and music can be shown to provide training in all of them. It is odd that I should be saying this in response to Cloonan and Williamson's chapter, however, because this is precisely the argument that Cloonan himself put forward in 2005: after explaining that PMS courses are not a route to employment in the industry, Cloonan (2005, 85) writes that 'PMS *cannot* simply be about vocationalism.... It is incumbent on PMS practitioners to impart transferable skills (such as critical thinking) to their students'. But there is something even odder about Cloonan and Williamson's argument. If you believe – as they say – that the vast majority of students take university courses in music in order to get a job in that field, when there are far fewer employment opportunities than there are music graduates, then the right answer is not to tinker with your courses to give your students a competitive edge over others, nor to give them skills that will enable them to follow career paths they do not want to follow. It is to do what happens in medicine, where the government controls the number of places on medical degree programmes in accordance with the openings available. In short, the logical conclusion of Cloonan and Williamson's argument is that university provision for music across the UK should be slashed.

I doubt whether that is really what Cloonan and Williamson intend. They set up their chapter as a provocation. 'We do not expect this argument to win us many friends', they say, 'and have ourselves been accused of being government/business lackeys for making the sort of arguments we make here'. Perhaps their chapter is best read as an attempt to problematize what might be seen as the nostalgic or unrealistic harking back to the age of Robbins or earlier that characterizes many of the other chapters in this book. It is not that Cloonan and Williamson are advocates or apologists for the neoliberal university: 'We retain traditional Marxist ambivalence towards free market capitalism', they say. But they are the only contributors to this book who directly engage with it. As in the case of the music industries, what they advocate is a critical, indeed highly critical, approach – but one that is based on an informed understanding that facilitates effective resistance. As I read

Afterword 205

the chapter, it is about working effectively with the world we have rather than wishing we had a different one.

Read more literally, however, Cloonan and Williamson's chapter raises – but does not directly address – another fundamental issue for higher education in music in the twenty-first century: priorities. There are only 24 hours in a day, and only 365 days in most years, and only four years in a Scottish degree programme – and three elsewhere in the UK. We might all agree on the desirability of running courses on the music industry. That's a no-brainer, provided you have someone to teach them, and more generally, because all musics are conditioned by the social, economic and legal environment in which they take place, courses that focus on that environment are likely to play a particularly important role in a music curriculum that is predicated on pluralism. But if they are to be mandatory, what are you going to get rid of to make space for them? In other words – Heile's words from the Introduction – what should university study of music include, and what should it exclude? No prizes for guessing that I won't come up with any real answer to this question, but before I at least make the attempt, I should complete my overview of the areas and courses outlined – and by implication advocated – in the remaining chapters in this book. I shall do briefly, as my aim is not to engage deeply with the individual chapters but to put the areas they cover onto the map.

Heile's own chapter, then, explores the historiographical implications of the pluralist ethos that pervades the book, as reflected by the virtual disappearance of monostylistic or monogeneric listening. As he says, the aim is to go beyond the approach of the *Cambridge History of Twentieth-Century Music* which I co-edited with Anthony Pople, and which set (some) musical traditions side by side and so thematized their difference, but without seriously attempting to put them into dialogue with one another. (Perhaps a multi-author book was not the right medium for that.) Instead Heile traces responses to the countercultural ethos of the late 1960s across modernist composition, jazz and rock, arguing that in each case there were attempts to defamiliarize or critique iconic repertory, coupled with a transgressive emphasis on noise; in general this involved the undermining of traditional hierarchies of authority, though Mauricio Kagel found it hard to relinquish the role of *auteur*. Heile suggests that similar studies might be based on quotation and collage, and on the political uses of music. I would suggest that another fertile area might be the cross-pollination of performance style, where there is on the one hand influence – in the sense of features passing from rock to classical music, for example – and on the other hand the relational identity formation Heile describes, with styles becoming defined in terms of difference from other styles.

David Code's chapter is an attempt to reimagine the historiography and analysis of canonic classical repertory for music education in the early twenty-first century. He begins by asking why, in the aftermath of Amy Winehouse's passing, anyone would 'choose to base a song course, yet again,

206   *Nicholas Cook*

on the arch-canonical repertoire of the early German Romantics' and, though he doesn't directly answer the question, his chapter demonstrates the range of broad issues about music and meaning, text and context, that can be drawn out of Schubert's songs if you approach them – I am borrowing Heile's words – from a post- or para-canonic perspective. As Heile goes on to say, Code turns the relative strangeness for twenty-first-century students of both the repertory and the German language to advantage, using a range of textual translations to open up issues of poetic meaning and the role of Schubert's music in articulating or reshaping it. But the main way in which Code rethinks canonical approaches to this repertory is through seeing Schubert's songs not as fixed and enduring works, permanent repositories of authorial intention to be faithfully reproduced in performance, but rather as a form of cultural tradition in which both performers and composers interpret and so appropriate them for different aesthetic or ideological ends (as indeed do listeners, though Code does not enter into that). In this way, Code is doing the same as Heile: rethinking Western 'art' musicology for students to whom the classical tradition represents just one of an indefinite number of niche musics that jostle up against one another on their iPods.

If Heile and Code focus on how key areas of the traditional curriculum may be made meaningful for today's students, Eva Moreda Rodríguez focuses on the skills through which students can express their understanding. That largely means writing, of course, itself a particularly crucial transferable skill, and Moreda Rodríguez's focus is on the way in which acquisition of this skill can be enhanced by building on the web-based communication skills that now form so major an element of student experience, such as blogging and social networking. All this makes self-evident sense both practically and pedagogically, and I will simply elaborate on some ways in which digital technology can enhance the study of music as performance and the presentation of outcomes. Combined playback and annotation systems such a Sonic Visualiser make it possible to work with recordings in much the same way that musicologists have always worked with scores – for example flicking backwards and forwards to compare different passages – and in this way they create a new kind of study environment. This enables the development of approaches that are equally applicable to notated and non-notated musical traditions. In 'What is popular music studies?', Cloonan (2005, 79) emphasized the extent to which academic approaches to classical and popular music were irreconcilable, because 'a methodology based on notation and assessment of music on the printed page is ill equipped to deal with a medium in which notation plays little or no part'. That was over a decade ago: musicology's performative turn, increasing engagement with non-notated aspects of music and development of study environments for recorded sound, go far to place classical and popular musics (not to mention jazz and non-western traditions) on a level playing field. Digital technology in this way serves an essential role in delivering a curriculum based on a commitment to musical pluralism.

Afterword 207

But when it comes to priorities, the most contentious area is the 'Kapell-meister' skills Butt talks about in the opening chapter, or what is left of them in today's educational system. Secondary schools, responding to the same curricular pressures as higher education, offer much less preparation in this area than they used to, and more than that, such provision as still exists is concentrated in the private sector: for universities, requiring traditional skills in harmony and counterpoint runs contrary to widening participation, and can even promote a sense of class-based injustice among students. As Butt says, you can do what American universities do and teach the skills from scratch – but that of course only exacerbates the problems of finding space in the curriculum. And in any case the problems do not stop there. As Butt explains, the traditional 'Kapellmeister' training offered essentially vocational preparation for a career that has largely disappeared today. High-level score-reading skills served a practical function in the days before gramophones – not to mention combined annotation and playback software – in a way they do not now. And more broadly, when music was understood to mean tonal music of the classical tradition from Bach to Brahms, together with a pre-tonal introduction and a post-tonal conclusion, the rationale for extensive training in harmony and counterpoint was straightforward enough: it was the gateway to the musical mainstream, opening up the ability to manipulate the elements of music, to understand the music from the inside, rather than merely marveling at the results. But we no longer live in that world, and there are many musicians – or more generally people who make a career from music – who simply do not deal in augmented sixth chords or fugue. I find it hard to construct a convincing argument that such people would benefit more from training in tonal harmony and counterpoint than, for example, in jazz improvisation or the techniques of digital sound processing. To put it the other way around, why is it better to be ignorant about jazz harmony or digital sound processing than about tonal skills?

We can't do everything, so we have to prioritise. The traditional approach to this is to ask what is the irreducible core of a music degree. But that is surely the wrong question, because – like Cloonan and Williamson's claim that any degree programme which does not include mandatory courses on the music business is doing its students a disservice – it implies a degree of homogeneity in music programmes that hardly exists, and to the extent that it does, arguably should not. Yes, in an ideal world every student would learn all about tonal harmony, jazz improvisation, and digital sound processing as well as composition, performance, analysis, musicology, ethnomusicology, PMS and the music business; the result would be an informed understanding of the variety and complexity of music in today's world, together with the same flexibility to pursue all sorts of different musical activities that the 'Kapellmeister'-trained students of the post-war generation had within their own, highly constrained musical world. But doing the same for today's

208 *Nicholas Cook*

globalized musical world, and in three or four years, is simply undeliverable. This implies that – beyond critical thinking and the other transferable skills necessary not only for employment but also for lifelong learning – the idea of a core applicable across all music degree programmes is simply wrong-headed.

The key point is that core knowledge and competencies do not exist in the abstract. They exist in relation to – dare I say it – intended learning objectives, by which I mean the particular repertoires, approaches, skills and career paths (whether or not in music) around which any particular degree programme is designed. That is the context in which it makes sense to ask which of all these areas and courses can be dispensed with. In one context skills in digital sound processing may be irrelevant, in another tonal skills or even fluency in staff notation. In other words, the logical response to the situation Heile outlines on the first page of this book is a much greater degree of diversity between tertiary music degree programmes than is currently the case. And in this context Cloonan and Williamson's observation that there are many music departments which have a single popular music expert, but none in which popular music dominates and classical music is restricted to just one expert, is telling. They add that 'the latter scenario is almost impossible to imagine'. I disagree: I think it is perfectly easy to imagine. The question then becomes why, in that case, there aren't any – and answers might range from the skills base of teachers who trained a generation ago to lingering ideas that higher education in music should have a civilising function, and that some kinds of music are more suitable for that than others.

The point of this book is not to prescribe solutions but to offer an example of what happens when you think in a sustained manner about the problems. But of course, even sustained thinking can only take you so far. In the end the question of how you are to fit a quart into a pint pot remains. Answers to that one on a postcard, please.

Note

1 The term 'creativity of improvisation' is implied but not actually used in Ingold and Hallam 2007; I discuss this, and the idea of performance as a culture of repetition, in the Conclusion of Cook (2018).

Bibliography

Berry, Wallace. 1989. *Musical Structure and Performance*. New Haven, CT and London: Yale University Press.

Boden, Margaret. 2004. *The Creative Mind: Myths and Mechanisms*, 2nd edition. London and New York: Routledge.

Cloonan, Martin. 2005. 'What is Popular Music Studies? Some observations'. *British Journal of Music Education* 22: 77–93.

Cook, Nicholas. 2018. *Music as Creative Practice*. New York: Oxford University Press.

Glazer, Nathan. 1997. *We are All Multiculturalists Now*. Cambridge, MA: Harvard University Press.

Ingold, Tim, and Elizabeth Hallam. 2007. 'Creativity and cultural improvisation: An introduction'. In *Creativity and Cultural Improvisation*, edited by Elizabeth Hallam and Tim Ingold, 1–24. London and New York: Berg.

Payne, Emily. 2016. 'Creativity beyond innovation: Musical performance and craft'. *Musicae Scientiae* 20, 325–344.

RAE. 2001. 1999. *Assessment Panels' Criteria and Working Methods (5/99)*, www.rae.ac.uk/2001/Pubs/5_99/ByUoA/crit66.htm.

Rink, John, Helena Gaunt, and Aaron Williamon, eds. 2017. *Musicians in the Making: Pathways to Creative Performance*. New York: Oxford University Press.

Slater, Harry. 2013. 'Music graduates are more employable than you might think'. *The Guardian*, 11 October. www.theguardian.com/education/2013/oct/11/music-students-employability [accessed 21 December 2016].

University of Glasgow. 2016. 'Undergraduate Programmes: Music – BMus', www.gla.ac.uk/undergraduate/degrees/musicbmus/ [accessed 21 December 2016].

Index

Adorno, Theodor W. 45, 53n 57, 114, 118–21, 200
Analysis 1–2, 9n2 11, 15, 20–1, 23, 27n 77–101, 133, 170–1, 183, 199
Art Ensemble of Chicago 62, 66–7
Art song 77–111, 205–6
Assessment 4, 7–9, 128–32, 136, 138–52, 155, 158–9, 164, 167, 172, 184, 188; *see also* feedback

Bach, Johann Sebastian 190
Beethoven, Ludwig van 62–5, 69
Browne report 115, 196–8

Cage, John 151, 188–9
Canon 1, 4, 8, 11, 14, 77–8, 157–8, 179, 181–2, 206–7
Community of learners 5, 7, 9, 30–53, 128–9, 163–4, 166, 197, 199–200
Composition 2, 5, 7, 11, 21, 23, 38–9, 47, 50, 138, 140, 148–50, 170–7, 179–94, 197; stylistic 11–13, 20–1, 23, 181, 183–4
Constructivism 155–7
Counterpoint 11, 20, 24–6, 181, 183, 199, 207
Creative practice 8, 9, 38–9, 138–53, 155–68, 172–3, 201–2; *see also* composition, performance
Critical thinking (do search) 31–51, 145–6, 165, 208

Diversity 2–3, 25, 158, 182–3

Employability 8, 12, 15–16, 18, 160, 179, 187; *see also* music industries
Ethics 142–4
Ethnomusicology 1, 19

Feedback 129–32, 139, 166, 172; *see also* assessment

Generative practice 144–6
Graduate attributes 4, 113, 179

Harmony 11, 21, 24–6, 181, 183, 199, 207
Hendrix, Jimi 62–3, 65, 68–9
High modernism 20, 28n 51n4, 52n5, 56–7, 62–70, 186, 200–1
Historically informed performance practice 6, 11

Intended learning outcomes (ILOs) *see* Learning outcomes
Interdisciplinarity 18, 78, 139–40, 180, 195

Jazz 1–2, 55, 58–62, 62–70, 207

Kagel, Mauricio 62–9

Learning community *see* community of learners
Learning outcomes 9, 147, 159–60, 170, 194, 196–7
Lied *see* art song
Listening habits 57, 180, 200, 205

Marketization of Higher Education 5, 9, 12, 115, 176–7, 196–8
Messiaen, Olivier 182
Music history 7–8, 11, 55–75, 200
Music industries 2, 8, 12, 112–24, 202–5; *see also* employability
Musical analysis *see* analysis

New Musicology 12, 21, 43–5, 114; *see also* canon
Notation 11, 60–1, 179–80, 185, 187, 189, 190–2

212 *Index*

Performance 2, 5, 7, 12, 24, 47–50, 101–109, 150–3, 159, 163, 166–7, 202; of contemporary music 148
Popular music 1–2, 7, 20, 55, 62–70, 113, 122–3, 175
Project-based learning 138–9

Research-led teaching 6, 35, 136, 160–2, 194, 198, 201

Schoenberg, Arnold 104–5, 107, 184, 188, 200–1
Schubert, Franz 77–109

Skills 11, 22–3, 25, 122, 160–1, 179, 204, 206–7; transferable 4, 18
Sonic Arts 155, 157, 160–1, 163, 167, 190, 193, 200–1
Subject benchmark statement for music 1–3, 22–3, 25, 28n12

Technology 3, 8, 2–5, 58–62, 158–9, 179, 191–3, 200, 206; *see also* Web 2.0
Traditional musics 1–2, 55

Web 2.0 126–36, 206; *see also* technology